BOLD DREAMS

SENIOR AUTHORS
Virginia A. Arnold
Carl B. Smith

LITERATURE CONSULTANTS
Joan I. Glazer
Margaret H. Lippert

READING
EXPRESS
MACMILLAN

Macmillan Publishing Company
New York

Collier Macmillan Publishers
London

ACKNOWLEDGMENTS

The publisher gratefully acknowledges permission to reprint the following copyrighted material:

"The Adventure of Eustace" is from Chapter VI in THE VOYAGE OF THE "DAWN TREADER" by C. S. Lewis. Reprinted with permission of Macmillan Publishing Company and Collins Publishers. Copyright 1952 C. S. Lewis Pte. Ltd. Copyright renewed 1980.

"All the Money in the World" is abridged and adapted from pages 109-119 in ALL THE MONEY IN THE WORLD by Bill Brittain. Text Copyright © 1979 by William Brittain. By permission of Harper & Row, Publishers, Inc.

"Amy's Capital Idea" is adapted from HOW TO GROW A HUNDRED DOLLARS by Elizabeth James and Carol Barkin. Copyright © 1979 by Elizabeth James and Carol Barkin. By permission of Lothrop, Lee & Shepard Books (A Division of William Morrow & Company).

"Associations," from THERE IS NO RHYME FOR SILVER by Eve Merriam. Published by Atheneum Publishers. Copyright © 1962 by Eve Merriam. Reprinted by permission of the author. All rights reserved.

"The Ballpark" is from THE BALLPARK: ONE DAY BEHIND THE SCENES AT A MAJOR LEAGUE GAME by William Jaspersohn. Copyright © 1979, 1980 by William G. Jaspersohn. By permission of Little, Brown and Company.

"Between Birthdays" is from CUSTARD AND COMPANY: POEMS by Ogden Nash, selected and illustrated by Quentin Blake. Copyright © 1961, 1962 by Ogden Nash. By permission of Little, Brown and Company and Penguin Books, Ltd.

"Bicycle Riding" by Sandra Liatsos appeared originally in *Cricket* Magazine. Reprinted by permission of the author.

"Biography of a Komodo Dragon" is an adaptation of BIOGRAPHY OF A KOMODO DRAGON by Alice L. Hopf. Text Copyright © 1981 by Alice L. Hopf. Reprinted by permission of G. P. Putnam's Sons and Larry Sternig Literary Agency.

"The Borrowers Are Found" is adapted from THE BORROWERS by Mary Norton. Copyright 1952, 1953, 1980, 1981 by Mary Norton. Reprinted by permission of Harcourt Brace Jovanovich, Inc. By permission also of Harold Ober Associates Inc.

"Cindy and Jennifer" is adapted from CINDY: A HEARING EAR DOG. Text by Patricia Curtis and illustrations by David Cupp. Text Copyright © 1981 by Patricia Curtis, illustrations Copyright © 1981 by David Cupp. Reprinted by permission of the publisher, E. P. Dutton, Inc.

"The Dragon and the Tiger" is from JANE AND THE MANDARIN'S SECRET by Jean Lewis. Copyright © 1970 by Jean Lewis. Reprinted by permission of McIntosh & Otis, Inc.

"Earn Your Own Money" is from "Easy Money Making Projects." Copyright © 1979 by Creative Education, Inc. and reprinted with their permission.

"The First Roads" is from FROM TRAILS TO SUPERHIGHWAYS by Adrian A. Paradis. Copyright © 1971 by Adrian A. Paradis. Reprinted by permission of Julian Messner, a division of Simon & Schuster, Inc.

"The First Transcontinental Railroad" is adapted from *Cobblestone's* May 1980 issue: *The Transcontinental Railroad.* © 1980, Cobblestone Publishing, Inc., Peterborough, NH 03458. Reprinted by permission of the publisher.

"Footprints" from SEE MY LOVELY POISON IVY by Lilian Moore. Copyright © 1975 Lilian Moore. Reprinted with the permission of Atheneum Publishers.

Macmillan Publishing Company
866 Third Avenue
New York, N.Y. 10022
Collier Macmillan Canada, Inc.

Printed in the United States of America

ISBN 0-02-160120-8

9 8 7 6 5 4 3 2 1

Contents

UNIT ONE
LEVEL 11

FAIR
EXCHANGE

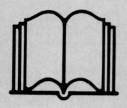

PREPARING FOR READING

Learning Vocabulary

1. Katya's mother had to repay a <u>loan</u> from Boris the moneylender.
2. Every month a <u>payment</u> was <u>due</u>.
3. Katya helped her mother pay the <u>debt</u> to Boris.
4. She <u>recited</u> her mother's words of <u>wisdom</u>.

loan	payment	due
debt	recited	wisdom

Developing Background and Skills
Cause and Effect

"A stitch in time saves nine" is an old saying. It still makes sense today. If you take the time to sew a small tear, it won't get bigger. If you sew one stitch today, you won't have to sew nine tomorrow.

This is an example of a cause-and-effect relationship. A **cause** is the reason something happens. An **effect** is the result, or what happens. A bigger tear is the result caused by not sewing a smaller one.

To find an effect, ask yourself "What happened?"
To find a cause, ask "Why did it happen?"

Look for words such as *because*, *so*, and *in order to*.
They can help you to find statements about cause and effect.

Read the sentences below. Find a cause and an effect in each.

1. Because there were no banks in some places, people went to moneylenders to borrow money.
2. In order to make money, the moneylenders charged interest, or a fee for lending their money.

Did you figure out the cause and effect in each sentence? The words *because* and *in order to* may have helped you.

CAUSE	EFFECT
1. no banks	people went to moneylenders
2. to make money	moneylenders charged interest

In the story "My Mother Sends Her Wisdom," there are many cause-and-effect relationships. As you read, see if you can find them.

My Mother Sends Her Wisdom

Louise McClenathan

"Mama," cried Katya, as she peered through the cottage window, "Old Boris, the moneylender, is coming down the road in his horse cart."

"Let him come, little one," answered Katya's mother, as she worked warm dough for bread.

Boris and Alexei (ə lek′ sē), the small boy who kept his accounts, drew up before the cottage. "Widow Petrovna," Boris shouted, "I have come to collect your monthly rubles (rü′ bəlz) due me from the loan of silver to your late husband."

Mama stood behind Katya, slowly wiping her hands on her apron. "Tomorrow, Old Boris," she said, "I shall send you a fine fat goose and gander. My daughter will bring them to your house in the city. They will be my payment to you this month."

"Very well then, but no later than sundown tomorrow," Boris said.

After his horse and cart disappeared down the road, Mama and Katya sat down for the evening meal. Katya ate her soup slowly, thinking about Old Boris. He was hated in the countryside, for he would lend money to the farmers but charge a very high interest rate. He would make them pay it even if the harvest was poor. When the farmers could not pay, he took over their farms.

"Do not worry, Katya," said Mama, as she looked across the table. "I have a plan for Old Boris. If it works, we shall keep our land." While the clock ticked softly and the firelight cast shadows on the walls, Mama told Katya what to do.

The next morning Katya ate her bowl of baked cereal and put on a warm coat. Mama sent her off: "Remember to repeat to Old Boris everything I told you. Especially to say, 'My mother sends her wisdom.' Do not forget his answer."

With a fat white goose under each arm, Katya set off through the forest. The trees were thick and the woods were silent. She walked quickly, and soon came out of the forest and into the city.

An old woman showed her the way to the moneylender's house, which stood on a corner surrounded by a fence. Katya opened the gate and went up to the door and knocked. Soon Boris came to the door and opened it wide. Alexei stood behind him. "So you have brought my birds," snapped the old man.

"Yes, here are the geese for payment, and my mother sends her wisdom," said Katya.

"Wisdom, is it?" said Old Boris with a laugh.

Katya's eyes were bright as she recited what her mother had taught her:

> "Two well-kept geese, so I've been told,
> May truly lay fine eggs of gold."

Boris shook his head. "What do I need with the wisdom of a peasant woman? Alexei, mark these geese in the book as payment. Then take them to the market to sell."

Katya started for home immediately. "Did Old Boris accept my wisdom?" asked Mama as Katya took off her coat.

"He laughed, Mama, and said he did not need the wisdom of a peasant woman. Then he ordered the goose and gander sold at the market."

"We shall see, we shall see," said Mama, as she warmed the child's feet before the stove.

The next month, on the day payment was due, Katya took two fat pigs through the forest to the moneylender. "Here are two pigs for payment, and my mother sends her wisdom," said Katya.

"What, your mother's wisdom again?" Boris asked. Katya drew a deep breath and spoke quickly:

"Five pink piglets, born anew,
Will squeal much more than old ones do."

The old man threw back his head and laughed. "If your mother were wise, she would not owe me money. Alexei, mark the book and take the pigs to market for sale."

Katya did not answer, but turned and quickly went on her way. When she returned home, she told her mother what Old Boris had answered. "Good," said Mama. "All is going well, little one."

When the next payment was due, one month later, Mama said, "Today, Katya, you will take a good sack of wheat to Old Boris," Mama said. "It is heavy, so you must pull it in the little cart and take the dog with you for company."

They loaded the small cart with the wheat, and again Katya set off. She entered the forest with the cart behind her and the dog leaping ahead.

At noon, Katya knocked on the moneylender's door and presented the grain. "Here is a sack of wheat for payment, and my mother sends her wisdom."

"What nonsense this time?" asked Old Boris, and Katya recited her mother's riddle:

"How is it that ten grains of wheat
Could give us all enough to eat?"

"I laugh at your mother's wisdom," snapped Old Boris. "She may keep it for herself. Alexei, mark the book for Widow Petrovna and take the wheat to market."

Once more Katya went home and told her mother what the old man had said.

"Now we shall see who is the wiser, daughter," said her mother with a smile.

The next month Katya did not visit the money-lender, and one day Old Boris and Alexei came to the cottage and knocked on the door. "You are late with your payment, Widow Petrovna," said the old man. "Do you have nothing to pay this month?"

Mama raised her eyebrows and spoke in a clear voice. "You must be mistaken, Old Boris, for my debt is paid off."

"Paid off, indeed! You still owe twenty rubles, either in money or in goods. Check the book, Alexei."

The boy turned the pages of the heavy book and read the figures. "Twenty rubles still owed."

The widow shook her head. "My debt is paid. The sack of wheat was the last payment, and you shall get nothing more. You must go to Judge Petruschka (pi trüsh′ kə) to ask for a hearing against me if you do not believe it, Boris."

"I shall, I shall," said the old man, nodding. "He will find that you are still owing, and I will take your land in payment," and he drove off down the road in a cloud of dust.

Soon the day came when Judge Petruschka held court. Old Boris and Alexei sat on one side of the room, while Katya and her mother sat on the other.

"What is the charge?" the judge asked quietly.

"This woman says she paid her debt, but she still owes me twenty rubles," said Boris.

"What has she paid you?" the judge asked.

"Two geese, which sold for six rubles. Two pigs, which brought ten rubles at market. A sack of wheat, which sold for four rubles."

"Is this true, Widow Petrovna?" the judge asked.

"No, your honor, it is only half true. My daughter will tell you what she offered Old Boris each time she took payment to him."

Katya stood before the judge and spoke out bravely. "When I took two geese, I offered him my mother's wisdom in this riddle:

'Two well-kept geese, so I've been told,
May truly lay fine eggs of gold.'

"He did not accept my mother's wisdom. If he had, he would have kept the goose and gander, collected many eggs, raised a flock of goslings, and sold them at market for three times what he received.

"When I took the pigs to him, I offered him more of my mother's wisdom in this riddle:

'Five pink piglets, born anew,
Will squeal much more than old ones do.'

"If he had kept the pigs and raised a litter of five piglets, he could have sold them for twice as much as the two pigs brought.

"The third time I offered my mother's wisdom in this riddle:

'How is it that ten grains of wheat
Could give us all enough to eat?'

"He could have sold half the wheat for payment, planted the rest, and had a field of wheat next year, two fields after that, and four the following year."

The judge looked at Old Boris. "Is it true, this story the child tells?"

Boris glowered angrily. "Wisdom is not the same as money," he said.

The judge sat for a moment, scratching some figures in his book with a long pen. "Such wisdom," he said slowly, "is what feeds us all. I find, Old Boris, that Widow Petrovna has overpaid you some thirty rubles in her wisdom, so it is you who owe her money. I order you to pay her."

The judge would not be moved, though the old man flew into a rage. Finally he took out the money and threw it on the table.

Soon all the countryside knew that Old Boris had been outdone by a peasant woman. Friends and family came to celebrate. "We share your joy, Widow Petrovna," they said. "May your land blossom with good fortune always."

Questions

1. What did Katya take to Boris as the three payments on the loan?
2. What would Boris do if Mama did not repay the loan?
3. What might have happened if Boris had followed Mama's good advice?
4. If you had been the judge, how would you have decided the case between Mama and Boris? How would you have explained your decision?

Applying Reading Skills

Number your paper from 1 to 3. Finish each cause-and-effect statement below. Write each complete statement on your paper. Then draw one line under each cause and two lines under each effect.

1. The farmers did not like Boris because _____.
2. Boris did not believe that Mama had paid all her debt, so _____.
3. The judge said that Boris had to pay Mama thirty rubles because _____.

PREPARING FOR READING

Learning Vocabulary

1. Money is anything that can be <u>exchanged</u> for goods and services.
2. Many different kinds of money have been used since <u>ancient</u> times.
3. The <u>origin</u> of the word *salary* can be traced to the Latin word *sal,* which means salt.
4. Salt was once used as money because it was <u>scarce</u>.
5. The <u>official</u> paper money of the United States is printed in Washington, D.C.
6. Putting a <u>design</u> on coins was done long ago and is still done today.

exchanged   ancient   origin
scarce   official   design

Developing Background and Skills
Cause and Effect
Figuring out cause-and-effect relationships is one way to understand what you read. You know that an **effect** is a result, or what happens. You also know that a **cause** is the reason something happens.

When you ask "Why did that happen?" you are looking for a cause. When you ask "What was the result?" you are looking for an effect.

Read the paragraph below. Find an effect and its cause.

Later, paper came to be used as notes of promise, or money. Carrying large amounts of gold and silver was difficult, so paper was used to represent coins. Some of the earliest paper money appeared in China. The Chinese had paper money made from mulberry tree bark. The oldest of this money was about the size of a sheet of notebook paper.

The word *so* may have helped you to find the cause.

CAUSE: Carrying large amounts of gold and silver was difficult.
EFFECT: Paper was used to represent coins.

In the next selection, you will read about many cause-and-effect relationships. Use what you have learned to figure out what they are.

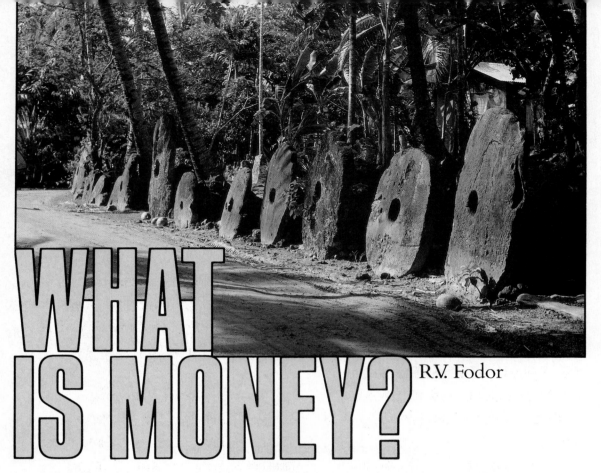

WHAT IS MONEY?

R.V. Fodor

What is money? What makes the coins and paper bills we use to buy things so special? After all, coins are made of the same metals used in stoves. Paper bills are not much different from magazine paper.

Money is anything that people give or take in return for goods and services. Anything can be used as money. The important thing is that people agree to use it.

Stones, Salt, and Shells

Money came into use at different times in different places. Some ancient people used money as we know it more than 2,500 years ago. Other groups used things that do not seem like money at all. The people of Yap were one such group. On this South Pacific island, stones were used for money. Some Yap money was made up of small stones. Other pieces were as large as six feet (two meters) high and twelve feet (four meters) across.

Many other unusual things have served as money. Some Roman soldiers were paid partly in salt. This practice is the origin of the English word *salary*, which means payment for one's work. Grains like wheat and corn were money in Egypt. The people of Fiji (fē′ jē) exchanged the teeth of whales for the goods they needed.

The seashell has been used as money in many places. An important kind of shell money in America was wampum (wom′ pəm), or strings of beads made from the shells of clams.

The name *wampum* comes from an American Indian word. The Indians cut the shells into pieces, made holes in them, and threaded them on strings. During the 1600s, many early settlers used wampum in their tradings with Indians.

Wampum served early Americans well until about 1750. Then some settlers learned how to make large amounts of the beads quickly.

American Indians made wampum from the shells of clams. Making the beads took a great deal of patience and skill.

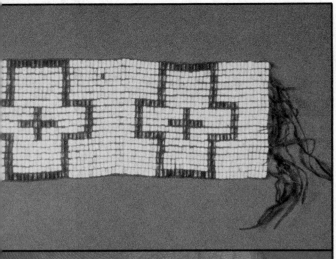

Factories were set up in New York and New Jersey, but the mass production of wampum made it worthless as money.

No matter what is used for money, it has to be scarce. If the object ever becomes too common, it is likely to lose its value.

Coins

The first metals that looked like coins were the ancient Chinese disks of about 500 B.C., known as *cash*. They were made of bronze and had a square hole in their center. The English word *cash* does not come from the name of this Chinese coin, however. Instead, it comes from the Latin word *capsa*, meaning box or money box.

The penny was introduced as a silver coin in England around 775 A.D. For a long time it was England's only coin. English money later developed into pounds, shillings, and pence. These coins were brought by the settlers

Top: part of a belt made from wampum

Middle: ancient Chinese coins known as *cash*

Bottom: an English penny

who crossed the Atlantic Ocean to the New World.

Spanish money was also found in the American colonies. Best known is the Spanish dollar, or piece of eight. This coin was often cut into smaller pieces, or bits, to make change. That word, *bits*, is still with us as slang: two bits is a quarter and eight bits is a dollar.

The first American coins were minted, or manufactured, in Boston in 1652. Shillings, sixpence, and three-penny bits were made. Many had a pine-tree design, so they were called pine-tree shillings.

For a long time, this money was used along with the coins of other countries. Then, in 1785, the new nation of the United States chose the dollar as its official money. New coins of gold, silver, and copper were made. There were eagles (worth ten dollars), half-dollars, dimes, and half-cents.

In 1792, the first official United States Mint was opened

Top: a Spanish dollar, shown in bits

Middle: a pine-tree shilling made in Mass-achusetts

Bottom: the first gold coins of the United States

in Philadelphia, Pennsylvania. This mint is still making coins today.

In the two centuries since the first coins were minted, money-making has changed. For example, two-cent, three-cent, five-cent, and twenty-cent coins were introduced during the 1800s. Only the five-cent piece, the nickel, has lasted. Gold coins, common in the 1800s, have not been minted since 1933. True silver dollars were stopped in 1935. Coin sizes change, too. The Susan B. Anthony dollar coin is smaller than other dollars minted this century.

Paper Money

Today, paper money is more important than coins. Its origins go back thousands of years, when traders first agreed to accept promises of payment. These promises to pay later in gold and silver were written on clay tablets.

Later, paper came to be used as notes of promise, or

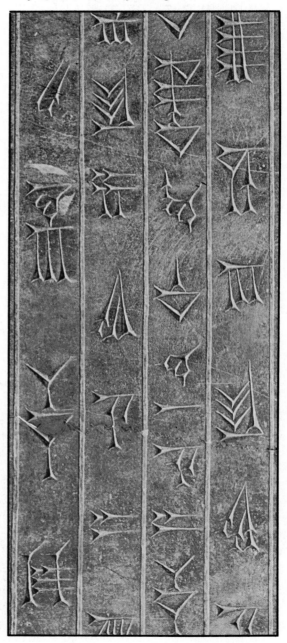

In ancient times, promises of payment were written in wet clay tablets. After the tablets were covered with writing, they were hardened by baking.

money. Carrying large amounts of gold and silver was difficult, so paper was used to represent the coins. Some of the earliest paper money appeared in China. The Chinese had paper money made from mulberry tree bark.

The oldest of this money was about the size of a sheet of notebook paper.

The United States Government printed its first official paper money in 1862. The Treasury Department needed money to pay for the Civil War. These greenbacks, as they were called because of their green ink, lost much of their value in a short time. People doubted that they were as good as gold. By 1864, the greenback dollar had dropped to only thirty-nine cents in gold value. The government did not get enough gold to return greenbacks to the same

Left: This Chinese bill was printed on bark paper in the early 1300s.

Bottom: a greenback dollar from 1862

buying power until 1879. All the dollars we have today were in use then, but the designs of the bills have changed.

Paper money in the United States is not manufactured in mints. It is made at the Bureau of Engraving and Printing in Washington, D.C. The Bureau uses secret-formula ink and special paper. Each bill is printed as part of a large sheet of thirty-two bills and has its own number. After the sheets are checked carefully, they are cut into thirty-two parts.

The next time you have a coin or bill, take a good look at it. Think about where it came from. You might just want to hold on to it for a while!

Questions

1. What are some things once used for money that are no longer used today?
2. How has the making of coins in the United States changed?
3. Why does the Bureau of Engraving and Printing use secret-formula ink and special paper to make paper money?
4. What do you think might be used as money in the future? Why do you think people would agree to use it?

Applying Reading Skills

Number your paper from 1 to 3. Finish each cause-and-effect statement below. Write each complete statement on your paper. Then draw one line under each cause and two lines under each effect.

1. Wampum became worthless as money because _____.
2. The dollars of the United States Government in 1862 were printed with green ink, so _____.
3. In order for something to be accepted as money, _____.

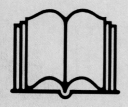

PREPARING FOR READING

Learning Vocabulary

1. Quentin Stowe's wish for all the money in the world was <u>granted</u> by a leprechaun.
2. Quentin's father stared in <u>wonderment</u> when the money appeared on his farm.
3. People could not receive <u>wages</u> for their work.
4. A <u>customer</u> could not pay for things.
5. All the people in the town were in <u>agreement</u> that something had to be done.

granted   wonderment   wages
customer   agreement

Developing Background and Skills
Sequence of Events

What would you do if you wanted to deposit some money in your savings account? First, you would have to find your account book. Next, you would probably go to the bank. Once you got there, you would have to fill out the form for depositing. Finally, you would be ready to see a bank teller and deposit your money.

After you turned in your money, account book, and form, your part would be over. Then the bank teller would begin to follow the steps needed to make the deposit.

Many things that you want or have to do must be done in a certain order, or **sequence.** Sometimes even though you know the sequence of steps you must follow, you meet with an unexpected event, or problem.

What would happen if you got to the bank and found that you had forgotten your account book, money, or both? Then you could not begin to follow the steps to deposit your money.

The events, or things that happen, in a story also have a sequence. In the next story, you will read about the events that take place when a group of people try to solve a problem. You will enjoy the story even more if you think about the sequence of events as you read.

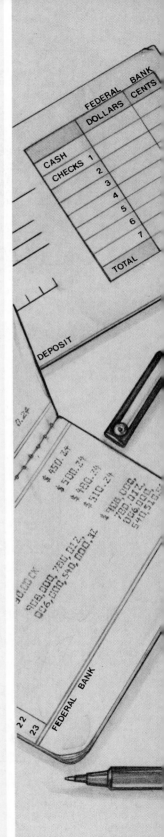

All The
M·O·N·E·Y
In The
W·O·R·L·D

BILL BRITTAIN

Quentin Stowe is just an ordinary boy from Cedar Ferry who likes to fish and bike and daydream— until one day he catches a leprechaun (lep' rə kon') named Flan and is granted a wish. When Quentin's wish comes true, and ALL THE MONEY IN THE WORLD is actually piled high on his family's farm, trouble begins. Without money, banks throughout the world have had to close, stores have had to shut down, and people can no longer buy the things they need. Can the people of Cedar Ferry do something to help get things running again? The Mayor calls a town meeting to find out.

All the grown-ups in Cedar Ferry were waiting inside the Volunteer Fire Department when Quentin and his parents arrived. They walked up the front steps, and Mayor Roscoe Peabody greeted them.

"Good afternoon, Mr. and Mrs. Stowe. Hello, Quentin. I see Flan decided to come, too."

Flan, perched on Quentin's shoulder, waved to the Mayor.

Inside, Quentin sat between his parents on a bench at the back of the large room. Mayor Peabody took his place at the speaker's table and rapped for order with a big wooden hammer.

"You folks all heard the President on TV yesterday," the Mayor began. "As long as we can't get any money, it's up to us to keep Cedar Ferry running properly without it. The question is—how are we going to do that?"

"Quentin Stowe's got all that money out on his farm," a woman yelled. "He'd just better give it back."

"Why don't we just go out there and take it?" shouted someone. "I don't believe all that stuff about how it keeps coming back to the farm."

Angry voices were heard all over the room. Quentin began to tremble. He looked up at Poppa.

Mr. Stowe stood up. "That's enough!" he said angrily. The people became silent.

"The money's out on my farm, and if anybody can take it away, he'd be thanked by me and my family. But I guess you've heard, we're having trouble getting it off the fields." Poppa shook his head in wonderment. "It keeps coming back."

"You mean it will be there forever?" Emma Hobson called out.

"You'd better ask Flan about that," replied Mr. Stowe. He bent down, picked up the little man, and held him up for everybody to see.

"Flan," said Mayor Peabody, "is what Mr. Stowe says true?"

"It is," Flan answered. "I gave Quentin just what he wished for."

"But if you brought the money, you must be able to return it."

Flan shook his head. "I cannot take back a wish once it's been granted. That's the Law of the Leprechauns."

"I say we put the green man in jail until he agrees to return the money," said Walt Milleridge.

"We can't do it," replied Sheriff Arbor. "He walks through walls."

"And if you try any rough stuff," Flan squeaked, "I'll turn the lot of you into mud turtles."

"I think he could do it, too, folks," added Mayor Peabody.

The room was silent. The people looked at one another in surprise. Then a man in one corner got to his feet.

"Some of us have made a plan about the money problem, at least here in Cedar Ferry," he said. "We think it will work, for the time being."

He and a second man picked up a large box and carried it to the front of the room.

"Folks," said Mayor Peabody, "you all know Bob Reese who owns the variety store. And Joe Ballard, the butcher. Tell them your plan, fellows."

Bob Reese reached down into the box. He pulled out and held up something that looked to Quentin very much like a stack of bills from one of the piles on the farm. But how could money be here?

"I've got four boxes of this down in the basement of my store," said Mr. Reese. "It's play money."

He pulled one of the bills from the stack. "Instead of a dollar, this is called a 'dilly.' There are bills in this box marked one, five, ten, and twenty dillies. It's our plan to turn this play money into real money."

"How?" asked Mayor Peabody.

"We all know about how much everybody in town earns. So we'd give everybody here a week's wages, right now. Only it would be in dillies, not dollars. We'd all agree that here in Cedar Ferry, we'd spend and receive the dillies just like real money."

"Mr. Reese?" Miss Draymore, who ran the jewelry store, got to her feet. "Your plan sounds well and good, as far as it goes. But what would happen if somebody found another supply of those . . . dillies? Someone could come in here from another village with a pocketful of dillies and begin spending them. We'd never know the difference. We'd just have a lot of dillies that weren't worth anything."

"We already thought of that," said Joe Ballard. From the pocket of his butcher's apron he pulled out a rubber stamp. He pressed the stamp against one of the dilly bills.

Bob Reese held the bill up for all to see. Stamped across its front in red letters were the words COLD CUTS.

"Our plan," Mr. Ballard went on, "is to stamp each bill with my COLD CUTS stamp. They would

be the only official money in Cedar Ferry. Any bills
that didn't have the stamp would be bad money,
and Sheriff Arbor would arrest anybody who tried
to spend it."

"Who'd guard the rubber stamp itself?" asked
Miss Draymore.

"It would be kept in a locked box at the
bank," said Mr. Ballard. "Mayor Peabody would
have the key. But even he couldn't get the stamp

unless Banker Sedgewick led him to the box."

Miss Draymore thought about this. "That seems
safe enough," she said finally. There were murmurs
of agreement from around the room.

"Then let's get going," ordered the Mayor. "I
call on Mr. Ballard, Mr. Reese, and Miss Draymore
to start stamping all the dilly bills in this box.
Sheriff Arbor, you keep an eye on them to see that
they do it right."

Finally, all the bills were printed with the COLD CUTS stamp. They were all put back into the big box.

"Now I want everybody who earns money to get into a line," ordered the Mayor. "Each one will come up and say how much you earn in a week. Banker Sedgewick will stand at the table here. If what you tell him sounds right, he'll give you that much in dillies. Let's start with you, Dr. Snow."

Dr. Snow went up to Banker Sedgewick. "It's hard to tell," he said. "Some weeks I have a lot of patients, and other times there aren't very many. I'd say about three hundred dollars, though."

Banker Sedgewick slid three hundred dollars in dilly bills across the table.

The second man was Wilber Vickers, who did odd jobs. He asked for seventy-five dollars.

For nearly an hour people went to the table to get money. When it was his turn, Mr. Stowe asked for ninety dollars. He received four twenty-dilly bills and a ten-dilly bill. "There's just about enough here to buy me a suit of clothes," he said to Quentin.

When everyone had his dillies, Mayor Peabody rapped the table for quiet. "Is everybody satisfied?" he called out.

"No, I'm not." Wilber Vickers stood up.

"What's the matter, Wilber?" asked the Mayor.

"I was thinking just last week about raising my prices for mowing lawns and cleaning windows," said Mr. Vickers. "You remember, Mr. Sedgewick. I spoke to you about it."

Banker Sedgewick nodded. "That's true. Maybe we should have given him more money, Mr. Peabody."

"Okay, Wilber," said the Mayor. "Will another twenty-five dillies be all right?"

"Fine." Mr. Vickers came forward and took the extra dillies.

"Wilber cleans the windows of my store," called out Mr. Hobson. "If I pay him more, I'll have to raise my prices. I should get more money, too."

"And me!" shouted Walt Milleridge.

Soon people were calling out all over the room. One person after another came up to get more dillies.

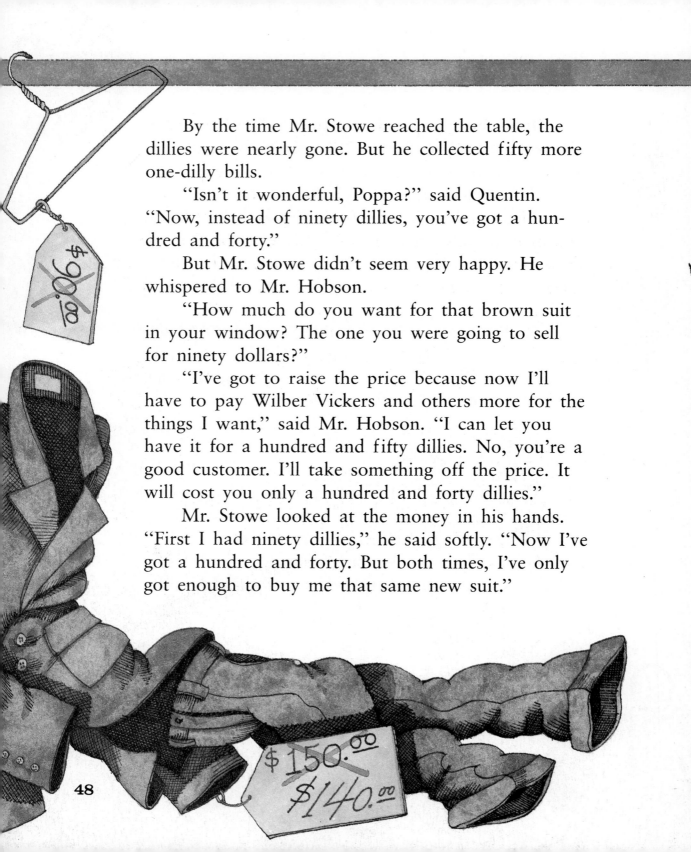

By the time Mr. Stowe reached the table, the dillies were nearly gone. But he collected fifty more one-dilly bills.

"Isn't it wonderful, Poppa?" said Quentin. "Now, instead of ninety dillies, you've got a hundred and forty."

But Mr. Stowe didn't seem very happy. He whispered to Mr. Hobson.

"How much do you want for that brown suit in your window? The one you were going to sell for ninety dollars?"

"I've got to raise the price because now I'll have to pay Wilber Vickers and others more for the things I want," said Mr. Hobson. "I can let you have it for a hundred and fifty dillies. No, you're a good customer. I'll take something off the price. It will cost you only a hundred and forty dillies."

Mr. Stowe looked at the money in his hands. "First I had ninety dillies," he said softly. "Now I've got a hundred and forty. But both times, I've only got enough to buy me that same new suit."

"If anybody's got debts to pay off," the Mayor called out, "now would be a good time to do it. The whole town is here, and we all have money."

There was a rustling of bills and the sound of low voices. And then, as if out of nowhere, a little pile of dilly bills appeared in Quentin's lap. The pile grew larger . . . and larger . . . and larger. Finally Quentin was almost buried beneath the huge mound of dilly bills.

"Look! The money disappeared!"
"What happened to it?"
"Over there in the back. See?"
"Young Quentin Stowe has all our money."
"How did that happen?"

"I don't know. But let's get it back."

All over the room, people began getting up. They began to crowd toward Quentin.

Flan scurried among their legs and got to the speaker's table. He climbed up on it and spread his arms wide.

"You fools!" he cried. "Don't you see what's happened?"

"What?" asked the Mayor. "What's happened?"

The people turned to listen.

"The dilly bills were fake money," said Flan. "But now you're using them to buy and sell things."

"Because now they're real money," someone said.

"Exactly," said Flan. "And since they're real money, Quentin gets them. Because now they're part of all the money in the world."

Questions

1. Why couldn't Quentin return all the money in the world?
2. Why did Mr. Hobson raise the price of the suit Mr. Stowe wanted to buy?
3. What made the dillies become real money?
4. What do you think Quentin will do next? What would you suggest he try?

Applying Reading Skills

The following events are from "All the Money in the World." Read the events. Then write them in the correct sequence on your paper.

As soon as the play money was used as real money, it all appeared in Quentin's lap.

Quentin made a wish and all the money in the world ended up on his family's farm.

All the people of Cedar Ferry who earned money received some of the play money to use.

The Mayor called a town meeting.

The Mayor told the people that now was a good time to pay off their debts.

The people of Cedar Ferry decided to use play money as real money.

Quentin Stowe caught a leprechaun who granted him a wish.

WRITING ACTIVITY

WRITE A FANTASY

Prewrite

Quentin Stowe had an interesting problem in the story "All the Money in the World." He made a wish, and the wish came true. You know from reading the story how the wish led to the problem.

"All the Money in the World" is a fantasy. A fantasy is a special kind of story. Magical things happen in a fantasy. Some characters, like Flan, have magical powers.

Like any other story, a fantasy has a setting. Where and when a story takes place makes up the setting. A fantasy also has a plot, or sequence of actions and events. Solving a problem can be an important part of a plot.

Look at the chart below. It shows the important parts of a fantasy. It also has examples for each part. You can use this information to write a fantasy, or you can make up your own information.

Setting	the town of Pennyville
Characters	Mayor Miller, Kirk, Maggie, Money (a talking dog)
Problem	Penny banks are disappearing from Pennyville.
Sequence of events	1. Mayor Miller tells Kirk and Maggie about the problem. 2.

Copy and complete the chart. You will have to write more sentences to complete the plan for the plot of the fantasy. What sequence of events will solve the problem of the disappearing banks?

Write

1. Read the information on your chart.
2. Think about how you will begin your fantasy. The first paragraph should introduce your characters and explain the setting.
3. The next part of the fantasy will probably explain the problem. Write about the events in the plot as you planned them in your chart.
4. When you write conversations, start a new paragraph for each different speaker.
5. Use your Glossary or dictionary for spelling help.

Revise

Read your fantasy. Did your characters solve the problem in your story? Did your sequence of events make sense? If not, rewrite parts of your fantasy now.

1. Did you use the correct punctuation in your conversations?
2. Did you use correct end punctuation for each sentence?
3. Did you capitalize the names of people and places?

PREPARING FOR READING

Learning Vocabulary

1. Coins in the United States are made in mints located in Philadelphia, Denver, and San Francisco.
2. Pennies are made from a mixture of two metals that are heated together.
3. The furnace tilts to pour the hot metal into a mold.
4. Glowing slabs of hot metal go through a mill to be flattened.
5. There is a raised rim around every penny.

located   mixture   tilts
glowing   mill   rim

Developing Background and Skills
Sequence of Events

A factory is a busy place where hundreds of people may work to produce or make something. In many factories, each worker or group of workers is responsible for only part of a job. They work on one step in a process, or **sequence** that involves many steps.

Pennies are made in factories. The process of making pennies involves many steps. The paragraph below describes part of the process. As you read it, think about the sequence of events.

The metals are heated until they melt. Then the furnace tilts and pours them into a mold. When the metal cools off, it takes on the shape of the mold. This huge piece of metal is 18 feet (5.4 meters) long and weighs about 6,000 pounds (2,700 kilograms). It is known as an *ingot* (ing′ gət).

Three steps in the process of making a penny are described. Can you name them?

1. metals are heated
2. furnace tilts and pours metals into mold
3. metal cools and takes on shape of mold

The word *then* may have helped you to keep the sequence straight. The order of the sentences should have helped, too.

As you read the next selection, you will discover all the steps in the process of making a penny.

The Money Factory

Mary Ann Castronovo

Everyone has heard of peppermint and spearmint. But there is another kind of mint: the United States Mint. This mint is a factory where coins are made.

Pennies, nickels, dimes, quarters, half dollars, and the Susan B. Anthony dollar—all the coins that you spend or save—usually come from three main mint offices. They are located in Philadelphia, Pennsylvania; Denver, Colorado; and San Francisco, California. In

addition to coins, these mints make medals at times to honor a famous person or a special event.

The Philadelphia Mint is so big that it covers one square city block. Inside this gray building, 30 million coins can be made each day.

If you want to see just how a money factory works, you can go to visit this mint. Inside the front door, you will step onto a long escalator. Along with other visitors, you will ride up to a glass-covered walkway. From here, you can look out over a huge room below. Hundreds of busy workers are running giant money-making machines.

All coins are made from huge pieces of metal. Actually, pennies are a mixture of two metals—copper and zinc. This mixture, or *alloy*, must have just the right amount of each. So first the metals are weighed.

It may be hard to imagine putting metal in an oven, but that is exactly what happens next. The metals are heated together in a huge furnace. Because this room is very hot, the workers here must wear suits made of aluminum. These suits make the workers look a little like astronauts.

The metals are heated until they melt. Then the furnace tilts and pours them into a mold. When the metal cools off, it takes on the shape of the mold. This huge piece of metal is 18 feet (5.4 meters) long and weighs about 6,000 pounds (2,700 kilograms). It is known as an *ingot* (ing′ gət).

Next, a big electric saw cuts the ingot in half. The two slabs must be heated again so they will be soft enough to work with. They are popped into a big toaster called a reheat furnace. Each slab is red-

hot and glowing like fire when it comes out of the furnace.

Next, the hot slab goes to the *rolling mill* to be rolled out like dough. After eleven squeezes through the mill's rollers, the slab is just one-half inch thick, but a whopping 114 feet (34 meters) long. That's longer than a basketball court!

The long metal strip is very hot now. To cool it down, it is sprayed with water. Then the top and bottom of the strip are shaved off to make it smooth. The metal shavings go back to be used all over again.

The metal strip is so long that it is hard to carry around. So it is sent to another machine that rolls it up like a giant roll of shiny copper ribbon. Then it is unrolled again and put through more rollers. Finally, it is flat as a penny and 800 feet (240 meters) long.

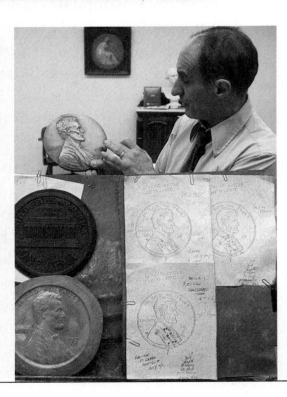

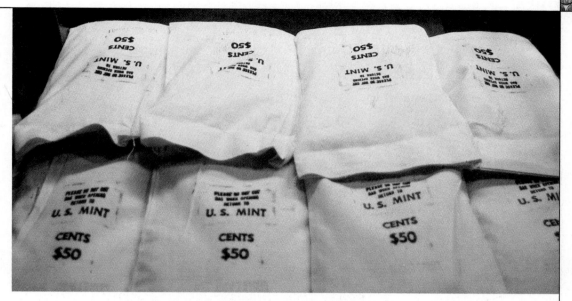

Now it is time to cut out the pennies. The *blanking press* punches out round blank coins. As they fall out of the machine, they sparkle like glitter.

All the blank pennies are dumped onto a net with penny-sized holes in it. Blanks made in the wrong shape or size fall through the holes. That is how the mint makes sure that all its pennies are the right size. The good blanks are cleaned, polished, and dried. Then they are fed into a machine which puts a raised rim around each one.

Finally, it is time to add the design that makes a penny look like a penny. Each blank goes into a special mold called a *die* that stamps the heads and tails designs on at the same time. On top is a picture of President Lincoln. On the bottom is the Lincoln Memorial. At last, the piece of metal is a real penny.

Questions

1. What is made at the mints in Philadelphia, Denver, and San Francisco?
2. What happens in the reheat furnace?
3. What do you think happens to the blanks that are not the right size?
4. Think of a process that has several steps; for example, making popcorn or building a model. Write each pair of steps in the correct sequence.

Applying Reading Skills

The following pairs of sentences tell about some of the steps in the process of making pennies. Read each pair of sentences and decide which step happens first. Then write each pair of steps in the correct sequence on your paper.

1. The metal takes the shape of an ingot.
   Metals are heated in a furnace until they melt.

2. The ingots are cut into two slabs.
   The slabs go through a rolling mill.

3. The metal strip is rolled until it is flat as a penny.
   A blanking press punches out blanks.

4. The blanks are stamped with the designs.
   The blanks are dumped onto a net with penny-sized holes in it.

Spendthrift

Norma Farber

Coins—coins—coins—
    a bushel to a breeze—
are pouring from the pockets
    of the elm in the square.

Gather up the money heaps
    as many as you please.
So rich an old tree
    doesn't count them or care.

PREPARING FOR READING

Learning Vocabulary

1. Aldo started a <u>fund</u> to save for an ice-cream freezer for his sister's birthday.
2. He read an <u>advertisement</u> about a sneaker contest being held by a local shoe store.
3. One boy, Trevor, had a pair of sneakers that were an <u>indescribable</u> color.
4. There were many <u>entries</u> in the sneaker contest.
5. Anyone who wasn't a <u>resident</u> of Woodside would be <u>disqualified</u>.

fund	advertisement	indescribable
entries	resident	disqualified

Developing Background and Skills
Main Idea

Suppose your friend is talking to you about a contest she had entered. What might she tell you?

She would certainly mention that she had entered the contest. Then she would probably tell you about the contest rules and the prizes. Maybe she would go on to tell you about how she planned to win.

The most important point your friend told you was that she had entered the contest. The details about the contest rules and prizes explain that point. Her plans for winning give you more information.

Writers have important points to make, too. They often organize their paragraphs around them. The most important point in a paragraph is called the **main idea.** The information that supports or explains the main idea is found in **supporting details.**

You can find the main idea of a paragraph by asking "What point is the writer trying to make?" You can also ask "What is the most important information in this paragraph?"

You can find the supporting details by asking "What words and sentences give more information about the main idea?"

The main idea is often in the first or last sentence of a paragraph. It can also be found in one of the other sentences.

As you read the next story, think about the important points the writer is trying to make.

THE GRUBBY SNEAKER CONTEST

JOHANNA HURWITZ

Aldo Sossi loves ice cream, so when his big sister Karen says she wants a machine to make ice cream, Aldo decides to buy it for her birthday. Aldo has the whole summer to earn money, but the machine, an ice-cream freezer, is expensive—$49.95. Aldo's job-hunting efforts are not successful. By August he has only $3.00 in the ice-cream-freezer fund. Then he starts to worry.

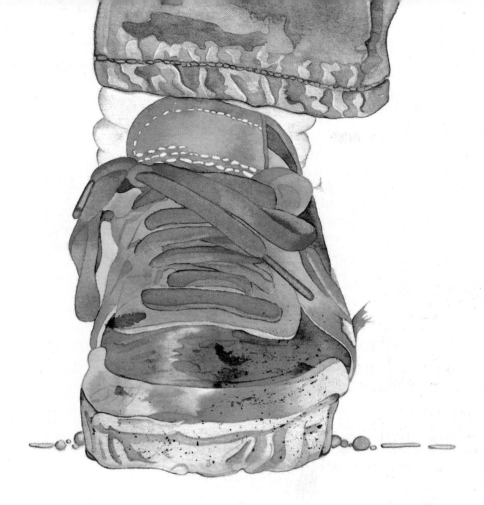

On the fifteenth of August, when there were only seventeen more days till Karen's birthday and twenty more days of school vacation, Aldo's luck seemed to change. He was looking through the *Pennysaver*, which had arrived that morning. He had given up looking for a job, but still he looked through the little newspaper out of habit. You never knew when you might find something interesting. Sure enough, midway through the pages, there was a large advertisement for the local shoe store.

Aldo looked down at his feet. His sneakers
were still caked with bits of dry mud. There was a
small hole where he had torn the canvas. The
sneakers were in bad shape, but Aldo decided that
he could make them worse.

He showed the advertisement to his mother.
"What a great way to save money!" said Mrs. Sossi,
laughing. "I think you have a fair chance to win."

Aldo got an idea. "If I won the free pair of
sneakers, would you add the money that you save
by not having to pay for new sneakers to the ice-
cream-freezer fund?"

So far there were only three dollars in his fund.
Sneakers could cost as much as twenty dollars. The
total amount would still be a lot less than he
needed for the ice-cream freezer, but it was worth
trying.

"Sure," agreed Mrs. Sossi. "I've got nothing
to lose."

During the days that followed, Aldo stepped everywhere and into everything: puddles, mudholes, and on rocks. He never stood still. He never sat still. He was determined that he would have the muddiest, grubbiest sneakers in the history of the world, or at least in the history of Woodside, New Jersey.

One day, Aldo saw two boys walking along on the main street of Woodside. One was wearing sneakers that looked much worse than Aldo's. He was a tall boy with red hair, and his sneakers had once upon a time been red, too. But now they were an indescribable color. The red-headed boy was walking with Michael Frank, who had been in Aldo's fifth-grade class.

"Hi, Michael," said Aldo.

"Hi, Aldo. This is my cousin Trevor," Michael said. "He's staying with me this week," he explained.

"When are you going home?" asked Aldo.

"Day after tomorrow probably," said Trevor.

"Oh," said Aldo. He almost said "good," but he caught himself in time. Trevor, with his worn-out sneakers, would be out of town before the grubby-sneaker contest.

"Well, see you around," said Aldo, hoping he wouldn't.

Trevor's sneakers worried Aldo. He saw that his own were not as bad as they could be. He started to work harder than ever. He hiked to the

park, and he climbed on some jagged rocks there. Then he went home and offered to run any errands his mother might have. Next he walked over to Mr. Puccini's house, instead of taking his bike, even though he had been there the day before. Wearing out his sneakers was turning out to be hard work.

Aldo's friend DeDe returned from her grandparents' six days before the grubby sneakers were to be judged. "I wish I had known about it," she complained to Aldo, when he brought her up-to-date on the local news. She was wearing a pair of new purple sneakers that her grandparents had bought for her. "My grandmother told me to throw my old ones away. She said they smelled."

"Not as bad as mine," said Aldo proudly. He removed his left sneaker and held it up to DeDe.

"Phew," she said, holding her nose. "If they judge by smell, you'll win for sure."

On the day of the contest Aldo wasn't so sure. About twenty kids were gathered at the Walk Well Shoe Store, and each of them was carrying a pair of old, worn-out, dirty sneakers.

DeDe had come along to watch the judging. "Yours look the worst," she assured Aldo.

One of the salesmen handed out tags to each of the children. "Tie your sneakers together," he told them, "and then put your name and address on the tag. Come back at noon. We'll have picked the winner by then."

"I sure hope I win," Aldo said to DeDe. "It's my last chance to earn some money this summer."

They saw two more boys coming down the street. The deadline for entering the contest was

10:30 A.M. These sneakers would probably be the last entries. The boys came closer. They were Michael Frank and his cousin Trevor.

"Hi, Mike," DeDe called out.

Aldo didn't say anything. He was too surprised to see Trevor to remember anything else. Hadn't he said that he would be going home in a couple of days? Why was he still here? Trevor was carrying his old sneakers. Even after all the hard work he had put in, Aldo could see that Trevor's sneakers looked worse than his own. Now he would never win the contest.

"I thought you were going home," said Aldo.

"I thought so, too," said Trevor. "But my little sister just got chicken pox, and my aunt and uncle said I should stay on here so I wouldn't catch it from her."

The cousins went inside the shoe store.

Aldo felt awful. "Let's take a walk," he said to DeDe.

When they reached the hardware store, there was a big sign in that window, too.

End-of-Summer-Sale!
$10 Off the Price of Any Lawn Mower, Sprinkler Set, Plastic Pool, Ice-Cream Freezer.

For a moment Aldo felt great. "Hey look! The ice-cream freezer will only cost thirty-nine dollars and ninety-five cents now." But then he remembered that he had only three dollars saved. Now that he wasn't going to win the contest there was no way in the world he could earn thirty-six dollars and ninety-five cents by tomorrow, which was Karen's birthday.

At noon, Aldo and DeDe walked back to the shoe store. Aldo rushed to see the display of old sneakers. He saw Trevor's old red sneakers right in front. He shouldn't have felt disappointed. He had known they would be there. As he stood at the window, the salesman brought Aldo's sneakers and placed them beside Trevor's. I guess I'm a runner-up, thought Aldo.

The salesman held a sign that said First Prize, and he placed it next to Trevor's sneakers. He recognized Trevor in the group and said, "Come along, young man. I'll give you any sneaker in the store." Aldo watched as Trevor proudly went inside and sat down to be fitted.

DeDe watched Trevor, too. Then she walked over to a contest poster. Aldo watched her reading it. He wondered why she was bothering now. Suddenly DeDe turned and grabbed Aldo. "Come with me," she said, pulling him into the store.

"It says on the sign that any kid who lives in Woodside can enter the contest."

"That's right," agreed the salesman. "But the contest is over now. The deadline for entering was ten-thirty this morning."

"I know that," said DeDe. "But did you know that this boy doesn't live in Woodside?" She pointed her finger at Trevor.

"What is your address?" the salesman asked Trevor.

"When I'm at home or when I'm visiting here in Woodside?" Trevor asked.

So that was how the first-prize sign was switched from Trevor's sneakers to Aldo's. Trevor was disqualified because he lived in Delaware, and visiting with his cousin in Woodside for two weeks didn't make him a resident.

Trevor's face turned as red as his hair. "I didn't mean to cheat," he said.

"That's OK," said the salesman. To show that there were no hard feelings, he gave Trevor a pair of green shoelaces as a consolation prize. Every boy and girl who entered the contest got a pair of shoelaces too, but thanks to DeDe's quick thinking, Aldo didn't get any. He got a brand-new pair of sneakers.

Mrs. Sossi was speechless when Aldo showed her the prize sneakers. When she heard that the ice-cream freezer was on sale, she did even more than she had promised. She not only added the twenty dollars that the sneakers would have cost to Aldo's three, but also paid the difference. The next day, Karen got the ice-cream freezer for her birthday and couldn't have been happier. Aldo was happy, too. He could have homemade ice cream at last!

Questions

1. Why did Aldo enter the Grubby-Sneaker Contest?
2. What were the rules of the contest?
3. If Aldo had not won the contest, how might he have tried to make the money he needed?
4. If your class wanted to have a contest, what kind of a contest would you suggest? What would the rules be? What might be the prize?

Applying Reading Skills

Number your paper from 1 to 4. Read each sentence below. Find the sentence in the story and read the paragraph it is part of. Then decide if the sentence is a main idea or supporting detail. Write your answers.

1. The sneakers were in bad shape, but Aldo decided that he could make them worse.
2. Then he went home and offered to run any errand his mother might have.
3. These sneakers would probably be the last entries.
4. I guess I'm a runner-up, thought Aldo.

PREPARING FOR READING

Learning Vocabulary

1. A person who wants to start a business has many decisions to make.
2. Asking for suggestions from other people in business may help.
3. Compare your rate with what others are charging to determine whether you are charging too much or too little.
4. When you accept a job, you are responsible for fulfilling your obligations.

decisions suggestions compare
determine responsible obligations

Developing Background and Skills
Main Idea
Read this paragraph from "Earn Your Own Money."

 Homeowners need help with some of their jobs almost all year around. In the summer, they are looking for help mowing grass and trimming hedges. In the fall, they might want someone to help rake and bag leaves. In the winter, clearing sidewalks of snow may earn you some money.

What is the **main idea,** or most important point, in the paragraph? What are the **supporting details**? The diagram below shows you.

Homeowners need help almost all year around.
mowing grass and trimming hedges in the summer
raking and bagging leaves in the fall
clearing sidewalks of snow in the winter

The main idea is the first sentence. The other three sentences have details that support the main idea.

In the paragraph, the main idea was in the first sentence. You know that the main idea can also be in the last or one of the middle sentences.

As you read the next selection, look for the main ideas. This will help you to remember the most important information.

EARN YOUR OWN MONEY

PATRICIA ELDRED

Right in the middle of dinner you find your mind wandering. You're daydreaming again about all the things you'd like to buy. . . . You hate riding your hand-me-down bicycle and you'd like a new one. . . . Your soccer team is ordering sweatshirts this year and you want to get one. . . .

There's just one problem. Your parents say that if you want those things, you'll have to earn the money yourself. So you go up to your room and get out your piggy bank. You have exactly $1.28. That won't even buy half

a sweatshirt! So what do you do? Give up?

Well, some people would. They'd say, "A kid can't earn that much money." Most people would really be discouraged.

HOW DO I START?

Instead of thinking about all the things you *can't* do, begin thinking about things you *can* do. Maybe you can't deliver papers. But even with a bike, you can run errands pretty fast. If you can't run a power mower, you can weed the garden.

There are many things you *might* do to earn money. All you need to do is figure out which of them you *can* do. You have to find the job that's right for you. First, figure out what skills and abilities you have. Then decide how they can help you earn money. You'll also need to discover the goods or services that people need and will pay for.

Stop and think for a moment about the people who live in your neighborhood. Think, too, about the kinds of help they might need. Then figure out how you can match your skills to their needs.

For example, walk slowly to the corner of your block. Do you see a tricycle parked in the middle of a driveway? Do you spot a stroller in a yard? These are clues that there are small children in your neighborhood. And that means there are parents who probably need babysitters. You may be too young to be an official babysitter. But you may be able to offer another kind of service. Parents often have things they would like to do without the help of their small children. If you like children, you may be able to earn money by offering to keep a child busy for an hour or so.

The large German shepherd who barks every time a stranger comes near his house may give you a clue to a job, too. If you like animals, why not knock on doors and ask to walk the dog? You might offer to take care of a pet while the owners go on a vacation, too.

If you have a bike or enjoy walking, you can offer your neighbors a one-person errand and delivery service. Be sure to seek out the older people in your neighborhood when you're looking for business. Many times it is difficult for them to get out to a store or to run an errand.

There are many other services you could perform for the people in your neighborhood. You could take clothes to the drycleaners. A more time-consuming job would be taking laundry to a laundromat, waiting for it, and then returning the clean clothes. You could take letters to a mailbox or packages to a post office. When you know there is a paper drive in your neighborhood, you could pick up newspapers and magazines and deliver them to the drop-off location. You'll probably be able to discover other errands to run if you study your own neighborhood.

Homeowners need help with some of their jobs almost all year around. In the summer they are looking for help mowing grass

and trimming hedges. In the fall, they might want someone to help rake and bag leaves. In the winter, clearing sidewalks of snow may earn you some money.

SOME BUSINESS TIPS

As you start your business, you'll find there are some decisions to make. You'll also find that it's important to keep your customers satisfied. The following suggestions may help you in both of these areas.

What To Charge

Knowing what to charge can often be difficult. It is hard to put a price on your own work. Also, rates and prices vary in different parts of the country. You should try to determine the going rate for the services you'll offer. Then compare what you are doing with what a person with more experience might do. For example, find out the average rate for babysitting. Then charge

83

25 cents an hour less for your entertaining of children.

When you are figuring out what to charge for an errand, you'll want to consider the time you spend and the distance you travel. If you ride your bike six blocks to the grocery store and pick up a loaf of bread, you might only charge 25 cents. But if you have to walk two miles to a laundromat and then wait for the clothes to be cleaned, you could charge 75 cents.

The wages for such jobs as grass mowing or snow shoveling will have to be determined by the job, too. The size of the yard or the length of the sidewalk will need to be considered. When you are shoveling snow, the amount of snow will be important. Shoveling one inch of light, fluffy snow is a lot different from shoveling four inches of heavy, wet snow.

The important thing is to try to come up with the price that is high enough to be worth your while and low enough to please your customers.

Letting People Know What You're Up To

Remember that an important part of getting a job is letting people know what's available to them.

Tell your neighbors about your babysitting service by delivering notices to each house and apartment on your block. If you're looking for work mowing lawns or taking care of animals, go around and introduce yourself.

People can tell from talking to you whether or not you're responsible. If they like what they see, they may give you a job.

You can also advertise in a neighborhood newspaper, or post a notice at your local supermarket.

REMINDERS

As soon as you enter the business world, even in a small way, you are taking on responsibility. If you want to be a success, you'll need to fulfill your obligations. Being on time is very important. Doing a careful and thorough job is, too.

The suggestions that have been given here should help you think of ways to earn money. If you're willing to use your skills to provide people with the services they need, you should be able to make enough to buy that new bike or team sweatshirt.

Questions

1. What should you do before you try to find a job?
2. Why would it be a good idea to find out what other people charge for doing a job?
3. How does advertising help business people and their customers?
4. What are some jobs that might need to be done in your neighborhood? How could you find out?

Applying Reading Skills

Number your paper from 1 to 4. Then write the correct answer for each question below.

1. What is the main idea of the second paragraph under "How Do I Start?"
2. What is one supporting detail from the same paragraph?
3. What is the main idea of the first paragraph under "Reminders"?
4. What are two supporting details from the same paragraph?

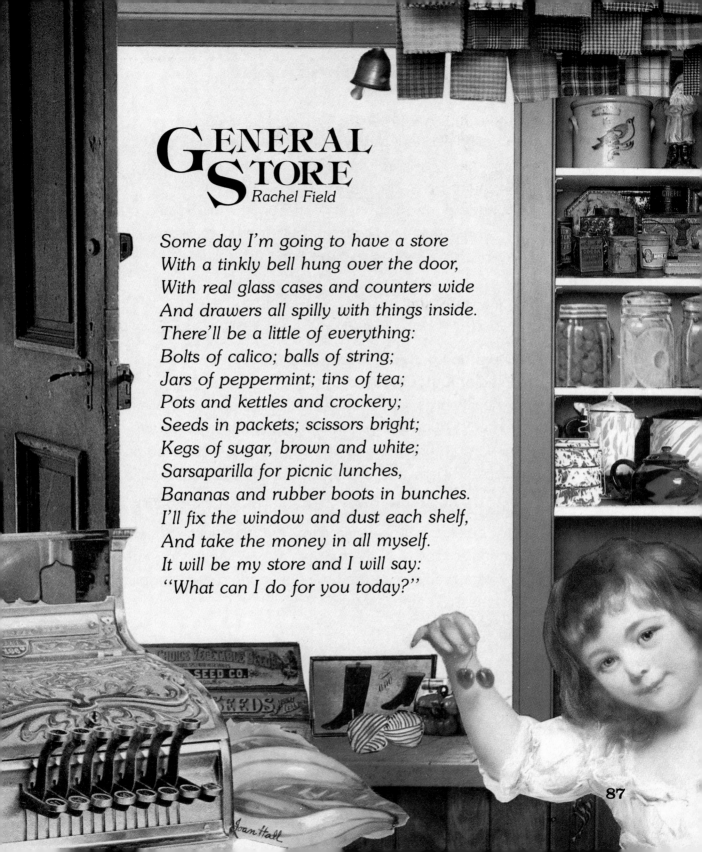

GENERAL STORE
Rachel Field

Some day I'm going to have a store
With a tinkly bell hung over the door,
With real glass cases and counters wide
And drawers all spilly with things inside.
There'll be a little of everything:
Bolts of calico; balls of string;
Jars of peppermint; tins of tea;
Pots and kettles and crockery;
Seeds in packets; scissors bright;
Kegs of sugar, brown and white;
Sarsaparilla for picnic lunches,
Bananas and rubber boots in bunches.
I'll fix the window and dust each shelf,
And take the money in all myself.
It will be my store and I will say:
"What can I do for you today?"

PREPARING FOR READING

Learning Vocabulary

1. Amy needed capital to start her new business.
2. She thought that terrariums made with fish bowls might be in demand.
3. Before investing in the fish bowls, Amy figured out an estimate of how much profit she would make.
4. Her goal was to make a hundred dollars.

capital   demand   investing
estimate   profit   goal

Developing Background and Skills
Predict Outcomes

When you go into a store that sells school supplies, you expect to find things such as notebooks, pens, and pencils. There are usually more of these supplies on display at the end of August than in the middle of July.

Store owners know that students usually return to school in September. They also know that students will need school supplies. Based on what they know, the store owners **predict** that they will sell more school supplies at one time than another.

Store owners make predictions all the time. They make predictions about what their customers will buy. Then they predict how much they will sell. Finally, they use their predictions to buy things for their stores.

Making predictions is an important business skill. It is also an important reading skill. You make predictions as you read when you think about what will happen next.

Based on what a writer tells you about a character, you can make predictions about what that character will probably do. Using information the writer gives you, you can predict what the next part of a story will be about.

In the next selection, you will meet a character named Amy. You will find out how Amy uses her business skills to make predictions. As you read, try to predict what Amy will do.

Amy's Capital Idea

Elizabeth James and Carol Barkin

Amy Collado looked around the dinner table at her family. "I've been thinking about that camping trip at the end of the summer," she said. "I sure wish I could go."

Her brother Danny helped himself to another piece of fruit. "But Amy, that trip costs a hundred dollars. Where are you going to get that much money?"

"I don't know," Amy said. "Do you have any ideas?"

Danny thought for a while. "How about making birdhouses like the one you made last summer? People would buy those."

"Great idea!" Amy said eagerly. "There's lots of scrap wood in the basement. I'll go see if there's any paint left over."

Amy ran down the stairs, but in a few moments she was back. "I just remembered," she said. "It took me almost all summer to make that birdhouse. I'll never make enough money that way."

Danny said, "I see what you mean. But how about that hand-painted scarf you made? That didn't take any time at all."

"Oh, Danny, no one's wearing those anymore. There's no demand—I couldn't even give them away! But wait—Suzie asked me to make her a necklace like this one. I could make a lot of them. Do you think I'd find many buyers?"

Danny laughed. "Sure! But don't you remember? You spent your whole allowance on beads and wire to make that necklace."

"I guess that won't work either," sighed Amy. "I'd have to charge too much and no one could afford them."

Standing up, Danny said, "Well, I've got to go. Keep thinking—you'll come up with something."

Amy's business goal is to end up with more money than she started with. This increase in money is called a *profit*. But of course, all the money received by a business is not profit. Some of the money must be used to pay the expenses of running the business and making the product. After all these expenses are paid, the money that is left over is the profit.

How can Amy decide what kind of business to start? She needs to produce something that other people want to buy. If she produces a large supply of things nobody wants, she won't be able to sell them for very much money. Her profit will then be very small. So Amy has to make sure there is a demand for whatever she decides to sell.

On her way to the library to look for a book on how to make money, Amy passed the pet store. Dozens of empty glass fishbowls were stacked everywhere. "Those are just like the bowl I used to make Mom's terrarium," Amy said to herself. "I wonder if I could make more terrariums and sell them?"

She went inside and found the owner, Mr. Buckley, sweeping up broken glass. "That's the third one I've broken today!" he exclaimed. "There's no room to turn around in this shop!"

"What are you going to do with all these fishbowls?" asked Amy.

"I don't know!" Mr. Buckley answered. "I ordered them for the town picnic, but they decided not to have the ping-pong toss. Now I'm stuck with them!"

"How much are you selling them for?" Amy asked.

"You can have them for what I paid for them— a quarter each. Do you want some?" he asked eagerly.

"Maybe," Amy replied. She ran out of the store and all the way home.

At home Amy pulled out a pad and a pencil. "Let's see," she said to herself, "I bet I could sell a whole lot of terrariums. All of Mom's friends thought the one I made for her was great. How much should I charge?" She thought a moment. "The flower shop sells terrariums just a little bigger for $5. If I sell mine for $3 each, that will be a bargain. If I sell 50 terrariums, I'll make $150. I'd better figure out how much these terrariums will cost to make."

50 fishbowls @ $.25	$ 12.50
potting soil and pebbles for 50 terrariums	5.00
plants for 50 terrariums	+ 10.00
total cost	$27.50
income from 50 terrariums @ $3	$ 150.00
expenses	− 27.50
profit	$ 122.50

"I'll have extra money after I pay for the camping trip," she thought happily. But before investing in 50 fishbowls, Amy decided to find out how much demand there was for her terrariums.

Amy spent the afternoon going around her block. By the end of the day she had found eight customers. That night she explained her problem to Danny. "Eight sales in one afternoon is pretty good," she told him, "but I've already covered our whole neighborhood. How am I going to find more customers?"

"Why don't you ask Mr. Buckley if you can use a corner of his store?" Danny suggested.

"He doesn't have any room. That's why he's selling the fishbowls so cheaply," Amy replied.

Danny had run out of ideas, but suddenly Amy exclaimed, "I'll go to the Saturday swap meet! People sell all kinds of things there!"

"Good idea," said Danny. "You'd better get started!"

The next days were busy ones for Amy. She wanted her terrariums to be beautiful and she spent a lot of time planning what plants to use. Suddenly she realized she only had $15 in her money jar. She couldn't buy all the bowls and plants and soil she needed for 50 terrariums with $15. She needed $27.50. "I guess I'll just buy half the stuff and make 25 terrariums first," she decided. "I forgot that I had to make the terrariums before I could sell them."

Any kind of business needs money to start with. This money is called *capital*. As Amy found out, the raw materials must be bought before the finished products can be made and sold. Amy had a total of $15 capital to invest in her business. When she spent $13.75 (half of $27.50) for raw materials, she invested almost all of her capital. This meant that until she made her first terrarium and sold it, she had only $1.25.

After Amy had enough materials for 25 terrariums, she quickly made the eight terrariums her neighbors had ordered. When she had delivered them, she had $24 from her sales to add to the $1.25.

"This is great," Amy said to herself. She worked harder than ever getting ready for the swap meet. By Saturday she had 12 terrariums all finished.

"They look great, Amy," said Danny. "You'll probably make a lot of money."

Amy was busy packing the terrariums in her wagon. "I hope so," she replied. "But I need some help getting them over to the swap meet. Will you take the back end of the wagon?"

"Sure," he said. "But it'll cost you a quarter. Labor isn't free, you know."

When Amy and Danny got to the swap meet, they chose a good spot and began unpacking the wagon.

Amy was putting up her sign

when the manager of the swap meet came up.

"Do you have a permit?" he asked Amy.

"No," answered Amy in surprise. "I didn't know I needed one."

"Oh, yes," the manager said. "It costs $2.25 but it's good for the whole summer."

As he walked away, Amy said to Danny, "I'll have to refigure my expenses when I get home. Here's your 25 cents, Danny."

"Thanks," said Danny. "And good luck."

Amy smiled and turned to greet her first customer.

As the afternoon wore on, Amy sold six, then seven, then nine of her terrariums. She was feeling happy but tired when she stepped backward and suddenly heard a crash. One of the three remaining terrariums had smashed to the ground!

"Oh, no!" Amy cried as she stared at the mess. Even the plants were broken beyond repair.

When Amy got home, she began to enter the day's expenses and sales.

Amy's Terrarium Business Record Sheet $15.00

ORIGINAL CAPITAL
EXPENSES
  25 fishbowls $ 6.25
  soil and pebbles   2.50
  plants   + 5.00   −13.75
                                 $ 13.75   1.25

CAPITAL   + 24.00
SALES 8 × $3.00 = $24.00 $ 25.25
CAPITAL

EXPENSES $ .25
  labor   + 2.25   − 2.50
  permit $ 2.50   22.75
                                             + 33.00
CAPITAL $ 55.75
SALES 11 × $3.00 = $33.00
CAPITAL

On another piece of paper Amy figured out how much money she would make from her terrarium business. When she started, she had figured she would make $122.50 profit from 50 terrariums. Now she had to change this estimate. Her new estimated profit sheet looked like this:

ESTIMATED INCOME
    50 terrariums @ $ 3.00
ESTIMATED EXPENSES
    raw materials $ 13.75 x 2 = $27.50 $150.00
    labor $.25 x 4 =   1.00
    permit   +   2.25
                                         30.75
                                                    - 30.75
    loss of 1 terrarium $119.25
ESTIMATED PROFIT   -   3.00
                                    $3.00 $116.25

What other kinds of costs does a business have? Like Amy, most business owners sometimes have damaged goods that cannot be sold. The money they expected to receive for these goods must be counted as a loss. Amy's finished product was a $3.00 terrarium, not just an empty fishbowl and some plants and a pile of dirt. When the finished terrarium was broken, she lost a $3.00 sale.

You may have already figured out that if Amy had broken all of the 20 terrariums she made, her business loss would have been $60.00. This is much more money than she had spent on business expenses. But Amy's time and labor are worth money, too—the selling price of her terrariums must repay her for the work as well as the capital she has invested.

Danny peered over Amy's shoulder. "You're doing really well," he said. "You'll be able to go on that camping trip after all."

"I hope so," Amy replied, "but I'll have to be careful not to break anything else!"

Questions

1. Why did Amy decide to start a business?
2. Why did Danny suggest that Amy might want to make hand-painted scarves?
3. What is the difference between profits and expenses?
4. If you had a business, what kind would it be? What would you have to do before you started your business?

Applying Reading Skills

Number your paper from 1 to 4. Read each incomplete sentence below. Based on what you know from reading "Amy's Capital Idea," finish each sentence. Write each complete sentence on your paper.

1. Amy decided not to make birdhouses, because she predicted that ____.
2. Mr. Buckley bought 50 fishbowls because he predicted that ____.
3. Amy predicted that $3.00 would be a good price for the terrariums because she knew that ____.
4. Amy had to refigure her expenses after the swap meet because she had not predicted that ____.

PREPARING FOR READING

Learning Vocabulary

1. Marshall was <u>dependable</u>, so his parents said he could try to find a job.
2. Mr. Caldwell was <u>arranging</u> fruit when Marshall went to see him in his store.
3. <u>Professional</u> bike riders <u>participate</u> in bicycle races.
4. To win <u>championships</u>, they must often ride fast for long distances.

dependable   arranging   professional
participate   championships

Developing Background and Skills
Predict Outcomes

Mr. Rondo asked his students to write a paragraph about what they like to do in their spare time.

Susan wrote:

   I love the outdoors. My uncle has some horses, and I spend almost every weekend at his place. I get to ride the horses and take care of them. I'm learning a lot about them.

Martin wrote:

I play my guitar every day. Practicing is something I really enjoy. I get together with a few other players once a week to work on songs. We hope to play for a school dance this year.

Then Mr. Rondo asked the students to think about the kind of work they might like to do in the future. He told them to think about the jobs that were related to their interests.

Mr. Rondo wanted the students to make **predictions** about the kind of work they might enjoy doing. He asked them to list two or three jobs they might want to have.

What jobs do you think Susan and Martin listed? Some predictions for Susan might include these jobs: horse trainer, veterinarian, professional rider or racer. Martin's list probably included some of these jobs: musician, music teacher, song writer.

The next story is based on the life of a real person named Marshall. As you read, think about what was important to him. Then, before you read the conclusion, try to predict what Marshall might do when he grows up.

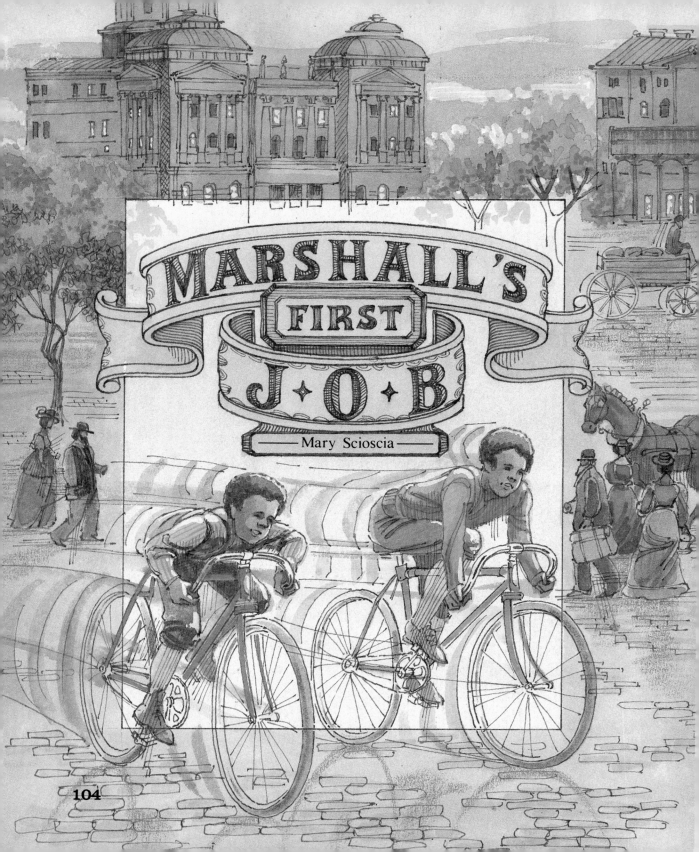

MARSHALL'S FIRST JOB

Mary Scioscia

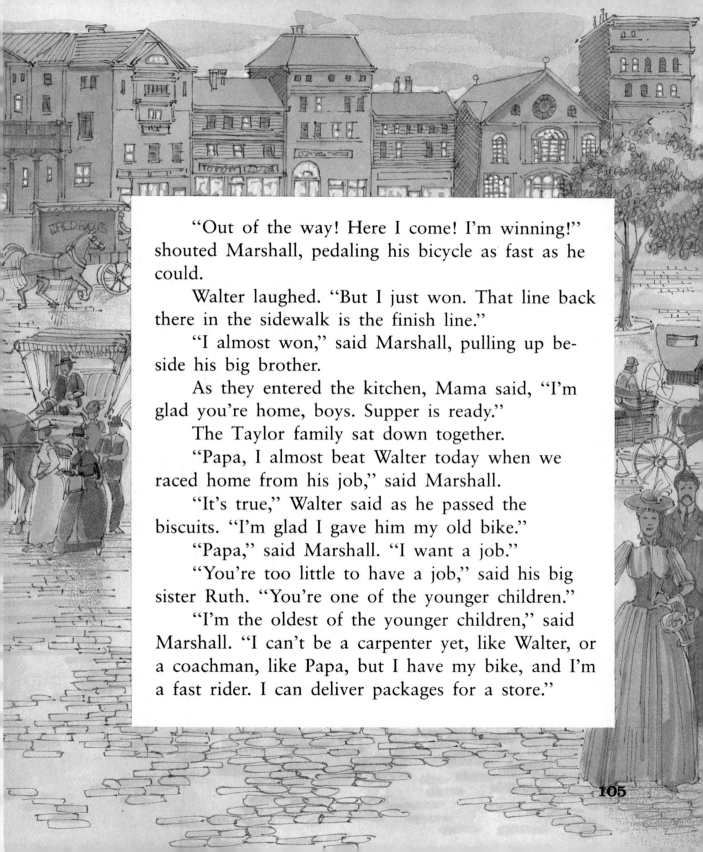

"Out of the way! Here I come! I'm winning!" shouted Marshall, pedaling his bicycle as fast as he could.

Walter laughed. "But I just won. That line back there in the sidewalk is the finish line."

"I almost won," said Marshall, pulling up beside his big brother.

As they entered the kitchen, Mama said, "I'm glad you're home, boys. Supper is ready."

The Taylor family sat down together.

"Papa, I almost beat Walter today when we raced home from his job," said Marshall.

"It's true," Walter said as he passed the biscuits. "I'm glad I gave him my old bike."

"Papa," said Marshall. "I want a job."

"You're too little to have a job," said his big sister Ruth. "You're one of the younger children."

"I'm the oldest of the younger children," said Marshall. "I can't be a carpenter yet, like Walter, or a coachman, like Papa, but I have my bike, and I'm a fast rider. I can deliver packages for a store."

105

"Maybe," said Papa.

"Can I try this Saturday?"

Papa looked at Mama. "What do you think?" he asked.

Mama nodded. "He's small," she said, "but he's a good bicycle rider, and dependable."

"Yes. You may try to find a job, son," said Papa.

"Not this Saturday," said his little brother, Carlton. "You promised to take me to the bicycle store, Marshall, and to teach me the bicycle tricks you made up."

"Those tricks? They don't amount to a hill of beans, Carlton."

"Marshall, you promised," complained Carlton.

"All right. We'll go to the bicycle store *after* I look for a job. I'll teach you the bicycle tricks, too."

On Saturday morning Marshall biked downtown. He went to Mercer's dry goods store, the biggest store on Main Street. Inside the store, Mrs. Mercer stood behind the counter.

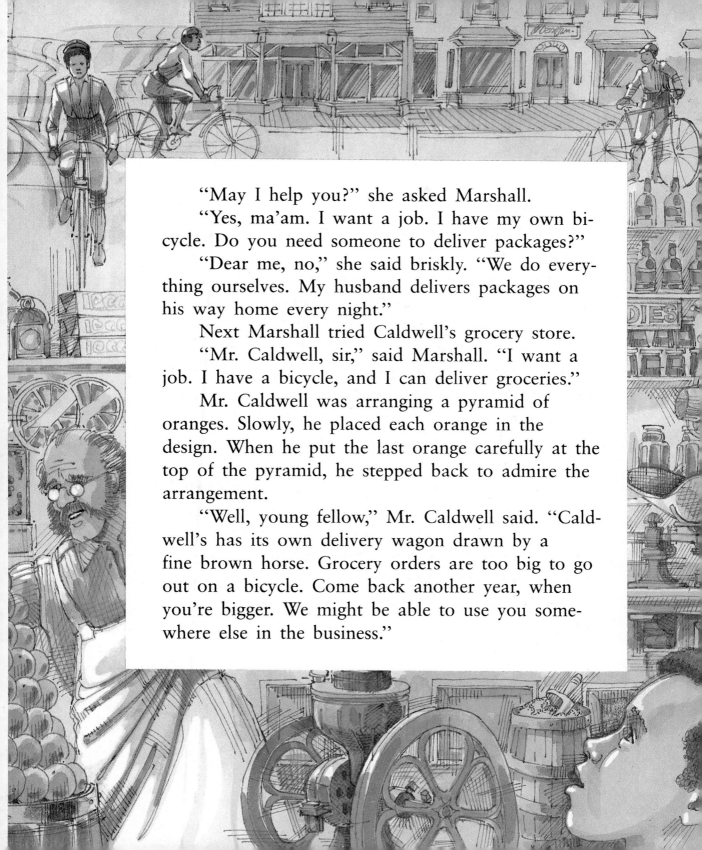

"May I help you?" she asked Marshall.

"Yes, ma'am. I want a job. I have my own bicycle. Do you need someone to deliver packages?"

"Dear me, no," she said briskly. "We do everything ourselves. My husband delivers packages on his way home every night."

Next Marshall tried Caldwell's grocery store.

"Mr. Caldwell, sir," said Marshall. "I want a job. I have a bicycle, and I can deliver groceries."

Mr. Caldwell was arranging a pyramid of oranges. Slowly, he placed each orange in the design. When he put the last orange carefully at the top of the pyramid, he stepped back to admire the arrangement.

"Well, young fellow," Mr. Caldwell said. "Caldwell's has its own delivery wagon drawn by a fine brown horse. Grocery orders are too big to go out on a bicycle. Come back another year, when you're bigger. We might be able to use you somewhere else in the business."

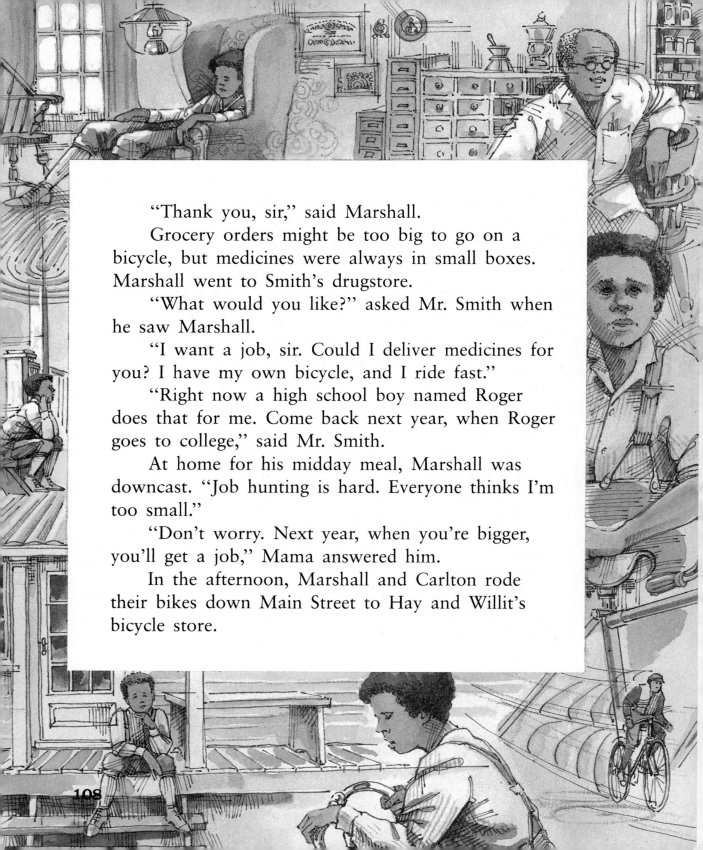

"Thank you, sir," said Marshall.

Grocery orders might be too big to go on a bicycle, but medicines were always in small boxes. Marshall went to Smith's drugstore.

"What would you like?" asked Mr. Smith when he saw Marshall.

"I want a job, sir. Could I deliver medicines for you? I have my own bicycle, and I ride fast."

"Right now a high school boy named Roger does that for me. Come back next year, when Roger goes to college," said Mr. Smith.

At home for his midday meal, Marshall was downcast. "Job hunting is hard. Everyone thinks I'm too small."

"Don't worry. Next year, when you're bigger, you'll get a job," Mama answered him.

In the afternoon, Marshall and Carlton rode their bikes down Main Street to Hay and Willit's bicycle store.

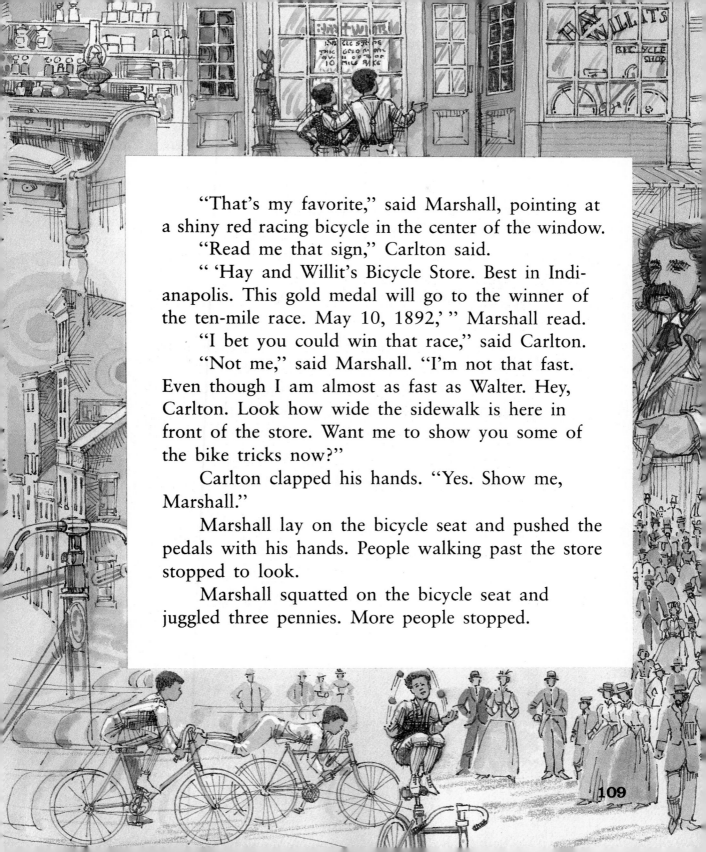

"That's my favorite," said Marshall, pointing at a shiny red racing bicycle in the center of the window.

"Read me that sign," Carlton said.

" 'Hay and Willit's Bicycle Store. Best in Indianapolis. This gold medal will go to the winner of the ten-mile race. May 10, 1892,' " Marshall read.

"I bet you could win that race," said Carlton.

"Not me," said Marshall. "I'm not that fast. Even though I am almost as fast as Walter. Hey, Carlton. Look how wide the sidewalk is here in front of the store. Want me to show you some of the bike tricks now?"

Carlton clapped his hands. "Yes. Show me, Marshall."

Marshall lay on the bicycle seat and pushed the pedals with his hands. People walking past the store stopped to look.

Marshall squatted on the bicycle seat and juggled three pennies. More people stopped.

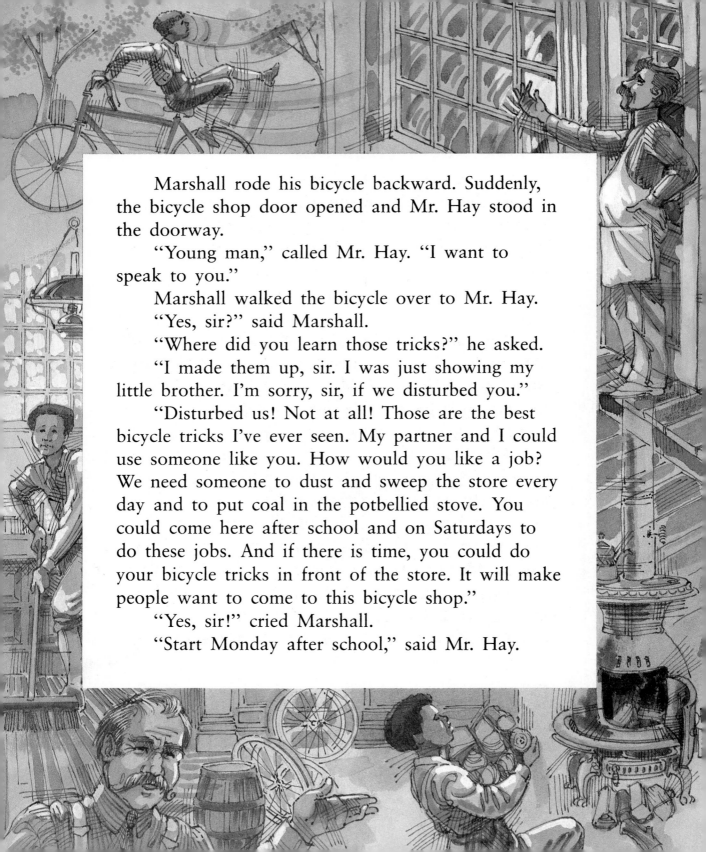

Marshall rode his bicycle backward. Suddenly, the bicycle shop door opened and Mr. Hay stood in the doorway.

"Young man," called Mr. Hay. "I want to speak to you."

Marshall walked the bicycle over to Mr. Hay.

"Yes, sir?" said Marshall.

"Where did you learn those tricks?" he asked.

"I made them up, sir. I was just showing my little brother. I'm sorry, sir, if we disturbed you."

"Disturbed us! Not at all! Those are the best bicycle tricks I've ever seen. My partner and I could use someone like you. How would you like a job? We need someone to dust and sweep the store every day and to put coal in the potbellied stove. You could come here after school and on Saturdays to do these jobs. And if there is time, you could do your bicycle tricks in front of the store. It will make people want to come to this bicycle shop."

"Yes, sir!" cried Marshall.

"Start Monday after school," said Mr. Hay.

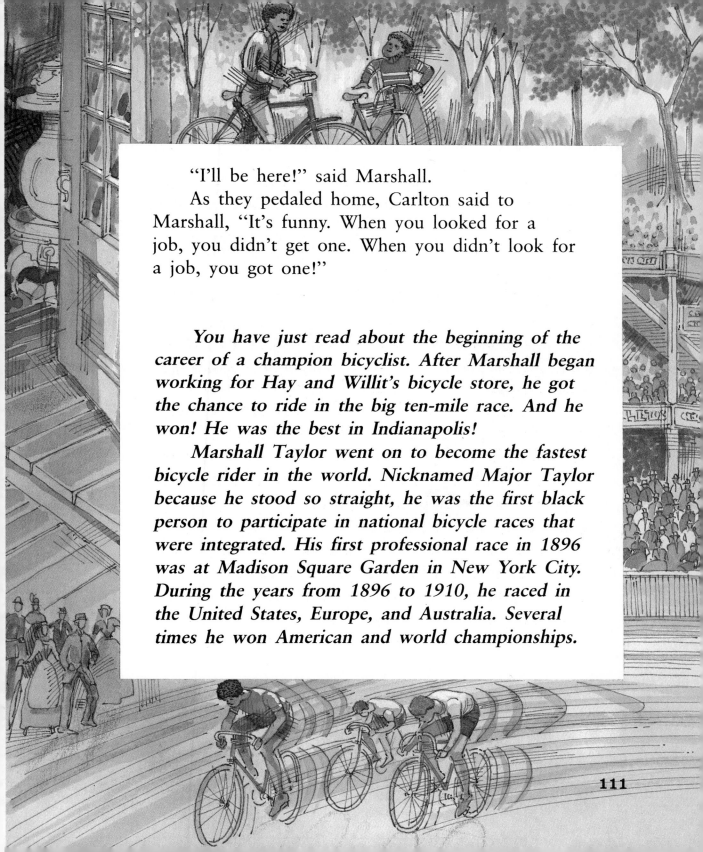

"I'll be here!" said Marshall.

As they pedaled home, Carlton said to Marshall, "It's funny. When you looked for a job, you didn't get one. When you didn't look for a job, you got one!"

You have just read about the beginning of the career of a champion bicyclist. After Marshall began working for Hay and Willit's bicycle store, he got the chance to ride in the big ten-mile race. And he won! He was the best in Indianapolis!

Marshall Taylor went on to become the fastest bicycle rider in the world. Nicknamed Major Taylor because he stood so straight, he was the first black person to participate in national bicycle races that were integrated. His first professional race in 1896 was at Madison Square Garden in New York City. During the years from 1896 to 1910, he raced in the United States, Europe, and Australia. Several times he won American and world championships.

Questions

1. Where did Marshall go to look for a job? Name the places in order.
2. How did Carlton feel about Marshall?
3. Do you think Marshall will help bring more business to Hay and Willit's Bicycle Store? Why or why not?
4. What are your hobbies or interests? What jobs can you think of that are related to your interests?

Applying Reading Skills

Number your paper from 1 to 3. Read each incomplete sentence below. Based on what you have learned about Marshall, choose the best ending for each sentence. Write each complete sentence on your paper.

1. If Marshall had not gotten a job at Hay and Willit's Bicycle Store, he probably would have _____.
   a. kept looking for a job
   b. given up
   c. waited until next year to try again

2. When Marshall won the ten-mile race, he probably _____.
   a. decided he didn't need to practice any more
   b. gained confidence in his ability to become a bicycle racer
   c. thought it didn't mean very much

3. As Marshall got older, he probably _____.
   a. entered many different bicycle races
   b. decided to become a professional bicycle racer
   c. both of the above

Bicycle Riding

My feet rise
off the planet,
pedal wheels of steel
that sparkle as
they spin me through
the open space I feel
winging out
to galaxies
far beyond the sun,
where bicycles
are satellites,
their orbits never done.

Sandra Liatsos

UNIT TWO

LEVEL 11

TEAMWORK

PREPARING FOR READING

Learning Vocabulary

1. The Marcoses expected Lila's <u>cooperation</u> when they needed help with the twins.
2. Lila didn't want to be <u>selfish</u>, so she planned to help out in the afternoons.
3. Even though birthdays usually made her happy, Lila was <u>depressed</u> on her birthday.
4. She was <u>positively</u> certain that no celebrations had been planned.
5. Lila tried to act <u>mature</u> and not show how upset she was.

cooperation   selfish   depressed
positively   mature

Developing Background and Skills
Draw Conclusions

Mr. Roberts was sitting on his porch when he saw Michael walking down the street. Michael often visited Mr. Roberts and ran errands for him.

"Can you stop for a minute, Michael?" called Mr. Roberts. "I have something for you."

"I'll be right there," Michael said.

Mr. Roberts went into the house and brought out a package wrapped in blue paper. He handed it to Michael. "I want you to take this," he said.

"Sure, Mr. Roberts," said Michael. "I'll be glad to deliver the package for you."

"No, Michael," Mr. Roberts laughed. "The package is for you. It's a present to thank you for all your help."

Michael was surprised when Mr. Roberts explained that the package was a present. Based on his past experience and on what Mr. Roberts said, he decided that Mr. Roberts wanted him to deliver the package. Michael was **drawing a conclusion,** or making a decision or judgment based on information.

Drawing conclusions is an important reading skill. As you read, you gather information about characters or events. You can use the information the writer presents to draw conclusions.

In the next selection, you will meet a girl named Lila. Notice how she uses information to draw some important conclusions about her family and friends.

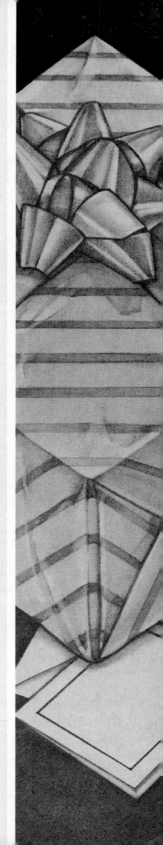

Happy Nothingday to Me

Marilyn Z. Wilkes

"I can't believe it! My own family!" Lila wailed into the telephone to Kim. "It's going to be my birthday, and they don't even care!"

"Sure they do," said Kim. "You've got a great family. They're just a little busy right now."

"Just because my mom had twins is no excuse," said Lila. "Who asked her to bring them home four days before my birthday? It's bad enough that I had to be born a week before Christmas. I might as well not even *have* a birthday!"

"Why don't you tell them how you feel?" asked Kim.

"I can't," said Lila. "My dad gave us this big speech about cooperation and teamwork. I don't want to seem selfish. I know it's a tough time for him and Mom. Taking care of the twins isn't easy. They never sleep at the same time. One of them is always hungry or wet or something. Roberto needs attention, too." Lila's brother was seven.

"I could call your parents and remind them, or ask my mom to do it," Kim offered.

"I don't want them to do something because they were reminded," said Lila. "It wouldn't be the same."

"Well, maybe you can sleep over Friday night," said Kim, "or I could come to your house."

"Grandma Celia is sharing my room for the next two weeks. She came to help out. I want to spend time with her, and I have to help, too."

Lila sighed and hung up. So much for her birthday.

"Happy nothingday to me," she muttered.

"Gee, I was sorry to hear about your birthday, Lila," Allison said the next morning. Allison's desk was next to Lila's in Mrs. Horst's fifth grade class. "Kim told me your mom and dad forgot all about it. How awful! I'd have a party for you, but I'll be busy this weekend."

"I will, too," said Lorraine. "Sorry."

"That's okay," said Lila. She sighed.

"Feel terrible about your birthday," Jessica scribbled to Lila during math. "I'll be thinking about you *all weekend*!!!"

Lila felt depressed. None of her friends would celebrate her birthday with her. A lump formed in her throat. Just then Mrs. Horst called on her to solve a long division problem on the board. Lila swallowed hard and walked to the front of the room. She'd try to be mature about the whole thing. After all, she was almost eleven, even if nobody cared.

On Friday morning, Lila picked at her breakfast. Across the table, Roberto was drowning his corn flakes in milk. Both babies were crying furiously in their cribs. At the stove, Grandma Celia was making scrambled eggs.

Lila's mother dashed in and out of the kitchen carrying babies, bottles, and diapers. "Hurry or you'll miss the school bus, kids," she said. "And take the bus home after school, Lila. I'll need help this afternoon."

Lila sighed and put on her jacket.

"Have a nice day," called Grandma Celia as Lila went out the door.

"Sure," thought Lila.

"Listen, everybody, are we all set for after
school?" asked Kim. She stood in the cafeteria lunch
line with Jessica, Lorraine, and Allison.

"My mom is picking us up so we can get to your house first and get things ready," said Jessica.

"I've got balloons and crepe paper in my desk," said Allison.

"I've got the party favors," said Lorraine.

"My mom and I baked the cake last night," said Kim. "Now all we have to do is get Lila to walk home with me instead of taking the bus after school."

"I still don't see why we couldn't just call the Marcoses and tell them we're having a surprise party for Lila," said Jessica. "Then they'd say she could come over."

"Lila didn't want me to call," said Kim. "Can you imagine parents forgetting their own child's birthday?"

"Shhh! Here she comes!" whispered Lorraine.

"Why didn't you wait for me?" asked Lila as she hurried up with her lunch tray.

"Sorry, Lila," said Allison. "By the way, happy birthday."

"Thanks a heap," muttered Lila. The other girls grinned at each other.

The afternoon went by fast enough. When the bell rang, Lila grabbed her books and ran to get her jacket.

"Mrs. Horst, my jacket is missing!" she yelled. She looked angrily around the room. She couldn't

believe it. This was positively the worst day of her
life. She could hear the school buses pulling away
as she searched the coat rack one more time.

"I'll help you look," said Kim. "Here it is," she
said after a few minutes, "behind this box of books.
How did it get there, I wonder?"

"Somebody probably thought it would be a
good joke," said Lila. "Now I've missed the bus."

"I guess you'll have to walk home with me,"
said Kim, grinning. "You can call your mom from
my house and tell her what happened. Let's go."

"SURPRISE!" everyone shouted as Kim and Lila walked into Kim's living room. Lila wasn't just surprised, she was stunned. There were balloons and colored streamers everywhere. Kim's mother brought in a big cake with candles on it. "Happy birthday, Lila," she said with a smile.

Lila smiled back. "Oh, thank you, Mrs. Park," she said. Then she started to cry.

"Cut it out!" yelled Jessica. "We went to all this trouble so you'd be *happy!*"

"I am," sobbed Lila. "You're the best friends anybody ever had."

"True," said Allison. "Now, blow out the candles." Lila blew.

"This is too good to be true," said Lila. "I'll just call my mom to let her know."

"But Mom," she said on the telephone. "It wasn't my fault."

"No buts, Lila," said her mother sternly. "Be home in one hour—no more!"

Even Mrs. Park was surprised. "I think we'll all drive Lila home," she said. "We'll take some balloons and birthday cake with us."

When she got to her house, Lila opened the front door. Something was odd. Except for the sound of a baby crying, it was totally quiet. There were no lights on either, even though the sun was beginning to set.

"I'm home," she called. "Where is everybody?"

"In here," Grandma Celia answered from the back of the house.

Lila, Mrs. Park, and the girls walked through the dark house. Suddenly the lights came on.

"SURPRISE!" yelled Lila's mother and father, Roberto, and Grandma Celia. Hanging on the den wall was a big sign that said, HAPPY BIRTHDAY, LILA. On the table was a big cake.

"You didn't forget!" said Lila.

"Forget? I could hardly keep from telling you when you left this morning," said Grandma Celia. "You looked so sad. But I promised your mama and papa I would cooperate."

"I helped color the sign," said Roberto.

"Everybody helped," said Lila's mother.

"We wanted you to know that no matter how many birthdays there are in this house, each one will always be important," said Mr. Marcos.

"Now she's going to cry again," said Jessica. But Lila just looked puzzled.

"What's wrong?" asked her mother.

"The twins," said Lila. "They're so quiet. Are they all right?"

Everyone tiptoed into the twins' room. The babies lay peacefully asleep in their cribs.

"It's the first time in four days!" said Mrs. Marcos gratefully. "Now, that's what I call cooperation!"

Questions

1. Why didn't Lila remind her family about her birthday?
2. What arrangements did Lila's friends make to surprise Lila on her birthday?
3. How did Lila probably feel when her mom told her to come home from the Parks' house in an hour?
4. If you wanted to surprise your friend on his or her birthday, what plans would you make?

Applying Reading Skills

Number your paper from 1 to 4. Then use complete sentences to answer each question below.

1. Why did Lila conclude that her family had forgotten her birthday?
2. Why did Lila conclude that none of her friends would celebrate her birthday with her?
3. When Kim found Lila's jacket behind a box of books, what did Lila conclude?
4. What part or parts in the story led you to conclude that Lila's friends were planning a surprise party for her?

Between Birthdays

My birthdays take so long to start.
They come along a year apart.
It's worse than waiting for a bus;
I fear I used to fret and fuss,
But now, when by impatience vexed
Between one birthday and the next,
I think of all that I have seen
That keeps on happening in between,
The songs I've heard, the things I've done,
Make my unbirthdays not so un-

Ogden Nash

PREPARING FOR READING

Learning Vocabulary

1. Before a baseball game begins, a <u>crew</u> works to get the field ready.
2. <u>Vendors</u> sell <u>souvenirs</u> and <u>refreshments</u> in the stands.
3. <u>Ushers</u> lead people to their seats.
4. The day's <u>attendance</u> is <u>computed</u> by counting the number of tickets sold.

crew   vendors   souvenirs   refreshments
ushers   attendance   computed

Developing Background and Skills
Graphs

Read the paragraph below and think of a good title for it.

There are 150 workers at Reed's Ballpark. Sixty people work as vendors, and forty work as ushers. There are twenty ground-crew workers and ten ticket takers. Twenty other people work at different jobs around the park.

Something like "Workers at Reed's Ballpark" may be the title you chose. All of the information in the paragraph is about the people who work at Reed's Ballpark.

A writer could have presented the same information about the workers at the ballpark on a graph.

A **bar graph** is one kind of graph. Reading a bar graph can help you to make comparisions.

The bar graph below presents the information you read in the paragraph on page 130.

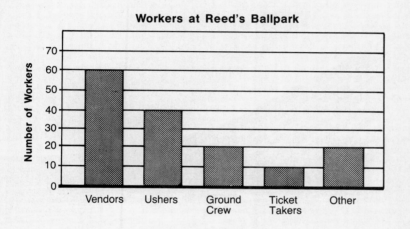

Workers at Reed's Ballpark

What do the numbers on the left side of the graph show? What does the bar above *Vendors* show?

How many ushers work at Reed's Ballpark? How many more ground-crew workers than ticket takers work there?

In the next selection, you will see two graphs. One is a bar graph. The other is a line graph. Study both carefully.

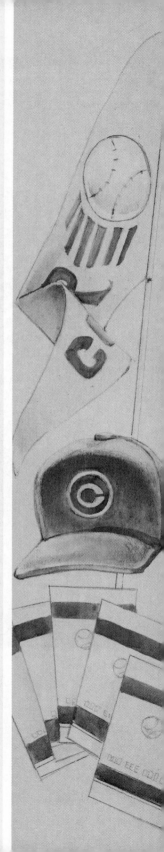

THE BALLPARK

WILLIAM JASPERSOHN

A ballpark is never quite empty. At 6 A.M., the pigeons in Fenway Park stir from the grandstands. Fluttering, they drop for bits of popcorn under the brightly painted seats.

The ballpark is quiet. But the hush will soon be broken because there is a baseball game today. At two-fifteen, the Boston Red Sox will play the Kansas City Royals. Thirty-five thousand people will view the game in the park. For Fenway Park's five hundred workers the day will be long and hard. But for the moment silence fills the seats.

The first workers to arrive are the ground-crew members. They are in charge of grooming the field and taking care of the ballpark overall. At seven o'clock, thirteen of them gather along the third baseline. They will "dump" the tarpaulin that had covered the infield all night. "Dumping the tarp" means getting all the water off it. The ground crew does this by folding the tarp over and carrying it into right field to dry. It takes at least six people to move the tarp.

At seven-thirty the commissary opens. That's where the refreshments and souvenirs are stored and prepared.

Soon the change for the vendors who sell souvenirs and refreshments arrives from a bank by truck. The man who brings in the money is in charge of the vendors. He gives them their selling assignments and looks over them during the game.

Minutes later, trucks start rolling up with all kinds of deliveries marked FENWAY PARK. Then the workers get busy preparing the food.

Meanwhile, the ground crew is hard at work. Every one of the forty workers has a special job. One worker drives the tooth harrow, a machine that digs up the soil on the basepaths. Then the soil is raked flat. The main job of the ground crew is to make the field as level and smooth as possible. At least every other day, the ground crew mows the infield grass to one-half inch. The outfield grass is mowed to one inch. Between mowings, the grass is watered and fertilized.

Once the infield has been raked, it is rolled and watered to pack it slightly. This keeps down the dust. Then the bases are set and the baselines drawn. Home plate gets painted.

The last big morning job for the ground crew is folding the tarpaulin and rolling it onto its steel cylinder. During games, the tarpaulin is stored along the first baseline. The ground crew sits nearby. If it rains during a game, they cover the infield quickly, before it gets soaked. The crew can spread the huge tarp in less than two minutes. By ten o'clock, the field is almost ready for batting practice.

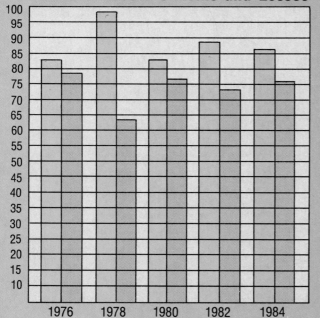

Red Sox Record of Wins and Losses

| | 1976 | 1978 | 1980 | 1982 | 1984 |

Number of Games Won: ☐
Number of Games Lost: ☐

While the outdoor work has been going on, a truck has arrived. It brings the uniforms, bats, and other equipment of the Kansas City Royals. The truck parks outside the visiting-team clubhouse. A crew quickly unloads the trunks and bags.

Inside the clubhouse, the visiting-team equipment manager unpacks the bags. He hangs each player's uniform in a locker. His job is to make sure that the visiting players have everything they need.

At ten forty-five, the ushers arrive. They will help people find their seats at today's game. In all, there are eighty ushers. They change into their red jackets, blue pants, and blue caps. In the commissary, the vendors start signing in for work, too.

The most important arrivals, of course, are the players. All the Red Sox players drive to work in their own cars. At eleven o'clock, they arrive and quickly enter a side door that leads to the Red Sox clubhouse.

At eleven-fifty, the whole team is dressed and ready. In ones and twos, they walk down the steps from the clubhouse, through a long tunnel, and out through the dugout to batting practice.

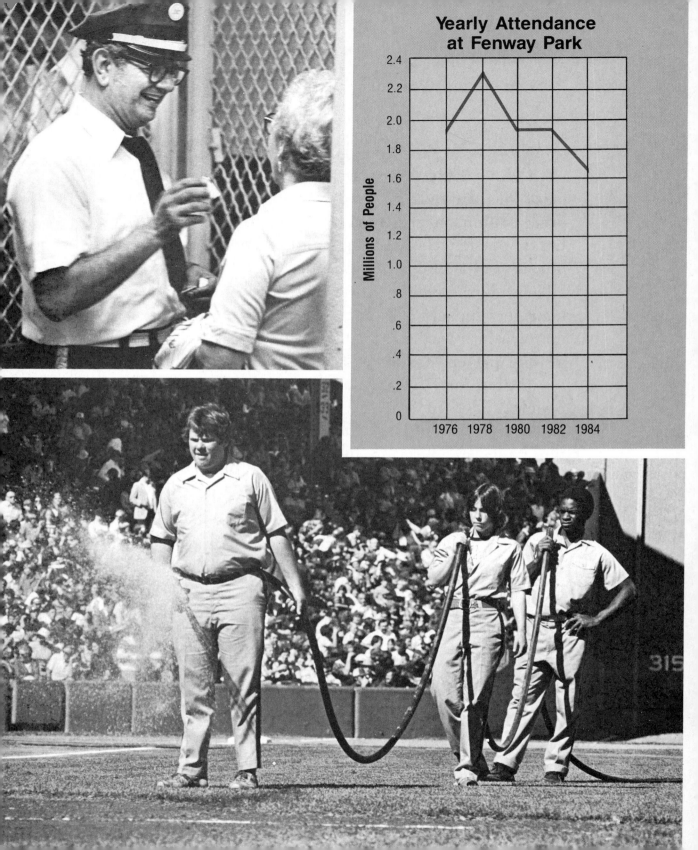

Yearly Attendance at Fenway Park

Finally, at twelve-thirty, managers around the park shout, "Open 'em up!" The ticket takers open the gates. The crowd starts to stream in. The day's attendance is computed from the number of tickets sold. But to keep track of how many people actually enter the ballpark, there are counting machines called turnstiles. They are located inside the gates. On a busy afternoon a single ticket taker may collect as many as three thousand tickets at one gate.

By twelve forty-five the Red Sox have finished batting practice. The Royals have taken the field. Most Red Sox players return to the clubhouse to change their uniforms, rest, and cool off.

The umpires wait upstairs in the locker room until game time. The umpires work for no team. They are paid by the American League of Professional Baseball. The home plate umpire is in charge of the game balls. These are always supplied by the home team. The home plate umpire gets sixty game baseballs. To make the baseballs easier to see and less slippery, he rubs them with a special mud.

It is almost two o'clock. The ground crew now grooms the field once more. They give the basepaths a final hosing. The crowd is seated, thirty-five thousand strong. Both teams are in their dugouts, warmed up and ready.

At two-fifteen the Red Sox take the field. Everyone stands and sings "The Star-Spangled Banner."

Then the umpire sweeps home plate with a tiny pocket broom. He snaps on his mask and shouts, "Play ball!" Finally, seven hours and twenty-one minutes after the ground crew dumped the tarp, the Red Sox pitcher steps up on the mound. The catcher waits for him to lean in, then gives him the sign: one finger, a fast ball. The pitcher winds up and throws the first pitch. It's a strike. The crowd roars. The game has begun.

Questions

1. What are two jobs of the ground-crew members?
2. Why does the ground crew have to stay during the game?
3. Why do you think the umpires do not work for any team?
4. If you could work at a ballpark, what job would you like to have? Why?

Applying Reading Skills

Number your paper from 1 to 5. Use the graphs on pages 138 and 140 to answer the questions below. Write the answers on your paper.

1. In what year did the Red Sox win the most games?
2. In what two years did they win the same number of games?
3. About how many people attended Red Sox games in Fenway Park in 1980?
4. During what two-year period did attendance at Fenway Park increase?
5. Use both graphs for this question. Why do you think attendance at Fenway Park was highest in 1978?

PREPARING FOR READING

Learning Vocabulary

1. The Blazers' pitcher and their catcher worked out a signal <u>system</u> to use during the game against the Cubs.
2. In the sixth inning, the Blazers took the coach's <u>advice</u> and <u>deliberately</u> let a runner reach first base.
3. The last of the sixth was filled with <u>confusion</u>.
4. Two of the Cubs ran home before Roger <u>recovered</u> the ball.
5. A <u>victory</u> in the game would mean the pennant.

system   advice   deliberately
confusion   recovered   victory

Developing Background and Skills
Facts and Opinions

If you listen to the fans as they are leaving a baseball stadium, you may hear some confusing conversation.

"The Cubs just didn't have it today. But they never do."

"The Cubs looked great today. If some of those close calls had gone their way, it could have been a victory!"

"I'm not sure what to think about those Cubs. They can make the greatest plays and the biggest goofs in the same game!"

How did the Cubs do? The fans have more than one opinion. The final score and the number of runs and errors recorded for the Cubs give the facts.

A **fact** is a statement that can be checked or proved. You can refer to the official score book to find the final score, the runs, and the errors.

An **opinion** is a statement about what someone feels or believes. People may have many different opinions about something. The three fans who talked about the Cubs game had three different opinions about it.

In the next story, the writer presents facts and opinions. Read carefully to be able to tell the difference.

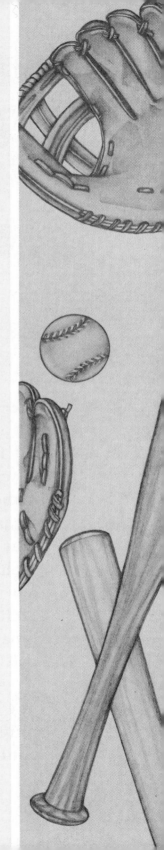

THE GOOF THAT WON THE PENNANT

Jonah Kalb

The Copley Blazers were a baseball team that had no place to go but up. Last season they had finished last in the league. This season, Coach Venuti told the players that they had it in them to win—if they could get it together as a *team*. The Blazers decided to give it a try. That meant no more arguing about who would pitch and who would play where. It also meant that Paco, the catcher, and Joe Ferguson, the pitcher, would have to work together on a signal system—even though they couldn't stand each other.

As the Blazers changed their losing ways, they found out for themselves that winning was something only a real team could do. But would that help them win the pennant?

The Cubs, the Cubs, the Cubs.

The Blazers were 11 wins, 2 losses. The Cubs were 11 wins, 2 losses. The two teams, tied for first place, were about to play the last game of the season. One team would win the pennant.

Coach Venuti took the team behind the stands for his final pep talk.

"Well," he began, "here we are, in the championship game. You made it. I'm very proud of you. But I also want you to know that this last game is *not that important!*" He paused.

"Someone's going to win, and someone's going to lose. Nobody deserves to lose a game like this. But it's only a game. It isn't a matter of life and death.

"I want you to go out there and have fun. Play the game, but enjoy it. If anyone is going to get nervous, let it be the other team."

"Don't you want us to win?" asked Paco.

The coach smiled. "In my book," Coach Venuti said, "you've already won. Every one of you is a winner. Remember that. If you win this last one, fine. But if you lose it, don't hang your heads. You were all great to get this far. You're already champions."

"I'd still like to win this one," J. C. said, a little confused.

The team broke, and returned to the field for "The Star-Spangled Banner." Every seat in the stands was filled.

The Cub pitcher was good. Really good. The Blazers were having a terrible time getting anyone on base.

But Joe Ferguson matched him, inning for inning, at the start. He had the Cub hitters swinging off stride, lunging at slow pitches, and handcuffed by the fast ones. It was as if they could never tell when Joe was going to throw fast.

It was 0-0 after three and a half innings, just like a championship game should be.

Then, the Cubs got on to something. After three of Joe's pitches to the first batter in the bottom of the fourth, the Cubs' first-base coach stage-whispered "change!" Joe threw a changeup, just as Paco had signaled, and the Cub hitter slashed the ball to deep left field. Roger made a fine catch for the out.

Again, with the second hitter of the inning, the Cub coach stage-whispered "change!" just before Joe threw his changeup, and again, a Cub hitter

timed it perfectly. The Blazer centerfielder caught the
long drive on the run, right in front of the wall.

And then, the next Cub hitter hit one out of
the park. Over the fence. Home run.

The Cubs weren't swinging at Joe's fast ball.
They were just standing there, waiting for the
changeup. And because of that first-base coach,
they seemed to know every time it was coming.

The inning was finally over, but the Cubs had
hit three pitches really hard, and had a run.

"They're guessing right," Joe complained.
"Every time I used my slow ball, they were
waiting for it."

Coach Venuti pulled his pitcher and catcher to
the corner of the bench. "They're not guessing," the
coach told them. "They're reading Paco's signals.
When he wiggles his finger for the changeup, he's

wiggling a little of his wrist, too. And they know
what that wiggle means."

"Let's change signals," Paco said.

"O.K." said Coach Venuti. "But let's change
them in a certain way. From now on, one finger is
still the fast ball. But now, two fingers means
changeup. The wiggle doesn't mean anything."
He turned to the rest of the team. "Let's get some
runs!" He clapped his hands.

Roger walked, but after two strikeouts, he was
still on first base. Then it happened, the miracle the
Blazers were waiting for. The Cub pitcher reared
back and fired his best fast ball, over the heart of
the plate, waist high.

Phantom Baxter Snow, who had been pretending all year, took his marvelous imaginary swing,
but this time, it was real. This time, for the first
time in his life, the ball really did jump off his bat,

flying on a high arc for the distant fence. When Phantom shielded his eyes from the sun to watch— as he had done for thousands of imaginary home runs before—this time, he really did see the flight of the ball out, out, out over the wall. His dream— his thousand dreams—had come true.

Home run. Home run. The Blazers were leading 2-1. But the game was not over. The Cubs still had two more times at bat.

Paco was a very smart catcher. Guessing that the Cubs were still laying back, waiting for the changeup, he called three straight fast balls on the first hitter in the bottom of the fifth inning. The batter took them all, and he was called out on strikes. One out.

The Cub coach was talking furiously to his next batter, as he stepped up to the plate. The coach was pleading with him to swing the bat! Joe threw a medium-fast ball on the first pitch, the Cub swung, and lifted a harmless pop fly to Phantom at second base. Phantom waved wildly, yelled, circled, waved some more, and made the catch. Two out.

But what Paco did to that third batter of the inning was worth the season. He was one of their heavy hitters, and he fouled the first pitch deep into left field. But foul is foul, and it was just a long strike. Strike one.

Joe's next pitch was a fast ball, right on the corner. The umpire called it strike two.

Then . . . Paco put one finger down for the fast ball, and, remembering it didn't mean anything any more, he wiggled. The Cub first-base coach stage-whispered "change!" The Cub hitter got ready for the slow ball, and Joe Ferguson reared back and threw the hardest fast ball of his entire life.

The Cub hitter looked surprised. He hardly got the bat off his shoulder, as he tried a useless poke at the ball. But it was too late. The ball was in Paco's mitt. Strike three. Three out.

Paco was laughing out loud when he came back to the bench. He, at least, was taking the coach's advice. He was having fun.

There never was a sixth inning like the sixth inning of the Cub-Blazer game. First of all, the Blazers did nothing in their half of the sixth. And the Cubs came to bat one more time, trailing by one run. This was their last licks. Unless they scored, the Blazers were the champs.

The first Cub walked. The second Cub grounded to Bunky at shortstop, who flipped the ball to Phantom at second, for the force out. One out, man on first.

The next Cub doubled, putting men on second and third, one out. But the batter after him popped up, so there were two outs. Coach Venuti strolled out to the mound.

"Look, Joe," he said, trying to keep calm, "this guy coming up is the big Cub pitcher, and he's a pretty good hitter, too. First base is open. Why don't we put him on base on purpose? Then, they'll have the bases loaded, so we have a force at any base."

Joe nodded, and when Coach Venuti returned to the bench, he threw four wide pitches deliberately, and walked the bases full.

That's when the confusion started.

Bases loaded, two out, last of the sixth, championship game. Joe threw a fast ball. The hitter leaned in and slammed it, on the line, to left centerfield. A clean hit. The Cub on third scored easily. The Cub who was on second, running at the crack of the bat, rounded third and also scored before Roger had even recovered the ball. That, of course, was the winning run.

But the big Cub pitcher on first, knowing that his run "didn't matter," just stood between first and second bases. And when he saw his teammate from second going all the way home, he leaped into the air and clapped his hands. He then held up his first finger in a victory salute! He didn't bother running to second base.

The stands emptied onto the field. The Cub pitcher's father ran to him and hugged him. His mother danced around him. He was jumping for joy.

Roger, in deep left field, realized something that nobody else did. He knew that if he got the ball to second base before the Cub pitcher got there, then it would simply be a force out, three outs, and the runs wouldn't count. He yelled to Phantom, and then threw a floating fly ball, way over his head.

The fans were now in the infield, lifting the Cubs, dancing, cheering. The overthrown baseball, therefore, went into the crowd, where it was picked up by a fan.

From deep left field, Roger came running into
the crowd, looking for the ball. He elbowed his
way past the screaming fans and found the fan,
who had put the ball in his pocket.

"Give me the ball," Roger demanded angrily.

"Why?" said the fan, as he took it out of his
pocket, and held it up. "It's a souvenir!"

Roger grabbed for it, and the fan dropped the
ball. Roger picked it up, and taking no chances
with the crowd, ran himself, dodging the fans, over
to second base. He jumped on the base with both
feet, held the ball up, and looked for the umpire.

The umpire was right there. He had watched
the whole thing. He raised his right fist, and
shouted to be heard over the crowd.

"*Out*! The runner is *OUT* going to second."

And now, only Roger and the umpire knew that the Blazers had won the championship. For if the runner was out going to second, then it was a simple force play, and none of the runs counted. The Cub on first had to reach second, and he never did.

It was the greatest goof in the history of Copley baseball. It was the goof that won the pennant . . . for the Blazers!

Once the Blazers, and their fans, realized what had happened, the riot started all over again. This time, it was the Blazers who were dancing, and shouting, and carrying on. Roger was picked up by Paco, J. C., Joe, and Phantom and pounded on the back until he cried through his laughter.

The Blazers had won the championship. The Blazers!

The Goof That Won the Pennant was based on a real baseball goof made by New York Giant Fred Merkle. Merkle made his mistake in a game between the Giants and the Chicago Cubs on September 23, 1908.

The score was 1-1 in the bottom of the ninth inning. With two outs, Merkle was on first base and another Giant player was on third. When the Giant batter got a hit, the player on third ran home. Like the pitcher in the story, Merkle didn't touch second base after his teammate scored. The Giants thought they had won the game. When a Cub player realized what had happened, he got the ball to the second baseman, and Merkle was called out. The run did not count. With the score tied, the game was called off because of darkness.

At the end of the season, the Cubs and the Giants were tied for first place. A tie-breaker was played and the Cubs won. That gave them the pennant.

Merkle's failure to touch second base was, and still is, considered to be the greatest goof in the history of baseball.

Questions

1. What advice did Coach Venuti give the Blazers before the game?
2. Why did the Blazers change their signals in the middle of the game?
3. Who do you think was the hero of the game? Why?
4. What field position in baseball do you think is most important? Why?

Applying Reading Skills

Draw a line down the middle of your paper. Write the heading FACTS on one side of the line. Write the heading OPINIONS on the other side. Read the following sentences from the story. Then write each under the correct heading.

1. The Cubs weren't swinging at Joe's fast ball.
2. What Paco did to that third batter of the inning was worth the season.
3. From deep left field, Roger came running into the crowd, looking for the ball.
4. It was the greatest goof in the history of Copley baseball.
5. The Blazers had won the championship.

Associations

Home to me is not a house
filled with family faces;
Home is where I slide in free
By rounding all the bases.

A tie to me is not
clothing like a hat;
It means the game is even up
And I wish I were at bat.

Eve Merriam

PREPARING FOR READING

Learning Vocabulary

1. A film crew's job is to <u>record</u> action and sound.
2. Before a film is made, money must be raised to pay for its <u>production</u>.
3. The producer of a film is the person who <u>hires</u> the director.
4. Films can <u>communicate</u> thoughts or information in an interesting way.
5. The lighting helps to create the <u>mood</u> of a film.
6. The soundperson uses a <u>portable</u> tape recorder to listen to the sounds as they are recorded.

record   production   hires
communicate   mood   portable

Developing Background and Skills
Draw Conclusions

You know that a **conclusion** is a decision or judgment based on information. As you read, you can draw conclusions about the information a writer presents. All the information should support the conclusion.

Read the paragraph below. What conclusion can you draw from the information?

It takes a lot of people to make a movie. One person has to find ways to raise money for the production. Another must be able to direct the actors and the rest of the crew to make the kind of movie he or she wants. The cameraperson has the job of photographing the action. Others are experts in sound or lighting.

Which of the following conclusions is supported by the information given in the paragraph?

1. It takes a lot of time to make a film.
2. Movies are made by many people with different skills.
3. The cameraperson has the most important job in making a movie.

The second conclusion is best supported by the information given in the paragraph. It makes use of all the information given.

As you read the next selection, try to draw conclusions about the information the writer presents. Remember to base your conclusions on all the available information.

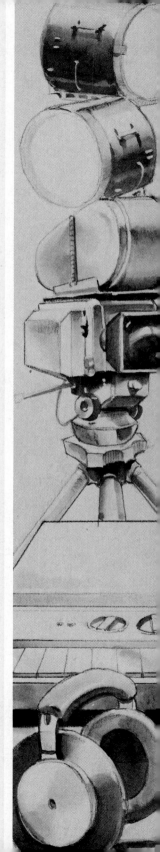

Putting it Together:

A Film Crew
George Ancona

Movies are made by people with different skills working together as a team. A film crew can be made up of many people or just a few. It depends on the kind of film being produced. No matter what its size, the crew's job is to record the action and the sound that are what films are made of.

The *producer* has the job of raising the money to pay for the production of the film. She hires the director and takes care of the crew's needs. She also guides the film through all the steps to the finish.

The *director* is in charge of the crew and the making of the film. She decides what to shoot, where to shoot it, and what the style will be. She will direct people to produce what is in her mind and what she wants the movie to communicate.

The *cameraperson*, working with the director, chooses the rest of the crew. He photographs the action. By using lights, color filters, and movement, he will create the mood that the director wants.

The *soundperson* records the sound as the cameraperson shoots. With headphones, she listens to the sounds as they are recorded on a portable tape recorder. Before the camera is turned off, the soundperson flashes a number, which the cameraperson shoots. This number identifies the recorded sound with the action just shot. In this way the sound can be found on the tape and put together with the right picture.

The *gaffer* lights the scene the way the cameraperson wants it. Using a light meter, the gaffer makes sure that there is enough light for the scene to be well photographed.

This crew is shooting a television documentary film about children who study dance. In a documentary, the people in the film are not told what to do or say. Actions are shot as they happen. The cameraperson carries the camera, so he can move quickly and follow the movements of the children. Meanwhile, the director watches for other actions that may be important for the story. The soundperson moves with the camera, recording the sounds. By using a microphone on a pole, she can bring it in close to get the best sound.

Later, more people take over the making of the film. Film labs develop the pictures. An editor chooses what should be kept and what should be taken out. The editor also puts the pictures together with the sound. A composer writes music. He may also conduct, or lead, musicians in a recording session. The sounds are then put onto one sound track. Finally, the lab will make the finished print we will see on television.

Questions

1. What jobs are described in "Putting It Together: A Film Crew"?
2. How does the cameraperson help the director?
3. Which crew member does the soundperson work most closely with?
4. The film described in the article was a documentary. What other kinds of films might a film crew work on?

Applying Reading Skills

Number your paper from 1 to 3. Choose the best answer for each question by drawing conclusions based on facts given in the article. Write each conclusion using a complete sentence.

1. Why is the job of producer very important?
   a. A producer is the first person to be hired.
   b. A producer is in charge of the crew.
   c. A producer raises money for the film, hires the director, and sees the film through to the finish.

2. Which person has the most control over the way a finished film appears to an audience?
   a. soundperson   b. editor   c. producer

3. Why aren't the people in a documentary film told what to do or say?
   a. A documentary film tries to show things as they happen in real life.
   b. A documentary film has no speaking parts.
   c. The people in documentary films do not want to memorize their lines.

PREPARING FOR READING

Learning Vocabulary

1. Allison and Andrew Potter were hoping that the closing of the zoo would be <u>postponed</u>.
2. They thought up a <u>scheme</u> to keep the zoo open.
3. Allison <u>confessed</u> that she was the "brains" of the <u>operation</u>.
4. Their mother, who was a <u>newscaster</u>, would prepare a story about the zoo.
5. The crowd listened in <u>disbelief</u> as Mrs. Potter told about the <u>incredible</u> events of the zoo story.

postponed   scheme   confessed   operation
newscaster   disbelief   incredible

Developing Background and Skills
Facts and Opinions

Most magazines and newspapers have advertisements. The ads give information. They also sometimes try to convince people to buy or support something.

If you read carefully, you will discover that most ads include facts and opinions. Remember that **facts** are statements that can be proved. **Opinions** are statements about what someone feels or believes.

Read the ad below. Look for facts and opinions.

RIVERDALE ZOO

Wonderful Riverdale Zoo is open every day this month
from 10:00 A.M. to 5:00 P.M.
You can ride in a tramway above miles of land where
wild animals roam freely.
Youngsters will love the Children's Zoo.
There's something for everyone at Riverdale Zoo!

Only one statement in the ad is completely factual.
That is the statement about the tramway. The first
sentence includes facts about the hours the zoo is open.
That sentence also includes an opinion. Riverdale Zoo may
seem wonderful to many people, but to others it may not.

As you read, you will find sentences that tell both facts
and opinions.

In the next selection, you will meet a newscaster. People
who report the news try to tell only the facts. Read to find
out if the newscaster does this. Look for facts and opinions
in what the other characters say, too.

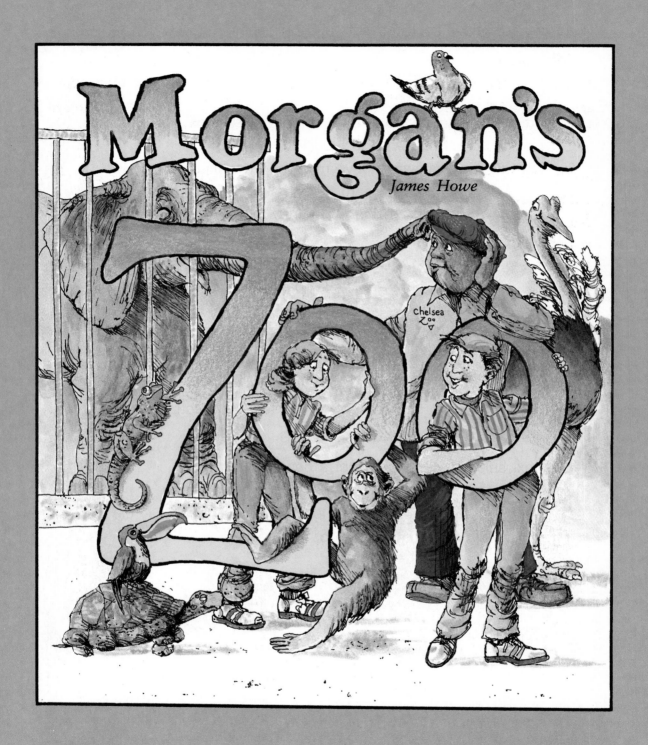

Morgan's

James Howe

Morgan is the keeper who feeds and cares for the animals, so the Chelsea Park Zoo is simply called Morgan's Zoo. Morgan does not own the zoo, however, and Mayor Thayer and head zookeeper Rollo Hackett, for different reasons, decide the zoo must close. For Morgan and the animals, the thought of being separated is heartbreaking. They must save the zoo!

Perhaps the twins, Allison and Andrew, have a plan that will work. With their mother's help, they think they can get the whole city interested in saving the zoo. But could it be that the animals themselves have a winning scheme to save the zoo? A discovery involving a trunk and two mysterious workers, made by Clarence the chimpanzee and his pigeon friend, William, lifts their hopes.

It was Tuesday, closing day of the Chelsea Park Zoo. The animals eagerly awaited the arrival of the twins' mother, Nan Potter, and her television crew. Only after the cameras began to roll could they put into action Clarence's plan.

A shadow crept slowly over the pavement. Six feet above, a red hat glowed in the morning sun. Both shadow and hat belonged to Rollo Hackett, come to bid the animals farewell. He looked at the animals with dry eyes and a satisfied smile. His smile vanished, however, as he approached the

seals' pool. For there, off to one side, was a huge banner that read: "SAVE OUR ZOO!"

"Morgan!" the head zookeeper shouted.

"Yes, Mr. Hackett?" called Morgan from a distance. His voice, traveling faster than his feet, arrived before the rest of him. "Is something wrong?" he asked.

Hackett was shaking a finger at the banner the twins had made. "What is the meaning of this?" he shouted.

"It's for the news program, Mr. Hackett," Morgan said.

"*What* news program!?"

"The news program about the closing of the zoo," he answered simply.

"But that was last week—"

"No," said Morgan. "It was supposed to be last week, but the television people never came. They were too busy covering the big jewelry robbery. So they're coming today instead."

Before Hackett could say anything, there came a low rumble of footsteps and voices, which grew and grew until all at once the zoo was filled with people. Allison and Andrew ran over to Morgan.

"Morgan!" cried Andrew. "Look at all the people!"

Rollo Hackett snorted like an angry bull and stormed off.

"I don't think Mr. Hackett's very happy about this."

"Maybe he'll be happier if we save the zoo," Allison said.

Morgan shook his head. "I don't think so," he replied. "I'm not sure what it would take to make Mr. Hackett a happy man, but I don't think saving the zoo would do it."

Clarence, who had been listening to this conversation with his friend, William, whispered, "Well, I guess *we*

know what would make Rollo Hackett happy, don't we?"

The pigeon's head bobbed up and down. "Yes," he said, "and soon everyone else will, too. Oh, dear, Clarence, I'm getting a little nervous."

"Now, don't worry," the chimpanzee assured him, "everything will be fine."

"But I have such an important part to play. What if … "

"They're here!" Lucy the elephant exclaimed from the next cage. Nan Potter and two men, one carrying a camera, were weaving their way through the crowd.

"Yes," said Clarence, "they are here. And that means it's almost time. Good luck, William."

William cooed, "Good luck to you, too, Clarence. Good luck to us all."

The twins, dragging Morgan by the hand, ran to greet their mother.

"This is Morgan," they called out.

Nan reached out her hand to the zookeeper. "Hello, Morgan," she said warmly. "I feel as though I know you already. The children never stop talking about you … and the animals, of course. You're

all awfully important to them, you know."

Morgan smiled at Allison and Andrew. "No more than they are to us," he said.

Nan Potter turned to her crew of two. "I'll start over here," she said, pointing to the seal pool. "Let's get the seals and that sign in the background. Then, I can move on to the chimpanzee's cage and the elephants. All right, guys?"

"Fine with me," replied the man with the camera. The other man nodded his head, as the two began to set up their equipment.

In a matter of minutes, they were ready to roll. Clarence and William were ready, too. They watched as Nan Potter took her position before the seal pool, with her microphone in hand, and faced the camera.

"Today is a sad day for our city," Nan Potter began. "The Chelsea Park Zoo, which has delighted thousands of people for many years, is closing.

"Many people have gathered here today," Nan went on, "to say goodbye not just to the animals but, perhaps, to a way of life as well." She turned slightly and looked at the banner behind her. "Some people don't want the zoo to close.

They are fighting to save it. But *can* it be saved? Perhaps. Perhaps if others care enough to join their fight." She began to move away now in the direction of Clarence's cage.

"This is it," Clarence said. "All set, William? Lucy?"

"All set," the pigeon and the elephant answered as one. William moved through the bars of Clarence's cage and flew to the railing before it.

Clarence suddenly found himself in front of the television camera. "This is Clarence," Nan Potter was saying, as she glanced over her shoulder at the chimpanzee. "The zoo is his home. But soon he will be crated off to a new home, one far from—"

All at once, a terrifying screech shattered the air and brought Nan's words to a halt. Everyone looked toward the cage next to Clarence's, where the awful sound had come from. There, Lucy was staggering about. She tottered from one side of the cage to the other. Then Lucy gave one final shriek and fell with a crash to the ground.

"Something's wrong with Lucy!" Morgan cried in alarm. "She's sick. Out of my way, please, out of my way." The zookeeper pushed forward, removing his keys from his

belt as he did so. This was William's cue.

"Keep the camera going," Nan Potter shouted. Then, in her hushed newscaster voice, she said, "It appears that one of the elephants has just been stricken. The zookeeper is coming to the—"

But before she could finish her sentence, even before Morgan could reach Lucy's cage, William took flight. He swooped down and caught Morgan's keys in his beak.

Morgan was so taken by surprise, he didn't realize at first what had happened. But Nan Potter saw it all. "Hard as it is to believe, a pigeon has just grabbed the zookeeper's keys right out of his hands," she reported. "And now...yes, he's turned them over to the chimpanzee."

As the camera recorded the amazing events, Clarence, keys in hand, rushed to his door and opened it quickly. He threw open the door, jumped down onto the pavement, and ran through the crowd.

"After him!" someone in the crowd cried out.

"Keep rolling!" Nan ordered her cameraman as they, along with everyone else, ran after the runaway chimp.

Morgan couldn't understand what had gotten into Clarence

and William. And he was worried about Lucy.

"Clarence is trying to tell us something," Andrew told Morgan. "We've got to go after him."

"I always knew he was smart," Allison said. "Come on, Morgan. Hurry!"

"But what about Lucy?" Morgan asked.

"She's fine!" Andrew shouted, grabbing Morgan's hand. "Let's go!"

And, indeed, when Morgan looked back at the elephants' cage, there stood Lucy, chewing on some straw, as if nothing had happened at all.

By the time Morgan and the twins reached them, the crowd had followed Clarence to the Jungle Playland area of the zoo.

"The chimp seems to know what he's doing," Nan said to the camera. "He's led us to another part of the zoo, one that looks as if it hasn't been in use for years. Now, he's... he's running to a trunk of some sort and..."

Clarence tugged at the lid of the old storage trunk near the children's zoo. As he threw back the lid, the crowd rushed forward. But William saw what was inside the trunk before they did.

"Rags!" he called out to his friend. "There's nothing but

rags, Clarence."

"What is the chimpanzee looking for?" Nan Potter asked the camera. "It appears he has led us to this trunk to show us something."

Morgan had worked his way through the crowd and was kneeling by Clarence's side. Clarence paid him no attention at first. He just stood, staring in disbelief at the emptied trunk. Under the rags, he had found nothing.

"How can this be!" he exclaimed. To the crowd, of course, his words sounded like gibberish, but to William they made perfect sense.

"I don't know," the pigeon replied, "unless we were wrong about—"

"We're *not* wrong," said Clarence. "I *know* we're not. Maybe they moved them. Maybe...maybe—"

Just then, Rollo Hackett appeared. "What seems to be the problem?" he asked Morgan sternly.

"I don't know, Mr. Hackett," Morgan answered. "It's Clarence. He—"

Without waiting for Morgan to finish, Hackett turned and faced the crowd. "All right," he said. "The show's over. Everybody can go home now."

"All right," Nan Potter called. Then, turning to her

cameraman, she said softly, "Keep the camera running. There's something funny going on here, and I want to know what it is."

The crowd began to leave. Morgan and Clarence, followed by the twins, moved slowly away from the trunk. It was as they were passing through the entranceway to the amusement area that the chimpanzee heard William say, "Well, we tried, Clarence. You can't say we didn't try."

"Where are you?" Clarence called out. "I don't see you."

William cooed. "I'm right above you," he said. "On the elephant."

Clarence looked up and couldn't believe his eyes. There, in the middle of the sign that read "Jungle Playland," sat William, perched on the wooden elephant's ...*trunk*.

"That's it!" Clarence cried.

Before the startled zookeeper knew what was happening, Clarence scrambled up onto his shoulders and from there took a giant leap to the elephant's head. William barely had time to get out of the way as Clarence grabbed hold of the trunk and swung back and forth, back and forth, until suddenly—

CRACK! The wood split

apart, and Clarence, holding tight to a piece of the trunk, fell to the ground. Jewels of every color and no color at all spilled from the elephant's head.

Suddenly, a voice cried out, "Hey, that's ours!"

Heads spun round, as did the camera recording the events, to discover a tall, thin man in the distance. The two men on either side of him began yelling at him. "You picked a fine time to start talking!" cried the man some recognized as Rollo Hackett. "What's the matter with you, anyway?"

"But they're ours," cried the tall man. "They can't have them. They're ours!"

"Gee," said Andrew to no one in particular, "I'll bet those guys are the jewel thieves!"

But Morgan was listening, and he nodded his head slowly. "You're right," he told Andrew. "They must be the thieves. But that would mean Mr. Hackett..."

Other people heard what Morgan and Andrew were saying. "Thieves!" someone called out.

All at once, the crowd began to move toward Rollo Hackett and his two companions. "Let's get out of here!"

Hackett shouted. Setting off in the direction of the animals' cages, they quickly turned their walk into a run as they looked back to see the crowd closing in on them.

Clarence, with Morgan's keys still in his hand, rushed ahead of the crowd and almost caught up with the escaping criminals. But he was not planning to catch them himself; no, he had something quite different in mind.

As the three men raced through the zoo, Clarence jumped up onto the ledge of the lions' cage. Looking for the right key, he said, "All right, Lance and Gwen, this is your big chance." Suddenly, a key slipped into the lock, turned, and the door swung open. Clarence, hanging on, swung with it, and cried out to the lions, "Go get 'em!"

Roaring ferociously, the two lions set off after Hackett and his friends. The sound brought a cheer from the animals but silence from the crowd, who stopped when they realized that two lions were on the loose.

Nan and her crew didn't miss a bit of the action. "Clarence, that incredible chimp, has freed the lions from their cages," Nan said. Her words spilled out rapidly as

she tried to keep up with what was happening. "And the lions are now chasing the three men attempting to escape. Wait, what's this? One of the men has turned around...he sees the lion...he—"

A scream came from the tall man's mouth. He stood frozen in his tracks as the two roaring lions came closer and closer. Hackett and the other man turned to pull him along. It was then that...

"All three men see the lions now," reported Nan Potter. "They look as if they don't know what to do. Well, who would in their shoes? After all, it's not everyday one finds

oneself being chased by lions! One of the men is pointing to a tree. I believe they're going to climb up...yes, yes... that's what they're doing... they're climbing the tree."

"The three men were led away by police some time later," Nan Potter told her viewers on the evening news. "The men admitted that they were the jewel thieves who have been robbing our city. Rollo Hackett, head zookeeper of the Chelsea Park Zoo, confessed to being the 'brains' of the operation."

Nan paused as a new picture appeared on the screen. In a little box over her left shoulder

was a picture of Clarence and Morgan. "What makes this story so remarkable," the newscaster went on, "is the fact that it was the zoo's animals, under the leadership of this chimpanzee, who found the stolen goods.

When told of today's incredible events, Mayor Thayer announced that the closing of the zoo will be postponed. The animals, who were going to be shipped off to other zoos starting tomorrow, can rest easy tonight. The Chelsea Park Zoo is still their home and, if all goes well, it will remain just that for a long, long time to come."

Questions

1. How did Mr. Hackett feel when he found out that a news program was going to be filmed at the zoo?
2. Why did Lucy the elephant pretend to be sick after Nan Potter began her news report?
3. Clarence and William overheard Mr. Hackett and the jewel thieves talking about hiding the jewels. Why were the animals confused about where the jewels were?
4. Think of a place you love to visit. How would you feel if it was about to close? What might you do to try to keep it open?

Applying Reading Skills

Divide your paper into three columns. Write one of these headings above each: FACT, OPINION, PART FACT/PART OPINION. Read the following statements from the story. Then write each under the correct heading.

1. It was Tuesday, closing day of the Chelsea Park Zoo.
2. Today is a sad day for our city.
3. Some people don't want the zoo to close.
4. There's something funny going on here.
5. What makes this story remarkable is that the zoo animals found the stolen goods.
6. When told of today's incredible events, Mayor Thayer announced that the closing of the zoo will be postponed.

WRITING ACTIVITY

WRITE A NEWSPAPER STORY

Prewrite

Nan Potter worked as a television newscaster in the story "Morgan's Zoo." A television newscaster, like a newspaper reporter, must give the facts about a news event and not opinions about it. Facts are statements that can be proved. Opinions are statements about what someone feels or believes.

Imagine you are a newspaper reporter. You are going to write a news story for your local newspaper. First you must think of an interesting event that happened to you or to someone you know in your school or town. You may want to report on a soccer game or a spelling bee.

Reporters use the Five W's to help them write.

The Five W's				
Who?	What?	Where?	When?	Why?

Choose the news event you will write about. Use the Five W's to make sure you include all the important facts. You may want to use the Five W's to write questions. Write an answer for each question, or use the questions to interview someone.

Write

1. Read your questions and answers.
2. Think about how many paragraphs you will write. Begin each paragraph with a main idea sentence. Make sure the other sentences in the paragraph give details that support or explain the main idea.
3. Use the sentences you wrote about the Five W's to write your news story. Be sure you write about the facts and not your opinions.
4. Write an exciting headline for your news story. The headline should be so interesting that it will make readers want to read the story.
5. Use your Glossary or dictionary for spelling help.

Revise

Read your news story. Did you use only facts and not give opinions? Can you find answers to the Five W's in your story? Does each paragraph have a main idea sentence? Did you write an exciting headline? Now is the time to rewrite parts of your news story that may be unclear.

1. Did you indent the first sentence in each paragraph?
2. Did you use adverbs that clearly described the action of the story?
3. Did you use correct end punctuation for each sentence?

PREPARING FOR READING

Learning Vocabulary

1. Paramedics, who are medical workers, are often called when there is an <u>emergency</u>.
2. They usually begin <u>treatment</u> of a patient before <u>transportation</u> to a hospital is arranged.
3. Paramedics are trained to <u>examine</u> patients using <u>techniques</u> doctors use.
4. The paramedic <u>profession</u> is a rewarding one.

emergency   treatment   transportation
examine   techniques   profession

Developing Background and Skills
Summarize

If you had to report an emergency, you would want to do it as quickly as possible. If there were a fire, you would not give details about how it started. You would tell where the fire is and say what is burning.

A report that tells the most important facts but leaves out unnecessary details is called a **summary.** You can give a summary of an emergency. You can also give a summary of a paragraph. A good summary is brief, but accurate.

Read this paragraph from "Paramedics on Call."

Today's paramedic does many things that only doctors did in the past. In a year, a paramedic may save as many lives as a doctor once did during a lifetime of medical practice. Besides this, paramedics are using medicines and techniques today that were unknown a few years ago.

To write a summary of a paragraph, you should first find the main idea. The main idea is that paramedics are now doing many things that only doctors did in the past.

Now look for the most important supporting detail. This is that a paramedic may save as many lives in a year as a doctor once did in a lifetime.

By restating the main idea and most important detail, you can summarize the paragraph.

Today, paramedics do many jobs once performed only by doctors. They may even save more lives than doctors.

As you read "Paramedics on Call," think about how you could summarize the information presented.

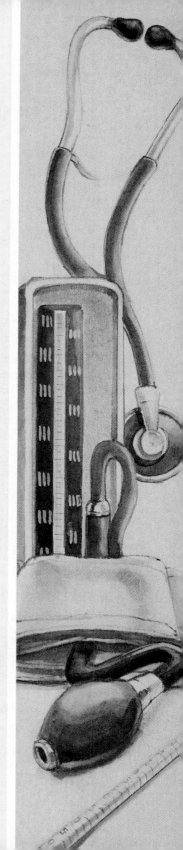

PARAMEDICS ON CALL

Kathy Pelta

Emergency!

Suddenly, a scream shatters the quiet of the afternoon. A man rushes from a building. He staggers down some steps and falls to the ground.

Immediately, the paramedics are at his side. They open special burn packs and put them on the man's face and arms. They measure the man's pulse and blood pressure. These are the "vital signs" they will report to the doctor.

Two paramedics continue to treat the patient. Another uses the radiotelephone to call base hospital. His message is a kind of code:

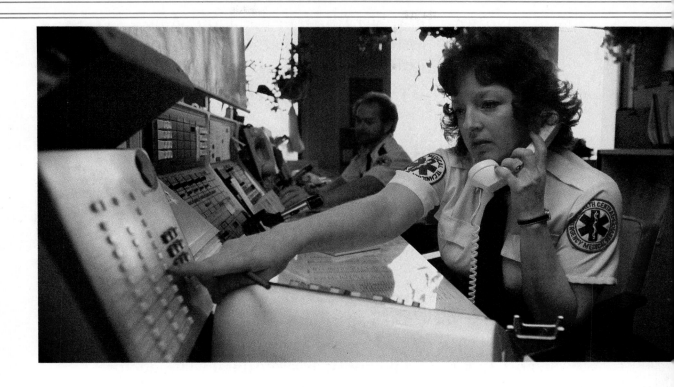

"General Hospital. This is Medic 17. Do you read me?"

"Medic 17. This is General Hospital. Go ahead."

"General Hospital. This is Medic 17. We have a twenty-three-year-old man involved in a gas oven explosion. He has second-degree burns on his face and arms. His vital signs are: pulse 80, B/P 120 over 70. We have applied a burn pack and started oxygen. Request permission to start an IV."

"Medic 17. This is General Hospital. We read you. Start an IV. Is transportation ready?"

No need, however, for transportation. This "burn victim" is not even injured. He is only play-acting. The burns are just make up. He and his "rescuers" are paramedic trainees. They are taking part in an exercise called a *simulation*. The person playing the doctor at General Hospital is their teacher.

Simulations are an important part of paramedic training. After weeks of classes, students get a chance to practice what they have learned. Everyone takes a turn being "paramedic." The teachers make the simulations as much like the real thing as possible.

In a real emergency, paramedics begin treatment as soon as they reach their patient. They find out as much as they can about the illness or injury. They report this to the doctor at base hospital. The doctor tells them what to do next. With their special equipment, the paramedics can give patients the kind of care they would get at the hospital. It's almost like bringing the emergency room to the patient.

What is a Paramedic?

Paramedics know a great deal about medicine, but they are not doctors. They are the link between the doctor at the hospital and the patient in the field. They examine the patient as the doctor would. They treat the patient after getting instructions by

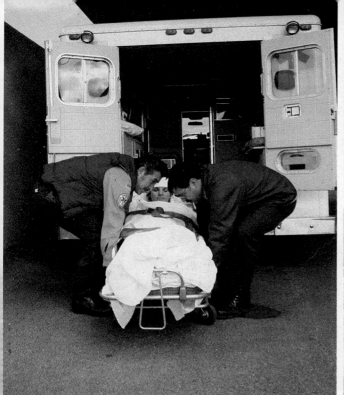
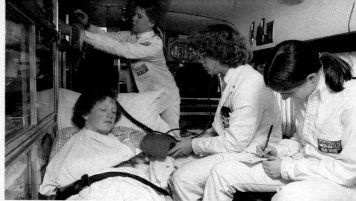

radiotelephone. The paramedics are the eyes, ears, and hands of the doctor.

When it was first suggested, in 1967, that someone who was not a doctor be given this job, many people were doubtful. "Impossible," they said. "How can you train someone to do things that only a doctor is supposed to do?"

The paramedics are proving that it *is* possible. Learning to be a paramedic takes lots of hard work and study. But thousands of men and women are doing it well, every hour of the day and night, all over the United States. Most paramedics are also firefighters. Some work for ambulance companies. There are police and lifeguard—and even forest ranger—paramedics.

Paramedic is defined in the dictionary as "a doctor who parachutes to areas where medical services are needed." That does not describe today's paramedic. A word closer in meaning is *paramedical*, which means "having to do with medicine."

In recent wars, doctors did parachute to areas to give medical help, but not often. Yet there are many war stories of the paramedics who took a doctor's place when there were not enough doctors to go around. Many were in charge of a hospital unit. But taking the doctor's place isn't the same as working with that doctor in a team effort. One-half of today's medical emergency team is at the hospital, and the other half is in the field. Between them is radiotelephone communication.

What Does a Paramedic Do?

What a paramedic does will depend on where he or she works. Paramedics in large cities have many different kinds of calls. There are lots of traffic accidents. Sometimes there are explosions or fires. In a city where many older people live, most paramedic calls are for heart problems. In a rural area, it might take an hour of driving just to reach the emergency. In our national parks, forest ranger paramedics make rescues that sometimes involve rock-climbing or a long trip by horseback.

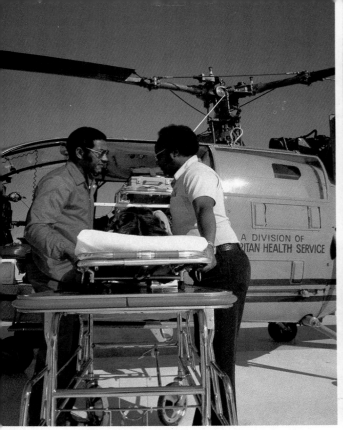

In small towns, paramedics sometimes work as doctors' assistants in the emergency room of a hospital. When a call comes, they head for the field. Some volunteer paramedics may work at a job that isn't related to medicine at all. These volunteers carry a "beeper" with them all the time, so they can respond to emergencies—night or day.

The Paramedic Profession

Before 1967, no one dreamed that anyone but a doctor could do part of a doctor's job. Yet today's paramedic does many things that only doctors did in the past. In a year, a paramedic may save as

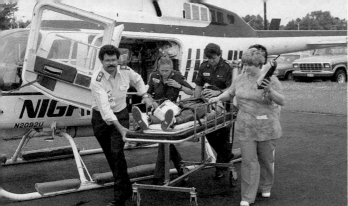

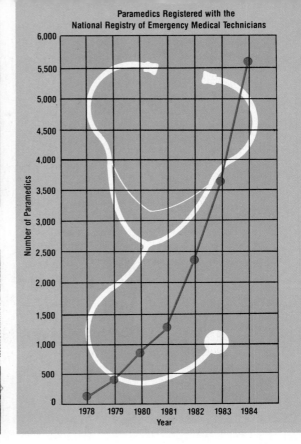

Paramedics Registered with the National Registry of Emergency Medical Technicians

many lives as a doctor once did during a lifetime of medical practice. Besides this, paramedics are using medicines and techniques today that were unknown, even to doctors, a few years ago.

The profession of paramedic is a respected one in the United States today. Calling a paramedic for a medical emergency is as common as calling the fire department for a fire. Because of the paramedics, lives have been saved that otherwise might have been lost. In fact, some doctors have paid the highest compliment of all to the paramedics. When there is an emergency in their office, they call the paramedics.

Questions

1. Where does the word *paramedic* come from?
2. How is the job of a city paramedic different from that of a paramedic working in a rural area?
3. Why do you think paramedics use code when they talk to doctors from the field?
4. What qualities do you think someone who wants to be a paramedic should have? Why?

Applying Reading Skills

Number your paper from 1 to 2. Choose the sentences that best summarize each paragraph referred to below. Write the answer on your paper.

1. The first paragraph under "What Is a Paramedic?"
   a. Paramedics examine a patient the way a doctor would.
   b. Paramedics and doctors know a great deal about medicine.
   c. Doctors depend on paramedics to give them information about patients and to follow their instructions for treating patients.

2. The last paragraph of the selection
   a. In case of an emergency, people can call the fire department or a paramedic.
   b. Paramedics have earned the respect of patients and doctors because their work has saved many lives that could have been lost.
   c. Doctors often call paramedics when they need help.

PREPARING FOR READING

Learning Vocabulary

1. Hearing ear dogs <u>alert</u> their deaf owners to the sounds around them.
2. Jennifer was <u>enthusiastic</u> about having her own hearing ear dog.
3. She had to work hard to win the <u>affection</u> of her dog.
4. Jennifer's dog had learned <u>obedience</u> from her trainers.
5. Now the dog had to be taught to <u>respond</u> to the <u>commands</u> and hand signals Jennifer gave her.

alert   enthusiastic   affection
obedience   respond   commands

Developing Background and Skills
Summarize

Read the notice below from the want ads section of a newspaper.

Wanted: Healthy, intelligent dogs to be trained to aid the deaf. The dogs will be well cared for and loved. They will be trained as hearing ear dogs and will be given good homes with responsible people.

People who place ads in the newspaper usually have to pay for every word or every line in the ad. They keep their notices brief to avoid paying too much. They summarize what they want to say.

If you wanted to tell a friend about the notice, you would probably summarize the information even more. Remember that a **summary** is a report of only the most important information or ideas.

You might summarize the notice by saying that it asked for healthy, intelligent dogs to be trained as hearing ear dogs. You might also say that the dogs will be well cared for and loved.

The next selection is about a deaf girl and her hearing ear dog. "Cindy and Jennifer" is a true story. As you read, look for the important information the writer presents about hearing ear dogs. Think about how you could summarize this information.

Cindy and Jennifer

PATRICIA CURTIS

WORK

FAST

"I'll take this one," said Mr. MacMunn to the woman at the animal shelter. He had chosen the small gray dog called Cindy to become a hearing ear dog.

Hearing ear dogs are trained to alert their deaf owners to sounds the owners cannot hear. From the start, Cindy was a fast learner. She worked well with her trainers, Lynn and Bill. But when the day came for her to meet her new owner, Jennifer, she didn't seem enthusiastic. Jennifer, who was deaf, had to win Cindy's affection before they could become a team.

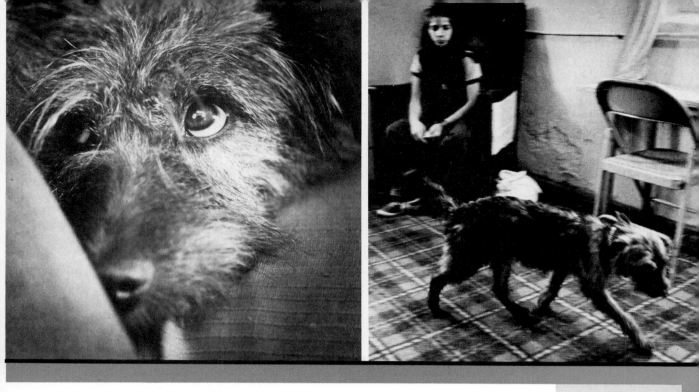

Cindy and Jennifer were to spend two weeks together getting to know one another. Jennifer would stay at the college where Lynn and Bill were students. Every day, she would work with Cindy in a special training cottage.

The big day arrived. Cindy, of course, knew nothing of the plans for her. She was taking a nap on the couch in the training cottage when Jennifer walked in. The dog opened her eyes and peeked out at the girl from between the pillows. Jennifer sat down and called Cindy to her. Cindy jumped off the couch and walked away, ignoring her. Jennifer was very disappointed.

WEEK

ONE ANOTHER

TIME

NEW

Lynn knew American Sign Language, which many deaf people use, so she could communicate with Jennifer. "Don't feel bad," Lynn signed. "It always takes a little time for one of our dogs to get to know its new owner. After you have been taking care of Cindy for a few days, she'll come to you."

Cindy let Jennifer hug her, but she looked as if she were saying "How long do I have to put up with this pushy girl?"

When Jennifer gave Cindy her dinner that night, the dog warmed up to her a little. But Cindy probably believed she was Lynn and Bill's dog.

As the days passed, however, Cindy spent more and more time with Jennifer. She slept on the floor in Jennifer's room. Jennifer took her for walks. Jennifer had brought her bicycle to the college, and

Cindy loved to run beside her when she rode it. Jennifer learned to bathe and brush the dog. Without thinking about it, Cindy began to accept Jennifer as her owner.

The next step was to teach Cindy to tell Jennifer instead of the trainers when the dog heard the sounds she had learned to respond to.

First they tried the doorbell. One trainer went outside the door while another stood behind Jennifer. When the bell rang, Cindy began to run back and forth between the door and the trainer.

"No, Cindy, *tell Jennifer!*" the trainer said.

They tried again. This time, Cindy ran to Jennifer. They kept up this lesson until Cindy always went to Jennifer when the doorbell rang. Then, they made the telephone ring, and sure enough, the dog

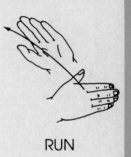

RUN

DOOR

WARN

JUMP

ran to the girl and brought her to the phone. It was clear that Cindy was beginning to team up with Jennifer.

One very important bell that hearing ear dogs are taught to respond to is a smoke alarm that warns of fire. In the kitchen of the training cottage, there was such a bell. Of course, it could be made to ring without smoke. Lynn went into the kitchen with Cindy while Jennifer sat in the next room. Lynn made the smoke alarm go off.

"*Sound*, Cindy!" exclaimed Lynn. "*Tell Jennifer!*" And Cindy dashed into the next room to Jennifer and led her out of the cottage.

Cindy's favorite bell was the alarm clock. She seemed to think it was so much fun to jump on the bed and wake up Jennifer.

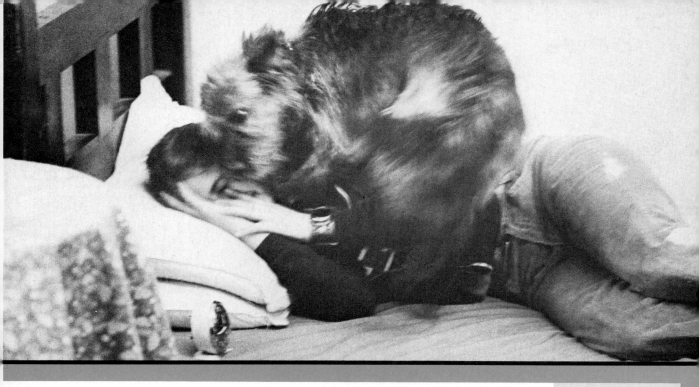

Jennifer of course had to learn her part, too. Lynn taught her to give Cindy all the obedience commands and hand signals. Whenever Cindy responded correctly, Jennifer hugged and petted her, just as the trainers had done.

The two weeks went by swiftly. The last few days, Jennifer's mother came and stayed at the college also. It was necessary for her to understand everything that Jennifer and Cindy knew. When they got home, Jennifer's mother would have to help Cindy do what she had learned at the college. She saw how Jennifer gave her dog the signals to come, sit, stay, lie down, and heel. She watched while Cindy ran and fetched Jennifer whenever the doorbell, telephone, alarm clock, teakettle, oven timer, or smoke alarm sounded.

SIT

LIE DOWN

LOVE

HOME

The trainers also told Jennifer to watch Cindy when they were outdoors together. If Cindy pricked up her ears and turned her head, it would mean she heard a noise. Jennifer should then look to see what Cindy heard. It might be a siren, an automobile horn, a person shouting, an object falling onto the sidewalk—something going on that Jennifer should know about.

Finally Jennifer packed up her suitcase, took Cindy by the leash, and walked out the door. Cindy at last had an owner who loved her. She was going to a home of her own, a home that really needed and wanted her.

The trainers, especially Lynn and Bill, would miss Cindy. But they had more dogs to teach to become hearing ear dogs for people who needed them.

Questions

1. How did Cindy react when she first met her new owner?
2. How did Jennifer win Cindy's affection?
3. How do you think Cindy will act when Jennifer takes her home? Why do you think she will act that way?
4. How is Jennifer's life different from the life of a person who can hear? How is it the same?

Applying Reading Skills

Number your paper from 1 to 2. Read each paragraph below. On your paper, write a brief summary of each paragraph.

1. A hearing ear dog can help its owner do everyday things. It can alert its owner when it hears an alarm clock going off, or when someone is at the door. The dog can even alert its owner to the sounds of an oven timer or a teakettle.

2. A hearing ear dog makes the life of a deaf person safer and more secure. Since the dog can hear sounds that its owner cannot hear, it might stop its owner from crossing the street when a car is coming. It can warn its owner when a siren or smoke alarm goes off.

Making A Friend

He wouldn't come at first.
But when
I stood quite still a long time,
Then

His tail began to move.
His eyes
Looked into mine, and in
Surprise

He sort of sniffed and showed
His tongue.
Then, suddenly, he moved and
Sprung

To where I stood. He smelled
My feet
And came up close so we could
Meet.

So then, I gently stroked
His head.
"Good boy—I'll be your friend,"
I said.

He licked me then, and that
Was good,
Because it meant
He understood.

Myra Cohn Livingston

THE
BORROWERS ARE FOUND

MARY NORTON

Have you ever lost something and never found it? That often happens in houses where Borrowers live. Borrowers are very small people who like to live in large, quiet country houses. They need places where they can go about their way unnoticed and where there is plenty to borrow. In such a house live the Borrowers named Pod and Homily and their daughter, Arrietty.

Although the Borrowers have a well-hidden, comfortable home under the floorboards, Pod and Homily are always afraid. They think terrible things will happen if they are ever seen by human beings (or "human beans," as they call them). Pod's brother Hendreary was "seen" once, and he and his family had to leave their home and make a new one in a nearby field.

Arrietty is not afraid, however. In fact, she meets a boy—a guest of the great house—and begins a friendship with him. When Pod finds out, he is very upset.

Pod did not speak until he and Arrietty reached the sitting room. Homily came running in from the kitchen, surprised to see them together. "She was in the night-nursery," said Pod, "talking to that boy!"

Homily moved forward, her hands clasped against her apron. "Oh, no—" she breathed.

"Oh, Mother," said Arrietty. "It isn't so bad. It really isn't. Look," she said, "here's a letter from Uncle Hendreary. I wrote to him and the boy took the letter—"

"You wrote to him!" cried Homily. "But whatever made you do such a thing, Arrietty? Whatever came over you?"

So Arrietty told them about being "seen." And how she had kept it from them not to worry them. And what the boy said about "dying out." And how important it had seemed to make sure the Hendrearys were alive. "Do understand," pleaded Arrietty, "please understand! I'm trying to save us!"

"Save us!" Pod repeated. "It's people like you, my girl, who do things sudden like with no respect for tradition, who'll finish us Borrowers once and for all. Don't you see what you've done?"

Arrietty met his eyes. "Yes," she said quietly, "I've—I've got in touch with the only other ones still alive. So that," she went on bravely, "from now on we can all stick together. . . ."

"All stick together!" Pod repeated angrily. "Do
you think Hendreary's family would ever come to
live back here? Can you see us going to live there,
two fields away, out in the open and no hot water?"

"Never!" cried Homily.

"But wait," Pod said as Arrietty tried to speak,
"that's not the point—as far as all that goes we're
just where we were. The point," he went on, "is
this: that boy knows now where we live!"

"Oh no," said Arrietty, "I never told him. I—"

"You told him," interrupted Pod, "about the
kitchen pipe bursting. You told him how all our
stuff got washed away to the grating. He's only got
to think," he pointed out. Arrietty was silent, and

Pod went on: "That's a thing that has never happened before, never, in the whole long history of the Borrowers. Borrowers have been 'seen'—yes; Borrowers have been caught—maybe. But no human being has ever known where any Borrower lived. We're in very grave danger, Arrietty."

"Oh, Pod," said Homily, "don't frighten her."

"Homily," said Pod more gently, "I don't want to frighten anyone, but this is serious."

"Yes!" exclaimed Homily. "Where's this letter?"

"It doesn't say much," said Arrietty, passing over the paper. "It just says, 'Tell your Aunt Lupy to come home.'"

"What?" exclaimed Homily, looking at the letter upside-down. "Come home? What can he mean?"

"He means," said Pod, "that Lupy must have set off to come here and that she never arrived."

"Set off to come here?" repeated Homily. "When?"

"It doesn't say when," said Arrietty.

"But," exclaimed Homily, "it might have been weeks ago!"

"It might," said Pod. "Long enough anyway for him to want her back."

"But something must have happened to her!" exclaimed Homily.

"Yes," said Pod. He turned to Arrietty. "See what I mean, Arrietty, about those fields?"

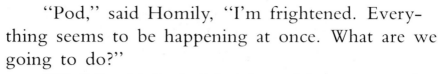

"Pod," said Homily, "I'm frightened. Everything seems to be happening at once. What are we going to do?"

"Well," said Pod, "there's nothing we can do tonight. That's certain. But have a bit of supper and a good night's rest." He rose to his feet.

"Oh, Arrietty," cried Homily. "How could you go and talk to a human bean? If only—"

"I was 'seen,' " cried Arrietty. "I couldn't help being 'seen.' Papa was 'seen.' I don't think it's all as awful as you're trying to make out. I don't think human beans are all that bad—"

"They're bad and they're good," said Pod. "They're honest and they're artful—it's just as it takes them at the moment. And animals, if they could talk, would say the same. Steer clear of them— that's what I've always been told. No matter what they promise you. No good ever really came to anyone from any human bean."

That night, while Arrietty lay straight and still under her cigar-box ceiling, Homily and Pod talked for hours. They talked in the sitting room, they talked in the kitchen, and later, much later, she heard them talk in their bedroom. She heard drawers shutting and opening, doors creaking, and boxes being pulled out from under beds. "What are they doing?" she wondered. "What will happen next?"

As it happened, Homily was only fidgeting, opening drawers and shutting them, unable to be still. She came to bed at last, and Pod with a sigh turned over and closed his eyes.

Homily lay for a long time staring at the oil lamp. It was the silver cap of a perfume bottle with a tiny, floating wick. She felt unwilling, for some reason, to blow it out. She gazed about the familiar room and thought: "What now? Perhaps nothing will happen after all. Perhaps Arrietty is right, and we are making a good deal of fuss about nothing very much. This boy, when all's said and done, is only a guest. Perhaps," thought Homily, "he'll go away again quite soon, and that," she told herself sleepily, "will be that."

Later (as she realized afterwards) she must have dozed off because it seemed she was crossing a field. It was night and the wind was blowing and the field seemed very steep. She was scrambling up it, sliding and falling in the wet grass. The tree branches were waving against the sky. Then there was a sound of splintering wood. . . .

Homily woke up. She saw the room again and the oil lamp flickering, but something, she knew at once, was different. There was a strange draft. Her mouth felt dry and full of grit. Then she looked up at the ceiling. "Pod!" she shrieked.

Pod rolled over and sat up. They both stared at the ceiling. The whole surface was on a steep slant, and one side of it had come away from the wall— this was what had caused the draft. And down into the room, to within an inch of the foot of the bed, was a huge bar of gray steel with a flattened, shining edge.

"It's a screwdriver," said Pod.

They stared at it, unable to move, and for a moment all was still. Then slowly the huge object swayed upward until the sharp edge lay against their ceiling and Homily heard a scrape on the floor above and a sudden human gasp. "Oh," cried Homily, "oh, no—" as their whole roof flew off and fell down with a clatter, somewhere out of sight.

Homily screamed then. She seemed almost to settle down in her scream, while her eyes stared up, half interested, into empty lighted space. There was another ceiling, she realized, way up above them—higher, it seemed, than the sky. Arrietty appeared in the doorway, scared and trembling, clutching her nightgown.

A great face appeared then between them and that distant height. There was silence and Homily sat upright, her mouth open. "Is that your mother?" asked a surprised voice after a moment, and Arrietty from the doorway whispered: "Yes."

It was the boy.

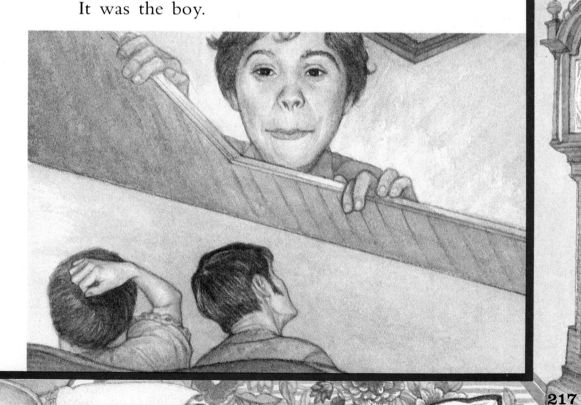

Pod got out of bed and stood beside it, shivering in his nightshirt. "Come on," he said to Homily, "you can't stay there!"

But Homily could. She had her nightdress on and nothing was going to move her. She glared at the boy—he was only a child after all. "Put it back!" she said, "put it back at once!"

He knelt down then, but Homily did not move as the great face came slowly closer. "But I've got something for you," he said.

Homily's expression did not change and Arrietty called out from her place in the doorway: "What is it?"

The boy reached behind him and, careful to keep it upright, he held a wooden object above their heads. "It's this," he said, as he lowered the object slowly into their hole. It was a doll's dresser,

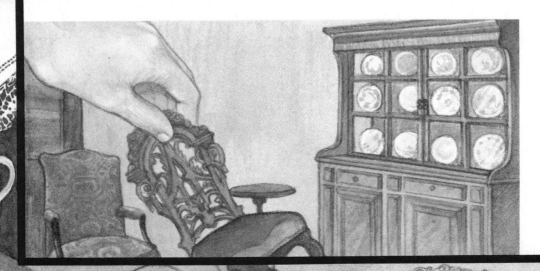

complete with plates. It had two drawers in it and a cupboard below. Arrietty ran around to see better.

"Oh," she cried happily. "Mother, look!"

Homily threw the dresser a glance—it was dark oak and the plates were hand-painted—and then she looked quickly away again. "Yes," she said coldly, "it's very nice."

There was a short silence which no one knew how to break.

"The cupboard really opens," said the boy at last, and the great hand came down amongst them.

"Yes," agreed Homily after a moment, "I see it does."

Pod drew a long breath—a sigh of relief as the hand went back.

"There, Homily," Pod said, "you've always wanted something like that!"

"Yes," said Homily—she still sat upright, her hands clasped in her lap. "Thank you very much. And now," she went on coldly, "will you please put back the roof?"

"Wait a minute," pleaded the boy. Again he reached behind him. Again the hand came down. And there, beside the dresser, where there was barely room for it, was a very small doll's chair, covered in red velvet. "Oh!" Arrietty exclaimed again and Pod said: "Just about fit me, that would."

"Try it," begged the boy, and Pod threw him a nervous glance. "Go on!" said Arrietty, and Pod sat down—in his nightshirt, his bare feet showing. "That's nice," he said after a moment. "It would go by the fire in the sitting room!" cried Arrietty.

"Let's try it," said the boy, and the hand came down again. Pod sprang up just in time to steady the dresser as the red velvet chair was taken away above his head and placed in the next room. Arrietty ran out of the door and along the passage to see. "Oh," she called out to her parents, "come and see. It's lovely!"

But Pod and Homily did not move. The boy was leaning over them, breathing hard, and they could see the middle buttons of his nightshirt. He seemed to be examining the farther room.

"What do you keep in that mustard-pot?" asked the boy.

"Coal," said Arrietty's voice. "And I helped to borrow this new carpet. Here's the watch I told you about, and the pictures. . . ."

"I could get you some better stamps than those," the boy said.

"Look," cried Arrietty's voice again, and Pod took Homily's hand, "these are my books—"

Homily clutched Pod as the great hand came down once more in the direction of Arrietty. "Quiet," he whispered. "Sit still. . . ." The boy, it seemed, was touching the books.

"What are they called?" he asked, and Arrietty reeled off the names. "Why couldn't you read me those?"

"Well, I could," said Arrietty, "but I'd rather read something new."

"But you never come," complained the boy.

"I know," said Arrietty, "but I will."

"Pod," whispered Homily, "did you hear that? Did you hear what she said?"

"Yes, yes," Pod whispered. "Keep quiet—" Pod looked up at the boy. "Hey," he called, trying to attract his attention. The boy looked down. "Put the roof back now," Pod begged him, trying to sound matter of fact. "We're getting cold."

"All right," agreed the boy, but he seemed to hesitate. He reached across them for the piece of board which formed their roof. "Shall I nail you down?" he asked, and they saw him pick up the hammer. It swayed above them, very dangerous looking.

"Of course nail us down," said Pod.

"I mean," said the boy, "I've got some more things upstairs—"

Pod looked uncertain and Homily nudged him. "Ask him," she whispered, "what kind of things?"

"What kind of things?" asked Pod.

"Things from an old doll's house there is on the top shelf of the cupboard by the fireplace in the schoolroom."

"What sort of things are there in the doll's house?" asked Arrietty from the sitting room.

"Oh, everything," the boy told her. "Carpets and rugs and beds, and there's a bird in a cage—not a real one—of course, and cooking pans and tables and five gold chairs and a pot with a palm tree—"

Homily leaned across to Pod. "Tell him to nail us down lightly," she whispered. Pod stared at her and she nodded, clasping her hands.

Pod turned to the boy. "All right," he said, "you nail us down. But lightly, if you see what I mean. Just a tap or two here and there. . . ."

Your glimpse into the miniature world of the Borrowers does not have to end! Find out more about the adventures of Pod, Homily, and Arrietty by reading **The Borrowers**, *the book from which this story was taken. There's a whole series of books about the Borrowers you can also read.*

UNIT THREE   LEVEL 11

SPIRIT
OF
AMERICA

PREPARING FOR READING

Learning Vocabulary

1. Little Wolf, the young Indian, made a <u>journey</u> to the great plains.
2. When he walked through the desert, he <u>shielded</u> his eyes from the bright sun.
3. Little Wolf met a creature that he thought might <u>destroy</u> him.
4. He was <u>ashamed</u> of his fear, and was determined to regain his <u>pride</u>.
5. Little Wolf felt <u>awkward</u> as he rode the creature for the first time.

journey   shielded   destroy
ashamed   pride   awkward

Developing Background and Skills
Cause and Effect

Janet was amazed to see her friend Louis carrying his raincoat on a sunny day. "Why do you have your raincoat on a day like today?" she asked.

Louis explained that he was on his way to practice for the school play. "I've got my raincoat because it's part of my costume," he said.

The answer Louis gave explained the **cause,** or reason, for what he was doing. Janet saw the **effect,** or result, of the cause.

Louis was carrying his raincoat because he needed it for his part in a play.

That sentence states a cause-and-effect relationship.

Signal words such as *because*, *so*, *since*, and *in order to* can help you understand cause and effect. But writers do not always use signal words. Then it's up to you to figure out cause-and-effect relationships.

Read the paragraph below. Look for a cause-and-effect relationship.

On the day of the young Indian's birth, someone had brought a wolf cub to the village. The boy was given the name Little Wolf.

First find the effect. Ask yourself "What happened?"

The young Indian was given the name Little Wolf. That is the effect, or result.

To find the cause, ask yourself "What caused this?" or "Why did it happen?"

The fact that someone brought a wolf cub to the village on the day of his birth is the cause. It is the reason the Indian was given the name Little Wolf.

In the story "The Sun Dog," there are many cause-and-effect relationships. As you read, ask yourself "Why did this happen?" or "What was the cause of this?"

THE SUN DOG

Clyde Robert Bulla and Michael Syson

After Columbus reached the Americas in 1492, Spain and other European countries began to claim the new land. The Indians who were living there could not stop the Spanish soldiers. They had brought weapons with them, and they had horses. The Indians had never seen horses before. They fled in terror at the sight of the armoured men who rode upon such strange animals. The Spaniards knew the value of their horses and took great care not to lose them. Still, some horses strayed away from the troops and wandered into the plains.

The young man stood alone in the desert. He was slim and straight; his skin was deep brown. He wore buckskin breeches, moccasins, and a necklace of seeds. With arms held high, he waited for his god.

Too long he had borne the name his mother had given him. On the day of his birth, someone had brought a wolf cub to the village. For no other reason, his mother had called him Little Wolf. As a child-name it had served well enough, but it was no name for him now.

Little Wolf had gone to the shaman, the medicine man of the tribe. He had asked, "Where shall I find my man-name? Set a time for my journey and tell me where to go. Give me a sign."

The old shaman had spoken: "Follow the grey goose south to the great plain beyond the mountains, farther than any of our people have been before, until you meet the sun-god face to face."

"And what then?" the young man had asked. But the shaman had not answered.

Little Wolf had made the journey. Now, in this land of scattered rocks and strange desert plants, he waited. Even the wind seemed to wait. The colors in the sky grew deeper, brighter. The sun-god rose over the hills. Little Wolf prayed: "Tell me what I seek to know. Give me a sign—"

A sound came to him, faint at first, then louder. It was like the beating of his own heart. He peered into the sun. The sound seemed to come from there. He shielded his eyes with his fingers. Out of the brightness came a rising, falling shape. An animal shape.

There were legs. There was a crooked hump. Little Wolf sank to the ground. The sun-god was angry. It had sent this

creature to destroy him! He closed his eyes. The thud of footsteps came nearer. Then there was stillness.

Slowly he opened his eyes. The creature was there, looking down at him. It had four legs, a head, a long, thick tail, and on its back that crooked hump. It wore a headdress—or was it a part of the animal?—that looked as if leather thongs were fitted to its head and looped over its neck.

Like a big, grey elk or a great dog, it stood and watched him. Its eyes were round and bright. It shook its head and made a jangling sound. The brush of hair on its neck lifted and fell. Its lips pulled back from its teeth, and it laughed. Then the animal took a step nearer.

With one hand Little Wolf reached for the bow slung on his back. With the other he reached into his bag for an arrow. He fitted it to his bowstring and took aim at the animal's chest. Its heart must

be there—if it had a heart.

The sun was in his eyes. His hand shook as he let the arrow fly. He had missed! But no— the arrow had struck home. It was deep in the crooked hump on the animal's back. But the animal did not fall. It did not cry out in pain. It seemed to feel nothing.

Little Wolf sprang to his feet and fled. But he did not go far. Ashamed of his fear, he stopped. Here he would make a stand.

The animal again came toward him. Its head was a little like that of a deer, but longer. There was pride in the arch of its neck. There was strength in the shoulders and hind quarters. It moved easily. Only the hump looked awkward.

Little Wolf was ready, knife in hand. The creature came closer. Little Wolf stepped aside, then flung himself forward in a long leap that carried him up behind the hump. If he moved quickly, he might finish the work of the arrow. He struck with the knife. The blade bit deep.

He heard a dull crack. He was falling. He was on the ground, his legs gripping the animal's hump. He twisted the blade, but no blood flowed. He looked up. The animal stood by, watching him. . . .

Little Wolf turned to face the creature. He was sure it was laughing at him. He looked down at the hump. Whatever it was, it was dead. Perhaps it had never been alive.

Little Wolf looked at the big, grey animal. Without its

ugly hump, it was beautiful. It had not harmed him. A thought came to him. Was this creature a gift of the sun-god—his to take back to the village?

The creature was moving away, and the young man moved beside it. The creature broke into a trot, then a lope. It left Little Wolf behind. He did not stop. His pace was slower, but it was steady. The big dog had been sent to him. He must not lose it. The creature was leading him on, waiting a few moments, then dashing off again. It started up a trail that led into the hills.

Little Wolf followed it and found it nearby, tearing at a clump of grass with its teeth. He gazed in wonder. Never before had he seen a dog eat grass.

He searched the desert floor. He found some dry, stiff grass and held it out to the big dog. The animal looked interested. It took a few steps forward.

Little Wolf waited. His eyes were on the headdress the

creature wore—the headdress made of leather thongs. Part of it lay over the animal's neck and was fastened to something the animal held in its mouth. Something that looked like a bar of metal. The big dog stretched out its neck. Its teeth closed on the handful of grass.

Little Wolf grabbed the leather thong near the animal's

mouth. The animal lunged and reared. Little Wolf was lifted off his feet and flung from side to side. The big dog stopped, legs braced, ears back. There was blood on its mouth.

If it lunged again, Little Wolf could not keep his hold on the thong. He knew it. He thought the animal knew it, too. One more lunge, and it would be free. But if he were

on the big dog's back—if he could wear down its strength and force it to its knees. . . .

He let go of the thong. In the same motion he grasped the thick hair on the creature's neck. His body twisted. He swung his leg up, and he was on the animal's back.

The animal was running. Little Wolf could hear the pounding hoofs beneath him as he bent forward. He gripped the animal's sides with his legs. Slowly he raised himself until he was sitting upright.

The desert was flying past him—the earth, the rocks, the growing things. Once this land had made him feel small, but no longer. From here to the distant mountains would hardly be half a day's journey!

On the back of the sun dog he could race the wind. He could race an eagle and leave it far behind. Never before had he known such power. He shouted, and his voice was strong above the thunder of hoofbeats. He lifted one hand

and waved to the birds, to the mountains, to the sun. He lifted the other hand and leaned into the wind.

Then he was falling. He saw the earth rushing toward him. He struck the desert floor and lay still.

His eyes opened. He felt bruised and numb, but his heart still beat with the wild joy he had felt when he was on the creature's back, flying between earth and sky. The world had grown quiet. He looked about him. The big dog was gone.

Little Wolf stood up and gasped at the stab of pain in his leg. The big dog's tracks were plain in the loose earth. He walked in the trail. Dragging his foot painfully, he kept on, stumbling, falling, rising again. Toward the mountains. Into the foothills. The creature's trail was still clear, but night was near. In the morning the sun dog might be gone forever.

He climbed up into a box canyon. On three sides it was closed in by high cliffs. The sun dog was there, standing still, its head lifted.

They faced each other, and suddenly he was filled with shame. This great animal had come from the sun-god, and he had fought it as he might have fought an enemy. He had wounded it, made it suffer. Now he was wounded and suffering in return.

The big grey dog looked as if it were waiting for something. But what? What was left for him to do? He could only go. He limped on. A sound came from behind him. The sun dog was following him! It came so near that he could feel its breath on his shoulder. He could have reached up and taken hold of the thong that lay on its neck, but he made no move toward it.

They walked together out of the canyon. The sunset cast arrows of light high into the sky. He said aloud: "Let this day be with me always. Let my man-name be He Who Rides the Sun Dog." And it seemed to him that the sun-god smiled.

The sun dog remained, and over the years others appeared. Under the Indians' care, they multiplied. On horseback, whole nations moved out of the barren mountains and into the grassy plains. On horseback, Indians could follow the buffalo herds that provided them with most of their needs. Thus they came to a golden age that was to last three-hundred years.

Questions

1. From where did the first horses in America come?
2. Why was Little Wolf frightened when he first saw the horse?
3. Do you think the "sun dog" followed Little Wolf all the way back to his village? Why or why not?
4. Have you ever been frightened of something because it was new to you? Describe your experience.

Applying Reading Skills

Copy the chart below on your paper. Fill in the missing information about cause-and-effect relationships from "The Sun Dog."

CAUSE	EFFECT
1.	Little Wolf went to the old shaman.
2. Little Wolf thought the creature was sent to destroy him.	
3.	Little Wolf stopped running from the sun dog.
4. Little Wolf was thrown from the horse.	

FRIEND

Friend,
My horse
Flies like a bird
As it runs.

Teton Sioux

WRITING ACTIVITY

WRITE A FRIENDLY LETTER

Prewrite

In "The Sun Dog," Little Wolf did not know that the animal he found was a horse. He had never seen such an animal.

Imagine that you have friends who live on another planet. On the planet, there are no dogs. Your friends write to you and say that they have heard about a creature called a dog. They want you to describe a dog. You decide to write a letter to your friends. Your letter must give a clear description of a dog for people who have never seen one. What will you write?

Your friends have helped you by sending some questions. Write sentences as answers for the questions. You may want to add other questions.

1. What does this creature look like?
2. Where does it live?
3. What does it eat?
4. Are all dogs the same? If not, how are they different? How are they alike?
5. What does a dog do?
6. Can a dog talk? If not, how do you know what a dog wants or how a dog feels? How does the dog know what you want or how you feel?

Write

1. Read the questions and your answers. Your audience, the people who will read your letter, does not know anything about dogs. Have you left out any important information?
2. Think about how many paragraphs you will have in your letter. You might try this plan:

   Paragraph 1: What a dog looks like, where it lives, and what it eats

   Paragraph 2: How dogs are alike and different

   Paragraph 3: What dogs can do and how people communicate with dogs
3. Write a main idea sentence for each paragraph and use your answer sentences for supporting details.
4. Use the correct form for your letter.
5. Use your Glossary or dictionary for spelling help.

Revise

Read your letter again. Will your friends get a good idea of what a dog is like by reading your letter? Have you left out any important information? Does each paragraph have a main idea sentence? Now is the time to rewrite any parts of your letter that are not clear.

1. Did you use the correct form for a friendly letter?
2. Did you use the correct punctuation in each part of your letter?
3. Did you indent the first sentence in each paragraph?

PREPARING FOR READING

Learning Vocabulary

1. Indian trails usually zigzagged uphill at a <u>gradual</u> <u>incline</u>.
2. The early <u>colonists</u> who settled America used the trails made by Indians.
3. Later, <u>merchants</u> sent their goods by wagon on post roads.
4. Stagecoaches were coaches that advanced by <u>stages</u>, covering a certain distance each day.
5. Not many towns had <u>paved</u> streets in the 1700s.

gradual	incline	colonists
merchants	stages	paved

Developing Background and Skills
Cause and Effect

When you read, you should think about how things go together or are related. One way that things are related is called **cause and effect.** In a cause-and-effect relationship, an event, the cause, results in another event, the effect.

Read the paragraph on the next page. Look for three cause-and-effect relationships.

In those days, coaches were called stagecoaches because they advanced by stages, covering a certain distance each day. The horses had to pull heavy loads, and they tired quickly. It was necessary to change teams often at a coaching stop.

Sometimes one sentence includes both cause and effect. Other times, you will have to find the cause of something and its effect in separate sentences.

In the first sentence above, the cause and effect are linked by the signal word *because*.

EFFECT: Coaches were called stagecoaches.
CAUSE: They advanced by stages.

The second example of cause-and-effect is in the second sentence.

EFFECT: Horses tired quickly.
CAUSE: They had to pull heavy loads.

The last cause-and-effect example is found in the second and third sentences.

EFFECT: It was necessary to change teams often at a coaching stop.
CAUSE: The horses tired quickly.

Notice that the effect in the second example is the cause in the third example.

As you read "The First Roads," look for cause-and-effect relationships.

THE FIRST ROADS

Adrian A. Paradis

The earliest roads in America were trails found on the plains in the Midwest and in the forests along the east coast. Those on the plains were trails worn through the tall grasses by buffalo and other animals. The animals took the easiest routes to reach their feeding grounds, water holes, or nearby streams.

Along the east coast, the trails were made by the Indians who lived in the forests. Most Indian trails or paths were eighteen or twenty inches (45 or 50 centimeters) wide. They seemed to wander from place to place without reason. As the Indians walked in single file along the narrow trail, they could stay hidden from their enemies.

An Indian path usually followed a stream. When the path came to a shallow pool, a person could wade through the water or jump across from rock to rock.

Then the trail led into the woods again.

The first settlers who came to America discovered that Indians did not walk straight up the steepest part of a hill. Instead, the Indians followed trails which wound snake-like through the woods along the side of a slope. This made climbing much easier because the incline was more gradual. An Indian hardly knew he was going uphill. In a short time, he would find himself at the top. Looking down through the trees, he could see how far he was from his starting point.

The early colonists used the Indian trails for roads as they went by foot or on horseback from village to village. Gradually the trails were made wider as trees were chopped down. Then they were called roads.

So travelers would know what kind of a road it was, the colonists marked each trail. A blaze, or ax

mark, was made on some of the trees where a road began. One ax mark meant it was a *one-chop road*, and only wide enough for horseback riders to use. When the road was widened so that two wagons could pass, two marks were cut into the trees and it was called a *two-chop road*. Later, if the roadbed was made smooth enough for coaches, it was known as a *three-chop road*. Then the trees showed three ax marks.

To build the first two-chop roads, rocks and tree stumps were removed. The earth was made as smooth and as hard as possible. But this did not help. No matter what the season, there was trouble traveling on these roads. In the summer, the horses' hoofs kicked up clouds of dust. During autumn, heavy rains soaked the dirt and turned most of the roads into muddy

paths. Throughout the winter, the roads in the northern
colonies were covered with snow. Then farmers had
to use wide shovels to clear paths. Many times they
had just finished shoveling when another storm dumped
more snow and blocked all travel again!

Spring was the worst season of all. For weeks,
melting snow and spring rains almost made roads into
swamps. Ruts a foot (30 centimeters) or more deep
were common. Drivers had to walk ahead of their
carts to guide the horse. They had to watch for the
safest ruts to use so the wheels would not sink below
their hubs.

Many of the roads that went through deep swamps
were made of logs laid side by side. Because they
looked like the striped lines of corduroy cloth, they

were called *corduroy roads*. The cracks between the logs were filled with earth, and for a few months there was a hard but uneven road. Then the wood rotted and sank into the swamp. The road quickly became unsafe to use until it was repaired.

In some places where the ground was dry but very uneven, the colonists built log or plank roads. They laid logs side by side just as they did on the corduroy roads. But instead of filling in the cracks, they covered the logs with dirt to form a hard smooth surface. However, heavy rains would usually wash away the dirt.

Some of the roads that stretched between Boston and New York City were known as *post roads*. Farmers and travelers who were going a short distance used

these roads. They were also used by riders who carried mail between a few towns. By 1673, riders could carry the mail on post roads all the way from Boston to New York City.

For many years, the post roads were used mainly by the mail riders and a few travelers. Some wagons and carts owned by farmers and merchants who shipped goods went along the bumpy roads, too. By 1722, the Boston post roads were made smooth and safe enough for stagecoaches.

In those days, coaches were called stagecoaches because they advanced by stages, covering a certain distance each day. The horses had to pull heavy loads, and they tired quickly. It was necessary to change teams often at a coaching stop. Here, fresh horses were hitched

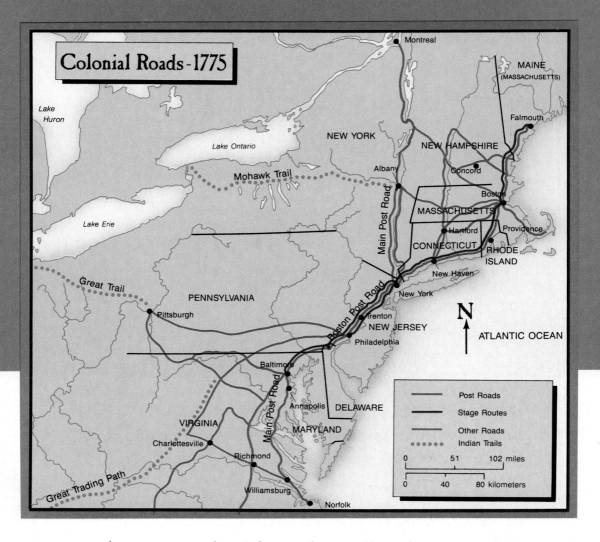

Colonial Roads · 1775

Montreal

MAINE
(MASSACHUSETTS)

Lake
Huron

Falmouth

NEW YORK

Lake Ontario

NEW HAMPSHIRE

Mohawk Trail

Albany

Concord

Lake Erie

Boston

MASSACHUSETTS

Main Post Road

Hartford

Providence

Great Trail

CONNECTICUT

RHODE
ISLAND

PENNSYLVANIA

New Haven

Pittsburgh

New York

N

Boston Post Road

Trenton

NEW JERSEY

ATLANTIC OCEAN

Philadelphia

Baltimore

Main Post Road

Annapolis

DELAWARE

VIRGINIA

MARYLAND

Charlottesville

Richmond

Post Roads

Stage Routes

Great Trading Path

Other Roads

Williamsburg

Indian Trails

Norfolk

0   51   102 miles

0   40   80 kilometers

to the stagecoach. After a long trip, the passengers were glad to reach a large town or city where the roads would be smoother. However, although these roads were better than those in the country, most of them became just as muddy in wet weather. Some towns paved their streets with bricks, blocks and planks of wood, flat stones, or gravel. But many years would pass before the streets in cities and towns were paved as they are today.

Questions

1. How did the early colonists mark trails?
2. Why did drivers have to walk ahead of their carts to guide the horse after heavy spring rains?
3. How is traveling by car today different from traveling by stagecoach in the 1700s?
4. Imagine you are living in the future. How might travel then differ from travel today?

Applying Reading Skills

Copy the chart below on your paper. Fill in the missing information about cause-and-effect relationships from "The First Roads."

CAUSE	EFFECT
1. The colonists marked each trail.	
2.	The earth was made as smooth and as hard as possible.
3. Roads made of logs laid side by side looked like the striped lines of corduroy cloth.	
4.	Stagecoach passengers were glad to reach a large town or city.

PREPARING FOR READING

Learning Vocabulary

1. The colonists protested against the <u>taxes</u> the English made them pay.
2. In the spring of 1775, English <u>troops</u> and <u>scouts</u> were seen near Boston.
3. Paul Revere was one of the <u>messengers</u> sent to <u>inform</u> the <u>citizens</u> of Charleston about the English.
4. As Paul Revere rode toward Lexington, two English officers tried to <u>overtake</u> him.

taxes   troops   scouts   messengers
inform   citizens   overtake

Developing Background and Skills
Sequence of Events

As you read, it is important to keep track of the order in which things happen, or **sequence of events.** When signal words such as *first*, *then*, *next*, and *finally* are not there to help you, it's up to you to figure out the correct sequence.

Read the paragraph about Paul Revere and the Sons of Liberty on the next page.

On December 16, 1773, Paul Revere and the Sons of Liberty dumped 10,000 pounds of tea into Boston Harbor. Pretending to be Indians, they marched on board English ships and hauled the chests of tea onto the decks. They broke open the chests with their axes.

What did the men do first? If you read the paragraph carefully, you probably figured out that the men first pretended to be Indians.

What did they do next? They marched on board the English ships and hauled up the chests of tea. After that? They broke open the chests.

The last thing the men did was dump the tea into Boston Harbor. The events in the paragraph were not written in the order in which they happened. The first sentence told you what happened last. In order to figure out the sequence of events, you had to do some careful thinking.

The next selection is based on events that actually happened. When you read about historical events, it is important to keep the events in order. Understanding the sequence of events can sometimes help you understand why things happened.

PAUL REVERE'S BIG RIDE

Jean Fritz

In 1735 there were in Boston 42 streets, 36 lanes, 22 alleys, 1,000 brick houses, 2,000 wooden houses, 12 churches, 4 schools, and 418 horses.

Along with the horses, streets, and alleys, there were, of course, people in Boston—more than 13,000. Four of them lived in a small wooden house on North Street near Love Lane. They were Mr. Revere, a gold- and silversmith; his wife, Deborah; their daughter, Deborah; and their young son, Paul Revere, born the first day of the new year.

Of all the busy people in Boston, Paul Revere would turn out to be one of the busiest. All his life he found that there was more to do, more to see, more to hear, more to say, more places to go, and more to learn than there were hours in the day.

There was plenty for Paul to do. When he was fifteen years old, his father died, and Paul took over the silversmithing business. He made beads, rings, lockets, bracelets, buttons, medals, pitchers, teapots, spoons, cups, shoe buckles, and candlesticks.

Still, Paul Revere wasn't always at work. Once in a while he just dreamed. There was one page in his daybook that he used simply for doodling.

Beginning in 1765, there was no time for doodling. The English were causing trouble. They were telling the colonies they couldn't do this and couldn't do that. They were slapping on taxes, one after another. First there was a tax on printed matter. When this was taken off there was a tax on tea, glass, printers' colors, and paper. The one tax England would never give up was the tax on tea.

What did Paul Revere do about it? He became a leader of the Sons of Liberty, a secret club that found interesting ways to work against the English.

One of Paul's busiest nights was December 16, 1773. He picked up his ax and joined other Sons of Liberty, all pretending to be Indians.

They were going to make sure that no one in Boston would pay taxes on the three shiploads of tea that had just arrived from England. So they marched

on board the ships, hauled the chests of tea onto the decks, broke them open with their axes, and dumped the tea—10,000 pounds of it—into Boston Harbor. It was all done in an orderly fashion. No one was hurt. The ships were not harmed.

When the Sons of Liberty finished, they marched home, washed their faces, and went to bed. But not Paul Revere. Someone had to ride to New York and Philadelphia and spread the news. Paul was picked to do it.

So off he galloped, his hat clapped to his head, his coattails flying. He rode from Boston to Philadelphia and back—sixty-three miles a day. He was back in Boston on the eleventh day. This was long before anyone expected him.

Paul Revere became Massachusetts' Number One express rider between Boston and Philadelphia. He also became a secret agent. In the winter of 1774 it looked more and more as if the English soldiers in Boston meant to make war on America. Paul's job was to try to find out the English plans.

He rode the streets at night, delivered messages to Philadelphia, and kept himself ready at all times to warn the countryside.

But all his rides, Paul knew, were small compared to the Big Ride that lay ahead. Nothing should go wrong with this one. In the spring, everyone agreed, the English would march into the countryside and really start fighting. When they did, Paul Revere would have to be ahead of them.

On Saturday, April 15, 1775, spring, it seemed, had arrived. Boats for moving troops had been seen on the Charles River. English scouts had been seen on the road to Lexington and Concord. A stableboy had overheard two officers making plans.

At 10:45 on Tuesday night, April 18, Dr. Joseph Warren, who was leading Patriot activities in Boston, sent for Paul Revere. Other messengers had been sent to Lexington and Concord by longer routes. Paul was to go, as planned, the same way the English were

going—across the Charles River. He was to warn the citizens so they could arm themselves. He was also to inform John Hancock and Samuel Adams, Boston's two Patriot leaders who were staying in Lexington.

He had already arranged a quick way of warning the people of Charlestown across the river. Two lanterns were to be hung in the steeple of the North Church if the English were coming by water; one lantern if they were coming by land.

So Paul rushed to the North Church and gave directions. "Two lanterns," he said. "Now."

Then he ran home, flung open the door, pulled on his boots, grabbed his coat, and off he went—his hat clapped to his head, his coattails flying. He was in such a hurry that he left the door open, and his dog got out.

On the way to the river, Paul picked up two friends, who had promised to row him to the other side. Then all three ran to a dock near the Charlestown ferry where Paul had kept a boat hidden during the winter. Paul's dog ran with them.

The night was pleasant, and the moon was bright. Too bright. In the path of moonlight across the river lay an armed English transport. Paul and his friends would have to row past it.

Then Paul realized his first mistake. He had meant to bring cloth to wrap around the oars so the sound would be muffled. He had left the cloth at home.

That wasn't all he had left behind. Paul Revere had started out for his Big Ride without his spurs. What could be done?

Luckily, one of Paul's friends knew a lady who lived nearby. He ran to her house, called at the window, and asked for some cloth. She gave him some.

Then for the spurs. Luckily, Paul's dog was there, and luckily, he was well trained. Paul wrote a note to his wife, tied it around the dog's neck, and told the dog to go home. By the time Paul and his friends had ripped the cloth in two, wrapped each half around an oar, and launched the boat, the dog was back with Paul's spurs around his neck.

Paul and his two friends rowed softly across the
Charles River. They slipped carefully past the English
transport with its sixty-four guns, and they landed in
the shadows on the other side—safely. There a group
of men from Charlestown who had seen the signal in
the church steeple had a horse waiting for Paul.

Off Paul Revere rode on his Big Ride. He kept
his horse on the road and himself on his horse. All
went well until suddenly he saw two men on horseback
under a tree. They were English officers. One officer
sprang out and tried to get ahead of Paul. The other

tried to overtake him from behind, but Paul turned his horse quickly and galloped across country, past a muddy pond, toward another road to Lexington. What happened to the officers? One galloped straight into the mud and got stuck. The other gave up the chase.

Paul continued to Lexington, beating on doors as he went, waking up the citizens. At Lexington he woke up John Hancock and Samuel Adams and advised them to leave town. Then, in the company of two other riders, he continued to Concord, warning farmers along the way.

For a while all went well. Then suddenly from out of the shadows appeared six English officers. They rode up with their guns in their hands and ordered Paul to stop. But Paul didn't stop immediately.

One of the officers shouted, "If you go an inch farther, you are a dead man."

Paul and his companions tried to ride through the group, but they were surrounded and ordered into a pasture at one side of the road.

In the pasture six other officers appeared. One of them spoke like a gentleman. He took Paul's horse by the reins and asked Paul where he came from.

Paul told him, "Boston."

The officer asked what time he had left Boston.

Paul told him.

The officer asked his name.

Paul answered that his name was Revere.

"What! *Paul* Revere?"

Paul said, "Yes."

Now the English officers certainly did not want to let Paul Revere loose. They put him, along with other prisoners, at the center of their group, and they rode off toward Lexington. As they approached town, they heard gunfire.

"What was that?" the officer asked.

Paul said it was a signal to alarm the countryside. With this piece of news, the English decided they'd like to get back to their own troops in a hurry. Indeed, they were in such a hurry that they no longer wanted to be bothered with prisoners. So after taking their horses, they set them free.

Then what happened? Paul Revere felt bad, of course, to be on his Big Ride without a horse. He felt uneasy to be on a moonlit road on foot. So he struck out through the country, across stone walls, through pastures, and back into Lexington to see if John Hancock and Samuel Adams were still there.

They were. They were just preparing to leave town in John Hancock's carriage. Paul and Hancock's clerk, John Lowell, went with them.

All went well. They rode about two miles into the countryside, and then suddenly John Hancock remembered that he had left a trunk full of important papers in a Lexington tavern. This was a mistake. He didn't want the English to find those papers.

So what happened? Paul Revere and John Lowell got out of the carriage and walked back to Lexington.

It was morning now. From all over the area farmers were gathering on Lexington Green. As Paul crossed the green to the tavern, there were between fifty and sixty armed men preparing to take a stand against the English. The troops were said to be near.

Paul went into the tavern, found the trunk, and carried it out, holding one end while John Lowell held the other. As they stepped on the green, the troops appeared.

Then what happened? Paul and John held onto the trunk. They walked right through the American lines, holding onto the trunk. They were still holding on when a gun was fired. Then there were two guns, then many guns firing back and forth. Paul did not pay any attention to who was firing or who fired first. He did not stop to think that this might be the first battle of a war. His job was to move a trunk to safety, and that's what he did.

The battles of Lexington and Concord did, of course, begin the Revolutionary War. And Americans have talked ever since about Paul Revere's ride.

Questions

1. Who were the Sons of Liberty?
2. Why were two lanterns hung in the steeple of North Church?
3. What kind of person do you think Paul Revere was?
4. If you had an important message to be delivered, whom would you pick to do it? Why?

Applying Reading Skills

The following sentences describe events from "Paul Revere's Big Ride." Read the sentences, then write them in the correct sequence on your paper.

Paul Revere and John Lowell carried John Hancock's trunk out of a tavern.
Paul escaped two English officers and rode to Lexington.
The English put taxes on many things the colonists used.
Paul had two lanterns hung in the steeple of North Church.
The Revolutionary War began.
The English took Paul's horse.
English troops were seen on the Charles River.
Paul rode from Lexington in John Hancock's carriage.

PREPARING FOR READING

Learning Vocabulary

1. The girls got into an old bed that was <u>propped</u> up with a stack of books.
2. Granddad <u>guaranteed</u> that the <u>tale</u> he was about to tell them was true.
3. The girls listened as Granddad recounted the ideas of a <u>genius</u> named Big Finn McReady.
4. McReady was <u>convinced</u> that he could change all rail transportation with his new invention.
5. As Granddad told every <u>detail</u> of the story, he <u>imitated</u> the actions of McReady and his friend.

propped	guaranteed	tale	genius
convinced	detail	imitated	

Developing Background and Skills
Sequence of Events

Have you ever wondered what things were like long ago? You might ask your parents or grandparents to tell you about the times when they were growing up.

Reading about the past is another way to find out about life long ago. Sometimes writers tell about events from the past in a story that is set in the present.

You may have seen movies or TV programs that did this, too. A character may be telling about something that took place in the past. As he or she talks, the scene changes. You see what happened long ago.

The **sequence of events** in a story that has events from the past and from the present can be tricky. The story starts. Some events take place. Then events from the past are described. Finally, the last events in the story take place.

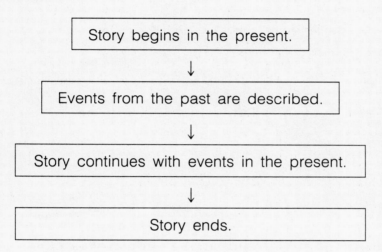

Story begins in the present.

↓

Events from the past are described.

↓

Story continues with events in the present.

↓

Story ends.

The next selection includes events from the past and from the present. As you read, notice how the writer describes both.

The Tale of the Wind Wagon

Nick Engler

Bedtime at my grandparents' house was 8:30 sharp, no arguments and no nonsense. So come 8:30, my grandfather would yell, "Time's up!" Off we'd run, my sister Deborah and I, up to the spare bedroom and into our pajamas. We were pretty tired by then, anyway. Life on a hog farm in Jackson County can do in two city kids pretty quickly when they aren't used to it. But that wasn't the point. The point was, time for bed meant time for a bed–time story, and my grandfather was the greatest storyteller of all.

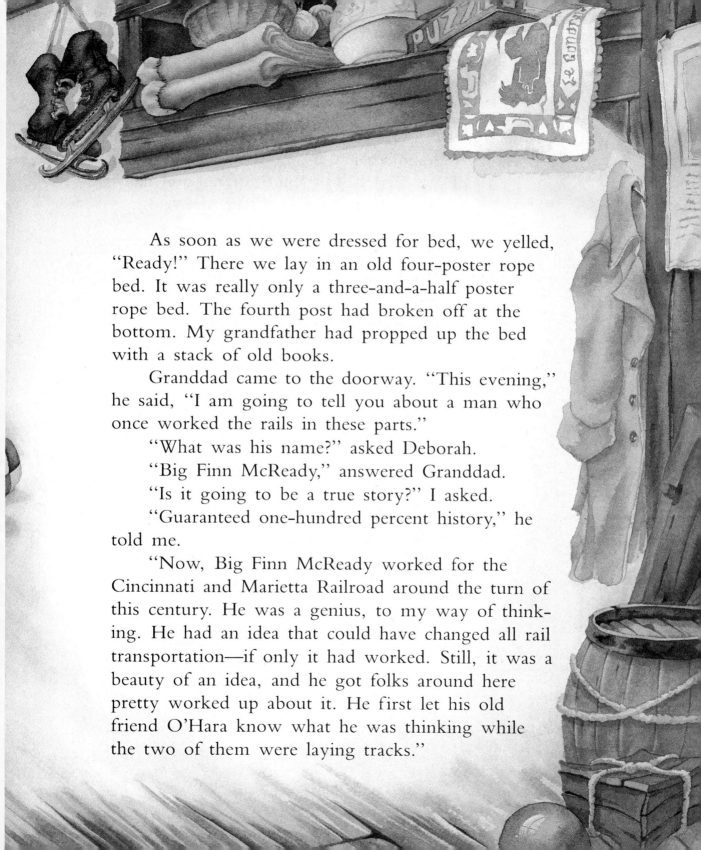

As soon as we were dressed for bed, we yelled, "Ready!" There we lay in an old four-poster rope bed. It was really only a three-and-a-half poster rope bed. The fourth post had broken off at the bottom. My grandfather had propped up the bed with a stack of old books.

Granddad came to the doorway. "This evening," he said, "I am going to tell you about a man who once worked the rails in these parts."

"What was his name?" asked Deborah.

"Big Finn McReady," answered Granddad.

"Is it going to be a true story?" I asked.

"Guaranteed one-hundred percent history," he told me.

"Now, Big Finn McReady worked for the Cincinnati and Marietta Railroad around the turn of this century. He was a genius, to my way of thinking. He had an idea that could have changed all rail transportation—if only it had worked. Still, it was a beauty of an idea, and he got folks around here pretty worked up about it. He first let his old friend O'Hara know what he was thinking while the two of them were laying tracks."

Next thing we knew, there were Big Finn McReady and his friend O'Hara, working away in the bedroom, just as if they had been there all along. Of course, both of them looked very much like my grandfather.

O'Hara carried in a length of rail and laid it down. "What's it been now, Finn?" he said. "Thirty-some years altogether?"

"Thirty-five this day. Watch your toe." Big Finn McReady swung his sledge hammer, driving a spike into place.

"Isn't it time they put you on retirement?"

"O'Hara," said McReady, "I just started to work for this man's railroad."

O'Hara lifted an eyebrow. "Now just what do you mean by that?"

McReady leaned on his hammer and let loose his secret. "I mean that for the last thirty-five years, I've been saving and figuring to build me a train engine that doesn't need wood or coal to run it."

"I'll be," said O'Hara in amazement. "What are you going to use to make it work?"

"Air," answered McReady and went back to swinging his sledge hammer.

O'Hara pondered while his friend pounded. At last he said, "McReady, I do believe you're past due for retirement."

McReady paused, thought about doing something with his hammer, and then thought better of it. Instead, he explained to O'Hara: "What I mean to do, O'Hara, is take the plans for one of those sailing ships and build it atop a flatcar. Then I'll just let the wind blow it along the tracks. I aim to call it the Wind Wagon."

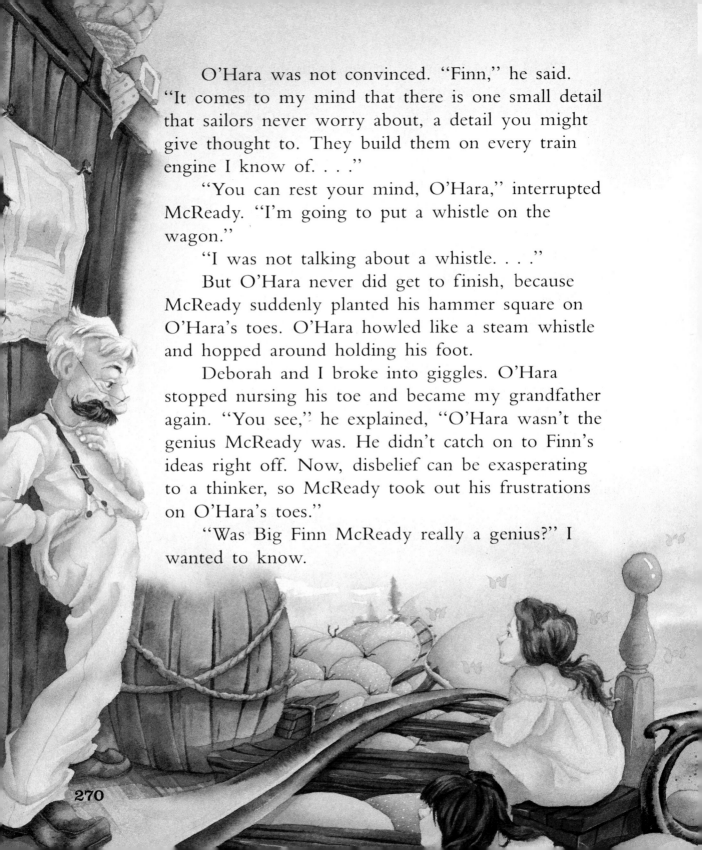

O'Hara was not convinced. "Finn," he said. "It comes to my mind that there is one small detail that sailors never worry about, a detail you might give thought to. They build them on every train engine I know of. . . ."

"You can rest your mind, O'Hara," interrupted McReady. "I'm going to put a whistle on the wagon."

"I was not talking about a whistle. . . ."

But O'Hara never did get to finish, because McReady suddenly planted his hammer square on O'Hara's toes. O'Hara howled like a steam whistle and hopped around holding his foot.

Deborah and I broke into giggles. O'Hara stopped nursing his toe and became my grandfather again. "You see," he explained, "O'Hara wasn't the genius McReady was. He didn't catch on to Finn's ideas right off. Now, disbelief can be exasperating to a thinker, so McReady took out his frustrations on O'Hara's toes."

"Was Big Finn McReady really a genius?" I wanted to know.

"Well," said my grandfather. "He had some big ideas. But the true test of a genius is not the size of the thoughts he thinks, it's whether or not he can keep himself from getting carried away with them."

"Did McReady get carried away with his Wind Wagon?" Deborah asked.

"That's the part I'm coming to," Granddad said.

"McReady retired that day to build his Wind Wagon. When it was finished, the Cincinnati and Marietta loaned him a stretch of track to try it out. The Wind Wagon was to set sail from Nelsonville Station. Folks came from all over to see her off. Oh, she was a sight to see! Three masts, four stories high, and yard upon yard of white canvas flapping in the wind. McReady was bursting with pride. He even let O'Hara ride along."

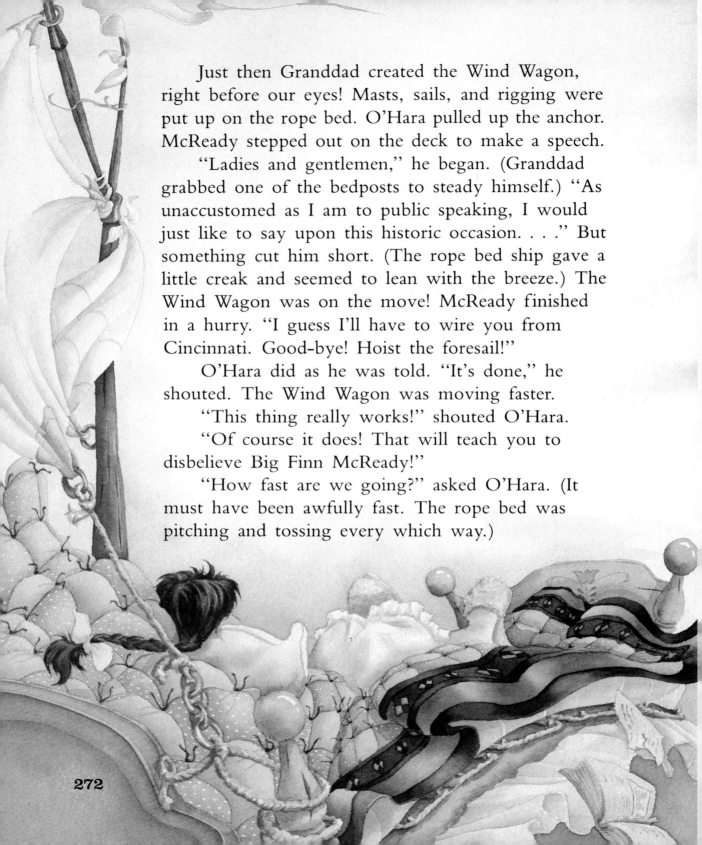

Just then Granddad created the Wind Wagon, right before our eyes! Masts, sails, and rigging were put up on the rope bed. O'Hara pulled up the anchor. McReady stepped out on the deck to make a speech.

"Ladies and gentlemen," he began. (Granddad grabbed one of the bedposts to steady himself.) "As unaccustomed as I am to public speaking, I would just like to say upon this historic occasion. . . ." But something cut him short. (The rope bed ship gave a little creak and seemed to lean with the breeze.) The Wind Wagon was on the move! McReady finished in a hurry. "I guess I'll have to wire you from Cincinnati. Good-bye! Hoist the foresail!"

O'Hara did as he was told. "It's done," he shouted. The Wind Wagon was moving faster.

"This thing really works!" shouted O'Hara.

"Of course it does! That will teach you to disbelieve Big Finn McReady!"

"How fast are we going?" asked O'Hara. (It must have been awfully fast. The rope bed was pitching and tossing every which way.)

McReady turned to look over his controls. "The gadget here says fifty-five miles an hour."

"Yahoo!" O'Hara cheered.

"Sixty-five!" called McReady, as the Wind Wagon picked up more and more speed.

"Seventy-five and still climbing," howled McReady. "We'll make a new world's record!"

O'Hara was scared stiff. "Finn," he begged, "why don't we hold it down to seventy? I only want to break one record at a time."

McReady saw the wisdom in this. "Maybe you're right, O'Hara. Better put on the brakes."

"The brakes," repeated O'Hara. "Right!" He disappeared below deck.

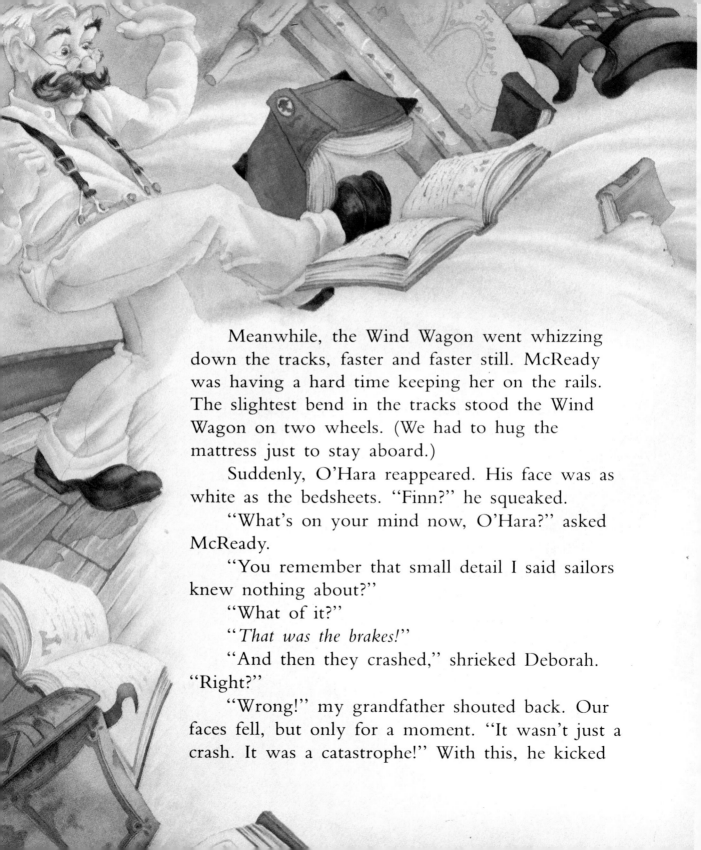

Meanwhile, the Wind Wagon went whizzing down the tracks, faster and faster still. McReady was having a hard time keeping her on the rails. The slightest bend in the tracks stood the Wind Wagon on two wheels. (We had to hug the mattress just to stay aboard.)

Suddenly, O'Hara reappeared. His face was as white as the bedsheets. "Finn?" he squeaked.

"What's on your mind now, O'Hara?" asked McReady.

"You remember that small detail I said sailors knew nothing about?"

"What of it?"

"*That was the brakes!*"

"And then they crashed," shrieked Deborah. "Right?"

"Wrong!" my grandfather shouted back. Our faces fell, but only for a moment. "It wasn't just a crash. It was a catastrophe!" With this, he kicked

the books from underneath the missing poster, and the bed tilted forward and to the side. My sister and I went tumbling down with the sheets and blankets.

"She jumped the tracks at the next bend," Granddad continued. "Plowed her way through fields and villages alike, skipped over ponds and streams just like a flat stone. She knocked down buildings, ruined crops, and came to rest, belly-up, in our great-granddaddy's pigsty, not a hundred steps from where you sit. The pigs took off in all directions. It took three days to find them all."

I found myself on the floor in a tangle of bed-clothes. Deborah freed herself and crawled up the tilted mattress, only to roll down it again. My grandfather, his part done, sat by and laughed.

We imitated the sights and sounds of buildings being knocked down, crops being ruined, and pigs being scattered every which way. Suddenly my grandmother appeared in the doorway.

"Wid," she said, "have you got them children all riled up again? What have you been doing?"

"I was just telling a story," said Granddad.

"Some story," huffed Grandmom. "Appears to me that you were about to tear the house down."

"Margret," my grandfather explained, as he began to put the rope bed back to rights. "You can't tell which way the train has gone by looking at the tracks."

The same holds for Wind Wagons.

Questions

1. Why were the girls always willing to go right to bed when they were at their grandparents' house?
2. Why did the girls have to hug the mattress when Granddad was telling his tale?
3. Based on Granddad's "true test," do you think McReady was a genius?
4. Part of the fun of a tall tale is being surprised by unusual events. Write about something that might have happened during McReady and O'Hara's Wind Wagon ride.

Applying Reading Skills

The sentences below tell about some of the events in "The Tale of the Wind Wagon." Read the sentences. Then write them on your paper in the correct sequence. Put a check mark beside each sentence that is part of Granddad's story.

The Wind Wagon jumped the tracks.
O'Hara and McReady laid tracks for the Cincinnati and Marietta Railroad.
Grandmom asked Granddad what he was doing.
Granddad said he was going to tell about a man who worked the rails.
The Wind Wagon set sail from Nelsonville Station.
McReady retired so he could build his Wind Wagon.
The Wind Wagon picked up speed.
Deborah and her sister rolled to the floor.
The Wind Wagon landed in a pigsty.

PREPARING FOR READING

Learning Vocabulary

1. On May 10, 1869, a crowd gathered at Promontory, Utah, to witness an important event.
2. A ceremony was being held because the first railroad across the United States had been completed.
3. This railroad had been very difficult and expensive to construct.
4. Today, the United States has a network of railroad tracks thousands of miles long.

witness   ceremony   expensive
construct   network

Developing Background and Skills
Maps

Imagine you and your family are planning a trip to a national park. You don't know how to get to the park or how far away it is. You only know which state the park is in. What should you do?

The best thing for you and your family to do is to read a **map.** A map can show you the exact location of the park. It can also show you in what direction you will have to travel.

If you use the scale on the map, you can even find out how far it is to the park. The **scale** is a line that shows how distances are represented on the map.

Look at the map and scale below. According to the scale, one inch represents 150 miles. Two centimeters represents 200 kilometers.

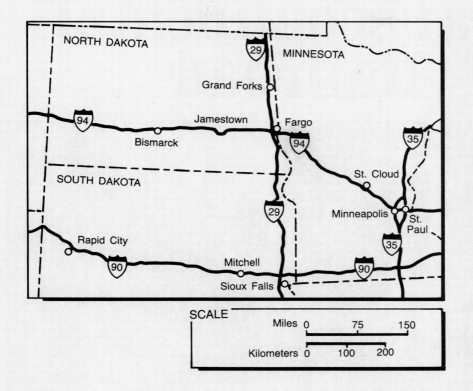

SCALE

Miles 0   75   150

Kilometers 0   100   200

Use the scale and a ruler to answer these questions.

About how many miles is it from Grand Forks to Fargo?

Which distance is greater: that from Mitchell to Sioux Falls, or that from Jamestown to Bismarck?

The next selection will tell you about the first railroad to cross the United States. Reading the maps in the selection will help you to understand the places the writer describes.

The First Transcontinental Railroad

I t was shortly past noon, May 10, 1869. The place was Promontory, a tiny settlement in Utah. A large crowd had gathered to witness an important ceremony. Telegraph wires waited to carry the news across the country. Two locomotives stood on their tracks nose to nose. One was from the East. The other was from the West.

The president of the railroad got ready to hammer in the last spike. He swung and missed. The vice president also missed! But the crowd cheered.

An ancient stone-paved road in Rome that is still being used today

A picture of an early ox cart

The first transcontinental railroad had been completed! The telegraph wires hummed their message.

The next day, Promontory was nearly empty. There were still a few tents, and of course, the railroad tracks. It was hard to picture the ceremony that had taken place the day before. What was it all about? Why was a transcontinental railroad so important? The answer is part of the story of railroads.

The Story of Railroads

The idea of a railroad began long ago. In ancient times, paved roads were built for carts and chariots. This was an improvement over dirt roads. The hard surface allowed the carts to roll more easily. Heavier loads could be moved. However, the paving was very expensive. It was also difficult to construct.

About the year 1000, miners found a way to push carts

281

1.

2.

3.

through tunnels. The tunnels were only as wide as the carts. (See Figure 1.) The carts were guided through the tunnels on wheels which ran on a track. The track was made from wooden rails nailed to cross-ties. Like the paved roads, the wooden tracks made a hard surface for easy rolling. Unlike the paved roads, they were much easier to build.

During the 1700s, carts carrying coal used a special track. A flange (flanj), or collar, was put on the inside edge of the rail. (See Figure 2.) This flange helped to keep the carts on the track. The tracks were mounted on stone blocks. It was difficult to keep them clear. If a branch or a rock lay on the tracks, the cart was easily derailed.

After much experimenting, an improvement was made.

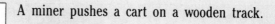
A miner pushes a cart on a wooden track.

An early steam-powered locomotive

The flange was placed on the wheel instead of the track. (See Figure 3.) The track was shaped like an I or T. The wheel's flange ran along its head. The rails were held in place by wooden crossties. This was an improvement because the rails were self-cleaning. They were also not too expensive to build.

Once the carts were rolling easily, people began hitching them together. A much larger load could be moved in one trip. But the horses or oxen that pulled the wagons could only move a few at a time. More power was needed to pull a train.

In 1769, James Watt invented a motor that was powered by steam. People began to work on a steam-powered locomotive. After 44 years of experimenting,

In 1830, a locomotive was tested by racing a horse-drawn carriage. The *Tom Thumb* broke down and the horse won, but people were convinced that trains would soon improve.

a locomotive finally pulled a train loaded with iron. The experiment took place in Wales. This first locomotive didn't work very well, but the idea caught on. It was not long before improvements were made.

The growth of railroads in America was amazing. In 1830, only 23 miles (37 kilometers) of track had been laid. By 1840, the network of tracks had grown a hundred times. By 1870, the tracks looked like a spider's web across the country!

Speed had increased as well. In 1830, the fastest train could only go from 12 to 18 miles (19 to 29 kilometers) per hour. In 1848, a train called the "Antelope" ran a 26-mile (42-kilometer) race in 26 minutes! The passengers were so scared, they laid down on the floor. No one knew that it was possible to travel so fast.

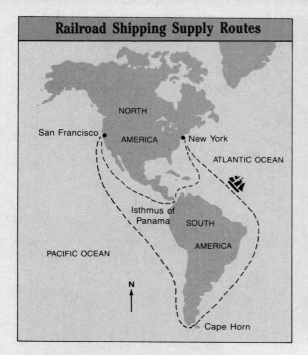

Railroad Shipping Supply Routes

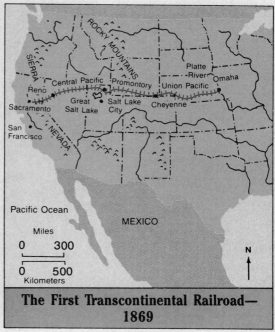

The First Transcontinental Railroad—1869

A Transcontinental Railroad

In the 1860s, settlers were moving into the West. A group of businessmen thought that a railroad between the East and the West would help trade.

The Central Pacific Railroad began construction in Sacramento, California, in 1863. The Union Pacific began in Omaha, Nebraska, in 1865.

Both companies had great difficulty getting their supplies. The Central Pacific had to ship their equipment from the Atlantic coast. They had to send it across the Isthmus of Panama or around Cape Horn. (See map of shipping routes.) This was very expensive. It also took a long time.

The Union Pacific had their own problems. At first, they had to ship their equipment up the Missouri River by steamboat. Then it was carried by stagecoach and in wagons. Later, they were able to send supplies along the tracks they

had laid. It took the work of hundreds of people to complete this huge job.

Work continued for many years after 1869. The land around the tracks had to be leveled or propped up. This had to be done to prevent landslides that would cover the tracks.

Ten years after the Golden Spike Ceremony, people were crossing America by train. Trains were a popular way to travel. They were also an inexpensive way to ship things.

Later, cars and trucks became more important than railroads. Many railroad companies were forced out of business. Today, you can see just as many unused railroad tracks as used ones. But the story of railroads does not end here. As we become more aware of the need to save fuel, perhaps we can look forward to using the rails once again.

Questions

1. What happened at Promontory on May 10, 1869?
2. Why were wooden tracks an improvement over paved roads?
3. Why was the steam-powered locomotive such an important invention?
4. Do you think trains will become a popular way to travel again? Why or why not?

Applying Reading Skills

Number your paper from 1 to 4. Then use the maps on page 285 to answer the questions. Write your answers in complete sentences.

1. If you were shipping railroad supplies from New York to San Francisco in the 1860s, which route would you take? Why?
2. Which railroad company laid more miles of tracks, the Union Pacific or the Central Pacific?
3. About how many miles is it from Sacramento to Reno?
4. About how many kilometers is it from Omaha to Cheyenne?

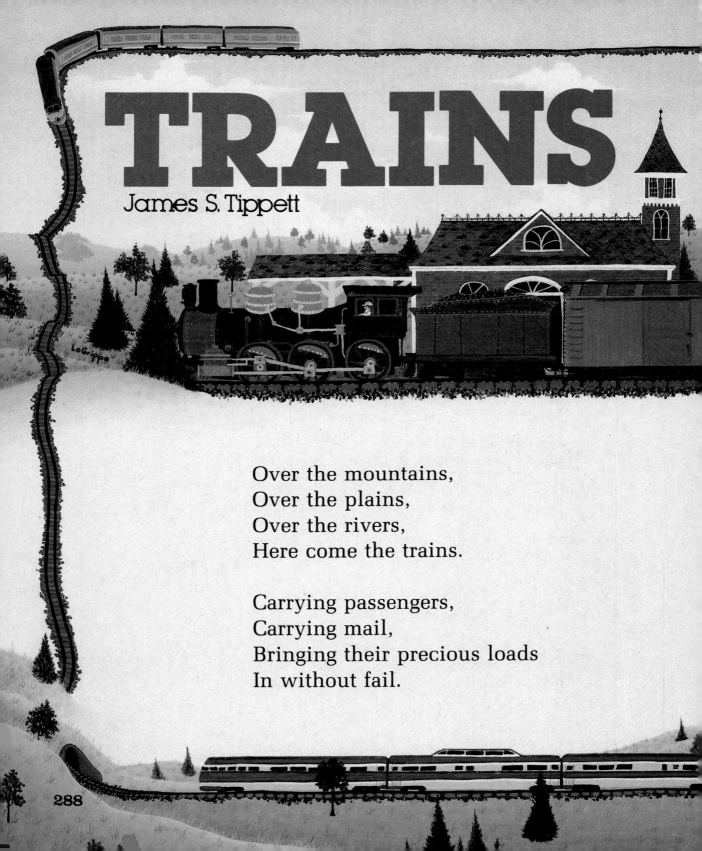

TRAINS

James S. Tippett

Over the mountains,
Over the plains,
Over the rivers,
Here come the trains.

Carrying passengers,
Carrying mail,
Bringing their precious loads
In without fail.

Thousands of freight cars
All rushing on
Through day and darkness,
Through dusk and dawn.

Over the mountains,
Over the plains,
Over the rivers,
Here come the trains.

PREPARING FOR READING

Learning Vocabulary

1. A <u>rumor</u> had started that there was a special way for slaves to escape.
2. Harriet and her father never <u>discussed</u> why he was teaching her all about the woods.
3. When Harriet ran away, she <u>hesitated</u> before stopping at a woman's house for help.
4. Harriet was careful not to look <u>suspicious</u>.
5. She didn't want people to <u>suspect</u> her of being a runaway slave.
6. A <u>patrol</u> had been formed to look for runaways.
7. It watched to see who would <u>emerge</u> from secret hiding places.

rumor   discussed   hesitated   suspicious
suspect   patrol   emerge

Developing Background and Skills
Sequence of Events

Imagine that you are planning a long and difficult trip. Before you begin the trip, you may want to carefully plan the route that you are going to take. It may be important for you to decide where you will travel each day and the order of the stops you will make. Otherwise, you may end up going miles out of your way.

Events in a story also have a certain order, or sequence. If the writer does not use signal words, you must read carefully to find the **sequence of events**.

As you read the paragraph below, think about the sequence of events.

In the morning, Harriet came to the house where her friend had said she was to stop. She showed the slip of paper that she carried to the woman who answered her knock at the back door of the farmhouse.

The first thing Harriet did was to find the house where her friend told her to stop. What did Harriet do next? If you read carefully, you found that after she came to the house, she knocked at the back door. Finally, she showed the slip of paper to the woman who answered the door.

The next selection is a biography of Harriet Tubman. Think about the sequence of events in Harriet's life as you read.

Harriet Tubman and the Underground Railroad

Ann Petry

Dorchester County, Maryland, was a fine place to live in the early 1800s—if you were free. Most blacks were not free, however. Slavery was common in the southern states, where large plantations grew cotton, tobacco, and other crops. Plantation owners had slaves to plant and pick their crops, and to do their housework and other chores.

Slaves did not have rights. They were considered pieces of property, and could be sold at any time. Slaves were often separated from their families, and some slaves were badly mistreated.

This was the world into which Harriet Tubman was born. She was part of a large family, and they all lived in a tiny, one-room shack. Their master allowed them to have very little, but he could not take away their spirit. It was a spirit shared by everyone who believed in freedom. Harriet would grow up to prove that this spirit would triumph.

In 1831, the year Harriet turned eleven, she kept hearing a strange story, told and retold in the fields. The story was about a slave named Tice Davids.

Tice Davids ran away from his master in Kentucky. He planned to cross the Ohio River at Ripley. But his master followed so close behind him that Tice had to jump in the river and swim across.

The master hunted for a boat, and while hunting, never lost sight of Tice. He kept watching his head, just above the water, as he swam toward the opposite shore. Once in the boat, the master followed him, and saw him plainly, swimming faster and faster. The master drew so near to him that when Tice stood up in the water and started to run, he could see the water splashing about his thighs. He saw him reach the shore. The master grounded the boat and jumped out—not more than five minutes behind the slave.

He never saw Tice Davids again. He searched the countryside; he searched the town of Ripley. He had heard that in Ripley there was a man named Reverend John Rankin who helped runaways. Even so, Tice Davids had disappeared right before his master's eyes.

The master went back to Kentucky and told about this strange disappearance. Puzzled, he explained this mystery by saying, "He must have gone on an underground road."

Harriet was also puzzled. She kept thinking about the story. Was there a road that ran under the ground? Was that how Tice Davids had escaped from his master? If Tice could find it, could other people find it, too?

People in the border states, who had been sheltering runaway slaves, helped further the mystery of an underground road. The new steam trains were being talked about everywhere. A rumor started, and spread, that there was an underground railroad, too.

The people who helped runaway slaves in Ohio, Pennsylvania, and New York started using phrases and words suited to the idea of a railroad. They called themselves conductors, stationmasters, and brakemen. Their houses and barns and haystacks, and the secret passages inside the big farmhouses, were called depots (dē'pōz) and stations. They called the runaways passengers, or parcels. Large parcels were grownups; small parcels were children.

In 1831 there were many people like the young Harriet, who believed that there really was a steam train that ran through a deep underground tunnel from South to North. They believed that a slave who could board it in the South, at some unknown point, would emerge a free person, in a free state, when the train came up out of the ground, snorting and puffing, leaving a trail of smoke behind it. Certainly the story of Tice Davids suggested that this was true.

Though Harriet was young when she heard it, she never forgot the story of the mysterious underground railroad. As Harriet grew, so did the idea of boarding that train to freedom.

When she was sixteen, her master, Doc Thompson, hired out Harriet and her father, Ben, to a builder named John Stewart. At first Harriet worked in his house, doing housework.

After three months, Harriet asked Stewart if she could work in the woods with the men. "I always did field work," she explained. "So I can swing an ax just like a man."

Stewart knew she was strong. He had seen her bring in big logs for the fireplaces. He did not have to pay her old master, Doc Thompson, very much for her hire because she was a woman. If she could do a man's work, felling trees, splitting logs, he'd be getting a bargain.

"We can try it," he said. "If it doesn't work out you'll have to go back to cooking and cleaning."

But it did work out. After a while Stewart even allowed her to "hire her time." This meant that Harriet could find jobs for herself, and would pay Stewart fifty or sixty dollars a year. Whatever she earned over and beyond this sum, she was allowed to keep.

Harriet found jobs that would keep her out of doors. She hauled logs, plowed fields, drove an ox-cart. During this period, she often worked with her father, Ben. John Stewart placed Ben in charge of the slaves who cut the timber which was to be sent by boat to the Baltimore shipyard. For weeks at a time Harriet swung a broadax in the woods as part of Ben's crew, cutting half a cord of wood a day just like a man.

Her father taught her about the woods: the names of birds, which berries were good to eat and which were poisonous, where to look for water lilies. Harriet was a good student. Ben taught her how to pick a path through the woods, even through the underbrush, without making a sound. He said, "Any old body can go through a woods crashing and mashing things down like a cow. That's easy. You practice doing it the hard way— move so quiet even a bird on a nest won't hear you and fly up."

Neither of them ever discussed the reasons why it was important to be able to go through the

woods soundlessly. Discussion wasn't necessary. Deep inside herself Harriet knew what her father was doing. He was, in his own way, training her for the day when she might become a runaway.

It was years before that day came. Harriet was 29 years old when one day a slave working beside her in the fields motioned to her. She bent toward him, listening. He said the water boy had just brought news to the field hands, and it had been passed from one to the other until it reached him. The news was that Harriet and her brothers had been sold to a Georgia trader, and that they were to be sent South with the chain gang that very night.

Harriet went on working but she knew she would have to run away. She would have to start as soon as it was dark. She could not go with the chain gang.

That night Harriet took some food and tied it up in an old bandanna. By hoarding the food, she could make it last a long time. With the berries and roots she could find in the woods, she wouldn't starve.

Harriet left quickly. Once she was off the plantation, she took to the woods, going toward Bucktown. She needed help. She was going to ask a white woman who often stopped to talk to her if she would help her. Perhaps she wouldn't. But she would soon find out.

When she came to the farmhouse where the woman lived, she approached it cautiously, circling around it. It was so quiet. There was no sound at all, not even a dog barking, or the sound of voices. Nothing.

She tapped on the door, gently. A voice said, "Who's there?" She answered, "Harriet, from Dr. Thompson's place."

When the woman opened the door she did not seem at all surprised to see her. She glanced at the little bundle that Harriet was carrying, and invited her in. Then she sat down at the kitchen table, wrote two names on a slip of paper, and handed the paper to Harriet.

She said that those were the next places where it was safe for Harriet to stop. The first place was a farm where there was a gate with big white posts and round knobs on top of them. The people there would feed her. When they thought it was safe for her to go on, they would tell her how to get to the next house, or take her there. For these were the first two stops on the Underground Railroad—going North, from the eastern shore of Maryland.

Thus Harriet learned that the Underground Railroad that ran straight to the North was not a railroad at all. Neither did it run underground. It was made up of a group of people who offered food and shelter, or a place of hiding to runaway slaves who had set out on the long road to the North and freedom.

Harriet made her way through the woods, crouching in the underbrush whenever she heard the sound of horses' hoofs, staying there until the riders passed. Each time she wondered if they were already hunting for her.

In the morning, Harriet came to the house where her friend had said she was to stop. She showed the slip of paper that she carried to the woman who answered her knock at the back door of the farmhouse. The woman fed her, and then handed her a broom and told her to go outside and sweep the yard.

Harriet hesitated, suddenly suspicious. Then she decided that with a broom in her hand, working in the yard, she would look as though she belonged on the place. No one would suspect that she was a runaway.

That night the woman's husband, a farmer, loaded a wagon with produce. Harriet climbed in. He threw some blankets over her, and the wagon started.

It was dark under the blankets, and not exactly comfortable. But Harriet decided that riding was better than walking. She was surprised that she

wasn't afraid. For all she knew, the man driving the wagon might be taking her straight back to the master.

The next morning when the stars were still visible in the sky, the farmer stopped the wagon. Harriet was instantly awake.

He told her to follow the river, to keep following it to reach the next place where people would take her in and feed her. He said that she must travel only at night, and she must stay off the roads because the patrol would be hunting for her. Harriet climbed out of the wagon. "Thank you," she said simply, thinking how amazing it was that there should be white people who were willing to go to such lengths to help a slave get to the North.

When she finally arrived in Pennsylvania, she had traveled roughly ninety miles (144 kilometers) from Dorchester County. She had slept on the ground outdoors at night. She had been rowed up the Choptank River by a man she had never seen before. She had been hidden in the attic of the home of a Quaker. She had been befriended by German farmers.

When she crossed the line into the free state of Pennsylvania, the sun was coming up. She said, "I looked at my hands to see if I was the same person now that I was free. There was a glory over everything. The sun came like gold through the trees, and over the fields."

*After her own escape, Harriet Tubman went back
again and again to the South, risking her life to
bring others to freedom. She rescued her family,
friends, and other slaves—more than three hundred
men, women, and children. Harriet was never
caught. She became one of the most famous conductors on the Underground Railroad. Years later,
Harriet would say proudly, "I never ran my train
off the track, and I never lost a passenger."*

Questions

1. How did the rumor of an underground railroad get started?
2. Why did John Stewart let Harriet do field work?
3. How do you think Harriet felt when she found out what the "Underground Railroad" really was?
4. Harriet Tubman is remembered for her courageous acts. What courageous people have you known, or read or heard about? How did they show courage?

Applying Reading Skills

The following pairs of sentences tell about some of the events from "Harriet Tubman and the Underground Railroad." Read each pair of sentences and decide which event happened first. Then write each pair of sentences in the correct sequence on your paper.

1. John Stewart allowed Harriet to "hire her time."
   Harriet's father taught her all about the woods.

2. Harriet decided to run away.
   Harriet learned that she was to be sent South with a chain gang.

3. Harriet came to the house where her friend had told her to stop.
   A white woman gave Harriet two names of people who would help her.

4. A man took Harriet to the river in a wagon.
   Harriet crossed the line into the free state of Pennsylvania.

THE WHIPPOORWILL CALLS

(For Harriet Tubman)

No one hears her
Coming
Through the woods
At night
For she is like
A whippoorwill
Moving through the trees
On silent wings.

No one sees her
Hiding
In the woods
By day
For she is like
A whippoorwill
Blending into leaves
On the forest floor.

And one night
The whippoorwill calls
And the warm air
Carries the haunting sound
Across the fields
And into the small dark cabins.

And only the slaves know
It is Harriet.

Beverly McLoughland

PREPARING FOR READING

Learning Vocabulary

1. Diana Vargas works as a television <u>commentator</u>.
2. Her job is to provide live <u>coverage</u> of important events.
3. The people of Launch Control <u>monitor</u> astronauts during their space <u>mission</u>.
4. The astronaut Neil Armstrong said that it is in the nature of human beings to face <u>challenges</u>.
5. Our interest in space <u>indicates</u> that we should see more missions into space during the next <u>decade</u>.

commentator   coverage   monitor   mission
challenges   indicates   decade

Developing Background and Skills
Context Clues

As you read, you may come across words that are unfamiliar to you. You can always look up their meanings in the dictionary, but you may not always have to.

You may be able to figure out the meaning of an unfamiliar word by using **context clues.** Nearby words and sentences may be clues to meaning. You can use the words you do know to figure out the meaning of the ones you don't know.

Read the paragraph below. See if you can use the other words and sentences in the paragraph to help you figure out the meaning of the underlined word.

The late President Kennedy thought our country should do whatever it could to put a man on the moon. He once said, "I believe that this nation should <u>commit</u> itself to landing a man on the moon and returning him safely to the earth." To set out for the moon was what he called "the most dangerous and greatest adventure on which man ever embarked."

What is the meaning of the word *commit*? The first sentence in the paragraph gives you a clue. The sentence tells you that President Kennedy thought our country should do whatever it could to put a man on the moon. The word *commit* must have something to do with pledging or promising what needs to be done. You can check the dictionary to see if that meaning is close to the definition.

You may find other words you do not know when you read "The Greatest Adventure." Use context clues to figure out what they mean.

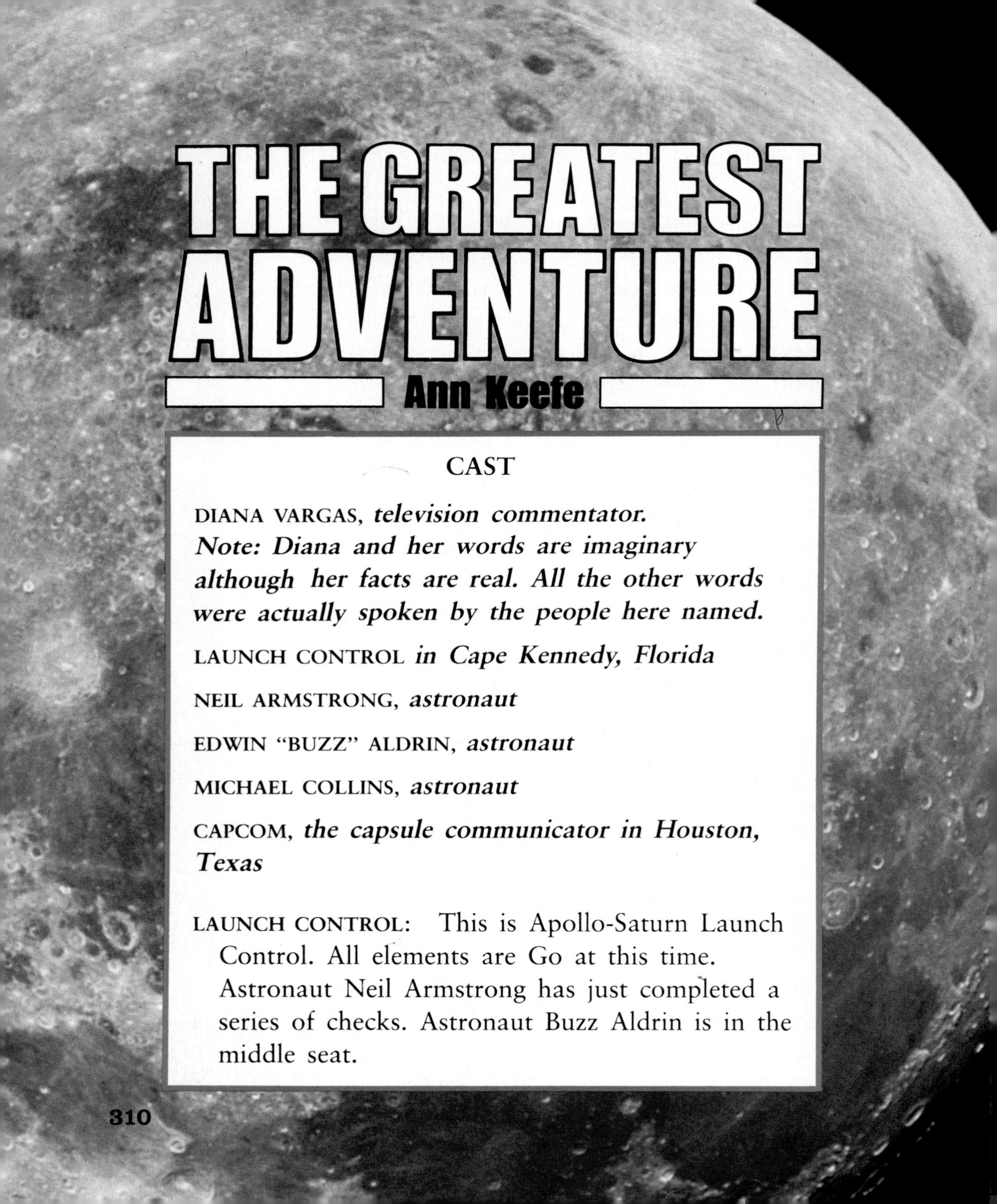

THE GREATEST ADVENTURE

Ann Keefe

CAST

DIANA VARGAS, *television commentator.*
Note: Diana and her words are imaginary although her facts are real. All the other words were actually spoken by the people here named.

LAUNCH CONTROL *in Cape Kennedy, Florida*

NEIL ARMSTRONG, *astronaut*

EDWIN "BUZZ" ALDRIN, *astronaut*

MICHAEL COLLINS, *astronaut*

CAPCOM, *the capsule communicator in Houston, Texas*

LAUNCH CONTROL: This is Apollo-Saturn Launch Control. All elements are Go at this time. Astronaut Neil Armstrong has just completed a series of checks. Astronaut Buzz Aldrin is in the middle seat.

DIANA: Good morning from Cape Kennedy, Florida. This is Diana Vargas bringing you live television coverage on man's flight to the moon. The third astronaut is Michael Collins.

LAUNCH CONTROL: On behalf of the launch team, good luck! Three minutes 25 seconds and counting. We're still Go at this time.

DIANA: The men receiving those good wishes are strapped inside *Apollo 11*, 45 stories above ground. Their 82-foot craft is sitting on top of *Saturn V*, the giant rocket that will launch it into space. *Saturn V* is the height of a football field set on end—about 300 feet. The men working beneath it look to be the size of ants.

LAUNCH CONTROL: When he received the good wishes Neil Armstrong said, "Thank you very much. We know it will be a good flight."

DIANA: The tension on this steamy morning is almost unbearable. The eyes of a million people are fixed on the launch pad here at Cocoa Beach. Hundreds of families camped out here last night.

LAUNCH CONTROL: Firing command coming in now. T minus 3—we are Go with all elements of the mission at this time.

DIANA: Just eight years ago the late President Kennedy said, "I believe that this nation should commit itself to . . . landing a man on the moon and returning him safely to the earth" before this decade is out. About to begin is what he called "the most . . . dangerous and greatest adventure on which man has ever embarked."

LAUNCH CONTROL: All is still Go as we monitor our status. Two minutes 10 seconds and counting. The target for the *Apollo 11* astronauts, the moon. At lift-off we'll be at a distance of 218,096 miles away. T minus 1 minute 54 seconds and counting. We continue to build up pressure.

DIANA: Neil Armstrong was asked the reason for this expedition at a press conference the other day. He said, "It's in the nature of the human being to face challenges. . . . Yes, we're required to do these things just as salmon swim upstream."

LAUNCH CONTROL: All information coming into the control tower at this time indicates we are Go. Forty seconds away from *Apollo 11* lift-off. Astronauts reported, "Feel good." T minus 15 seconds. 12, 11, 10, 9, ignition sequence starts, 6 (*rocket sound*), 5, 4, 3, 2, 1, zero, all engines running, LIFT-OFF. We have lift-off, 32 minutes past the hour. Lift-off on *Apollo 11*! (*crowd noises: cheers, applause, ahhs*)

DIANA: Rivers of flame, torrents of fire are gushing from the rocket! The noise is like thunder, more explosive than any sound I've ever heard, and the earth is shaking beneath our feet. *Saturn V* is trembling, wavering, climbing only a few inches a second. Now the speed is picking up. That fiery white tail is as long as the rocket itself. Now it's shooting skyward, faster and higher like an immense firecracker. Lift-off; we had lift-off at 9:32 A.M. this Wednesday morning, July 16, 1969!

DIANA: Good day from Diana Vargas, speaking to you now from Houston, Texas. After yesterday's lift-off, the astronauts went into orbit, circling the earth once every hour and 28 minutes while they tested their equipment. Then they fired off for the moon. This morning they breakfasted

on cinnamon toast cubes and ate tubes of fruit cocktail. Astronaut Michael Collins is reporting now to Capcom, the Capsule Communicator here at Mission Control headquarters.

COLLINS: It's really a fantastic sight. A minute ago you could see all of North Africa absolutely clear, all of Portugal, Spain, southern France, all of Italy. Just a beautiful sight. . . .

———————————

DIANA: It is Sunday, July 20, 1969, a day that Armstrong and Aldrin are about to record in history. This is Diana Vargas reporting to you as they squeeze inside the lunar module known as the *Eagle*. Now they are cutting themselves loose from the *Apollo 11* command module that Collins will continue to occupy as he orbits the moon and waits for their safe return.

CAPCOM: How does it look?

ARMSTRONG: The *Eagle* has wings. (*rocket sound*)

CAPCOM: You are Go for landing. Over. (*motor sound*)

ALDRIN: Roger. Go for landing. We're Go, 750, coming down at 23.

DIANA: Aldrin reports that his altitude is 750 feet and his rate of descent is 23 feet per second.

ALDRIN: Three hundred-fifty, down at 4. We're pegged on horizontal velocity.

DIANA: The men have taken over manual control. They are moving horizontally over craters and fields full of boulders, looking for a safe landing spot.

ALDRIN: Two hundred feet, $4\frac{1}{2}$ down. Things looking good.

DIANA: They appear to have selected their touchdown spot in the area known as the Sea of Tranquillity.

ALDRIN: Lights on. Forward 40 feet, down $2\frac{1}{2}$.

DIANA: The tiny, spiderlike craft is almost down now.

ALDRIN: Picking up some dust. Four forward, drifting to the right a little. Contact light. O.K., engines stop. (*silence*)

ARMSTRONG: Houston, Tranquillity Base here. The *Eagle* has landed.

CAPCOM: Roger, Tranquillity, we copy you on the ground. You've got a bunch of guys about to turn blue. We're breathing again. Thanks a lot.

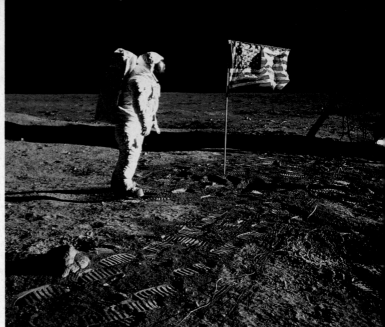

ARMSTRONG: The hatch is coming open.

ALDRIN: Neil, you're lined up nicely. O.K., down.

ARMSTRONG: O.K., Houston, I'm on the porch.

CAPCOM: Neil, we can see you coming down the ladder now.

ARMSTRONG: I'm at the foot of the ladder. I'm going to step off now. That's one small step for a man, one giant leap for mankind.

ARMSTRONG: The surface is fine and powdery. There seems to be no difficulty in moving around. It's quite dark here in the shadow and a little hard for me to see that I have good footing. I'll work my way over into the sunlight. It's like much of the high desert of the United States.

ALDRIN: Are you ready for me to come out?

ARMSTRONG: All set. O.K., you saw what difficulties I was having.

ALDRIN: Now I want to back up and partially close the hatch. Making sure not to lock it.

ARMSTRONG: A particularly good thought. Magnificent sight out here. We'll read the plaque that's on the front landing gear: HERE MEN FROM THE PLANET EARTH FIRST SET FOOT UPON THE MOON JULY 1969 A.D. WE CAME IN PEACE FOR ALL MANKIND.

The Apollo 11 *mission of 1969 was one of the most important events in the history of the space program. After the first astronauts walked on the moon, the United States continued to make "giant leaps" in space. In 1972, the astronauts of Apollo 17 spent 75 hours exploring the moon. They even had a special vehicle to drive on the moon's surface! In 1975, the United States and the Soviet Union participated in the first international space effort. Spacecraft from the two countries met and docked in outer space. In 1981, the space shuttle Columbia completed its first flight. Since then, the shuttle has made several more journeys into space. The Greatest Adventure continues.*

Questions

1. What were the names of the three astronauts on board *Apollo 11*?
2. Why didn't Astronaut Collins board the lunar module?
3. How do you think President Kennedy would have felt if he had lived to watch the *Apollo 11* mission?
4. Would you want to be a passenger on a space flight? Why or why not?

Applying Reading Skills

Number your paper from 1 to 3. Read the following sentences. Use context clues to choose the meaning of each underlined word. Then write the word and its meaning on your paper.

1. When Aldrin and Armstrong were 750 feet above the moon, Aldrin reported their altitude.
   a. way of thinking, acting, or feeling
   b. great surprise and wonder
   c. height above a surface
   d. distance from the earth

2. The lunar module was a separate spacecraft designed for the moon landing.
   a. a part of something that has a special purpose
   b. a small copy of a ship or a spacecraft
   c. control center
   d. laboratory

3. Aldrin and Armstrong used manual control when they directed the module themselves.
   a. made by people; not natural
   b. hand operated
   c. computer operated
   d. automatic

PREPARING FOR READING

Learning Vocabulary

1. Many thousands of <u>spectators</u> came to witness the beginning of the 1984 Summer Olympic Games.
2. One of the oldest Olympic <u>traditions</u> is the lighting of the flame, which is a <u>symbol</u> of the Olympics.
3. Runners ran in a <u>relay</u> to take the flame from New York City to the Olympic <u>site</u> in Los Angeles.
4. Many people <u>donated</u> money in order to carry the flame, even though one large company was the official <u>sponsor</u> of the relay.

spectators	traditions	symbol	relay
site	donated	sponsor	

Developing Background and Skills
Context Clues

As you know, **context clues** can help you figure out the meaning of unfamiliar words. It can often be easy to learn new words if you use nearby words and sentences as clues.

Sometimes it will take more than one sentence to figure out the meaning of a word. You need more clues than one sentence can give.

Read the paragraph below. Try to figure out the meanings of the underlined words. You may have to read the entire paragraph to be sure you have the right meanings.

The ancient Olympic games were held only in Greece. The modern Olympic games are an <u>international</u> event <u>hosted</u> by many different countries. The countries provide stadiums, swimming pools, and other sports <u>facilities</u> for the athletes.

You might have known that *international* meant "between or among nations," but the phrase "many different countries" might have helped you to be sure.

Did you figure out that *hosted* means "acted as a host, or someone who receives and takes care of guests"? The last sentence gave clues to the meaning of the word by telling what the countries did.

Stadiums and swimming pools are examples of *facilities,* or places that serve a special purpose.

In the next story, you may meet some words that are unfamiliar to you. Try to figure out their meanings by using context clues.

THE OLYMPIC FLAME Judith Nayer

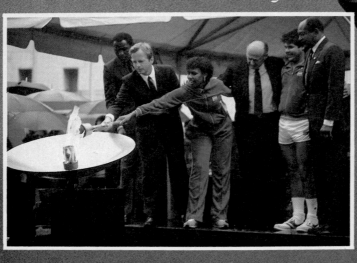

On July 28, 1984, the Los Angeles Memorial Coliseum was filled with thousands of the world's greatest athletes. They were ready for the 1984 Summer Olympic Games. Tens of thousands more filled the stands in the coliseum. They were gathered to witness the beginning of this 15-day sports event.

Before the games began, athletes and spectators observed one of the oldest Olympic traditions: the lighting of the Olympic flame. Cheers flooded the stadium as the final flame carrier ran up the 99 steps to light the main Olympic torch. This flame would burn until the Games ended.

The tradition of the flame dates back to ancient times. The first recorded Olympic Games took place in Olympia, Greece, in 776 B.C. In the ancient Games, the flame was lit by the rays of the sun. Later the Olympics became an international event. In 1936, the tradition of bringing the flame from Olympia to each Olympic site was begun.

The flame for the 1984 Summer Olympic Games was kindled at Olympia just as it was in ancient times. The first torch was lit. It was then flown by helicopter to Athens, Greece. There, three miner's lamps, each carrying a 12-hour supply of fuel, were lit. These lamps held the flame as it traveled to New York City in a United States government jet.

Left: Gina Hemphill, granddaughter of Olympic gold medalist Jesse Owens, lit the first torch from the Olympic flame in New York City.

325

Route of the Olympic Torch Relay

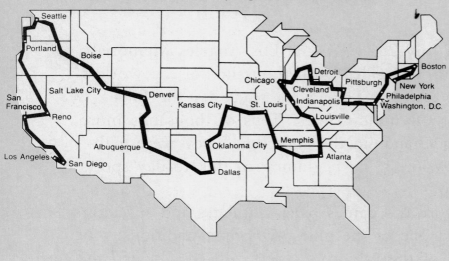

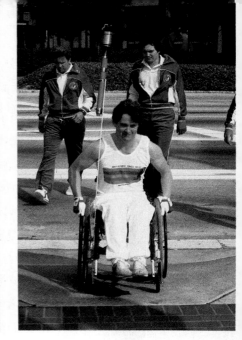

The original plan for the Olympic torch relay was a route that went through all fifty states and the District of Columbia. Officials changed this plan when they realized how long it would take to follow this route. The final route of the torch relay is shown on the map above.

On May 8, the flame began its 82-day cross-country journey to Los Angeles. The route was 15,000 kilometers (more than 9,000 miles) long. It passed through 33 states and the District of Columbia, including 41 cities and more than 1,000 towns. It was the longest torch relay in Olympic history.

The flame was carried by torches made of aluminum coated with a special finish. The torches were 22 inches (56 centimeters) high. Most of the torches weighed 2.5 pounds (1.1 kilograms). Some were designed to help keep the flame from blowing out in high winds. These torches weighed 4.4 pounds (2 kilograms). On all of the torches the Latin words *Citius, Altius, Fortius*—"Swifter, Higher, Stronger"—were written. This is the motto of the Olympics.

The flame was passed from torch to torch by a total of 4,200 runners. Four thousand people each paid, or had donated for them, $3,000. This allowed them to carry the flame 1 kilometer (.62 of a mile). The runners came from all parts of the country, all walks of life, and all age groups. Many earned the right to carry the torch by winning local raffles and races. Others spent weeks raising the money themselves by selling baked goods and crafts to the people in their towns. The $12 million raised went to athletic programs for youth clubs and to the Special Olympics. "The money," said Mayor Thomas Bradley of Los Angeles, "represents the spirit of people helping people."

The careful planning and hard work of many people made the Olympic torch relay a success. Computers helped to keep the relay on schedule. Trailers were set up to take care of people's needs along the way. Throughout the country, people came out to cheer for the runners.

The remaining 11,000 kilometers (6,500 miles) were covered by just 200 people. They were employees of American Telephone & Telegraph Communications (AT&T). AT&T was the official sponsor of the relay. These men and women were experienced runners. They had to be. To get to Los Angeles on time, the flame had to travel 180 kilometers (112 miles) a day. So the AT&T runners were called upon to run through the heat of the day, and into the darkness of the night. AT&T also provided a caravan of 47 vehicles. In the lead car, the Olympic flame burned in two miner's lamps. In case a runner's torch went out, it could be re-lit. The caravan followed the runners across the country. It also served as home for the AT&T running team.

Swiftly, the runners zigzagged their way across America. They held the torch high through city streets, cornfields, mountain trails, and long stretches of desert. They kept the flame going strong. But perhaps what really kept the flame—and the runners —going were all the people who cheered them on. About 30 million people came to see the torch passing. They filled the cities, flocked to the small towns, and lined the highways.

In cities such as Baltimore, Cleveland, Chicago, Atlanta, and St. Louis, huge crowds greeted the torch. There were high school bands and fireworks. People cheered "U-S-A! U-S-A!" In Oklahoma City, the people crowded so close to the runner that he could only walk his route.

In the smaller towns, school children waved paper torches and American flags. They asked the runners for their autographs and took pictures of them. Even in very small towns, such as Flat Lick, Kentucky; Rosebud, Missouri; Muleshoe, Texas; and Dinosaur, Colorado, the people came out to cheer the runners on.

The Olympic torch relay was like a parade from coast to coast. Everyone who was in it—those who ran, and those who cheered—felt they were a part of something special. "It's Us," they said. "Us. U. S."

When the flame finally reached the Los Angeles Coliseum on July 28, it became an Olympic symbol. But on the way across the country, it represented the spirit of America.

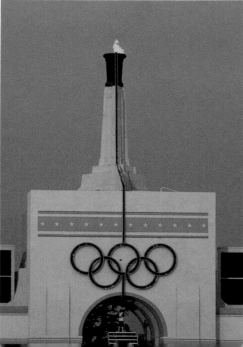

Former gold medalist Rafer Johnson carried the Olympic flame up a steep set of stairs to light a fuse. Fire raced through the five Olympic rings to the top of the main Olympic torch. The end of the relay marked the beginning of the 1984 Summer Olympics.

Questions

1. Where did the 1984 Summer Olympic Games take place?
2. Why did the 200 AT&T workers who carried the flame have to be experienced runners?
3. What do you think the writer meant by saying the Olympic flame "represented the spirit of America"?
4. Have you ever participated in a relay race? How did it feel to be part of that kind of team effort?

Applying Reading Skills

Number your paper from 1 to 3. Read the following sentences. Use context clues to choose the meaning of each underlined word. Then write the word and its meaning on your paper.

1. To kindle the flame at Olympia, a curved mirror was used. The mirror focused the sun's rays on a small area that became very hot.
   a. focus   b. create
   c. light   d. increase

2. To promote peace and cooperation among countries is the objective of the Olympics. It is something all who are involved in the games work for.
   a. motto   b. goal
   c. donation   d. meaning

3. The opening ceremonies of the 1984 Summer Olympic Games took place on July 28, 1984. The games commenced after the last runner lit the main Olympic torch.
   a. were completed b. changed
   c. continued   d. began

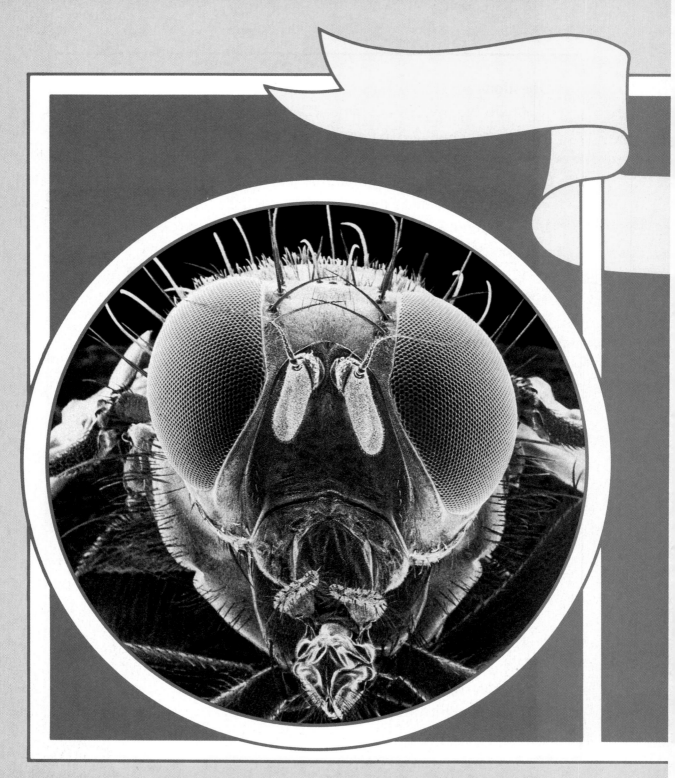

UNIT FOUR   LEVEL 11

MONSTERS

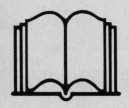

PREPARING FOR READING

Learning Vocabulary

1. Even though some animals may look <u>monstrous</u>, they are not harmful to humans.
2. The <u>male</u> chameleon uses the spikes on its body to push away other males when he is looking for a <u>female</u>.
3. The wolf spider is small but <u>savage</u>.
4. After it <u>pounces</u> on an insect, the <u>fierce</u> wolf spider kills the insect with its fangs.
5. If a lizard known as a gecko is <u>grasped</u> by its tail, the tail will usually break off.

monstrous   male   female   savage
pounces   fierce   grasped

Developing Background and Skills
Main Idea

You know that you can find an important point, or **main idea,** in most of the paragraphs you read. Sometimes the main idea is clearly stated in one sentence. At other times, the main idea can be stated only by using information from two sentences. You have to use the information to state the main idea in your own words.

Read the paragraph below. Think about what information you would use to state the main idea.

The spider is an animal that many people dislike. Spiders are not cute or cuddly looking. They are sometimes hairy and very large. But the spider will usually do no harm to humans. In fact, spiders help people by eating many insect pests.

Which of the following statements tells about the main idea of the paragraph?

1. Many people dislike spiders.
2. Spiders are not cute or cuddly looking.
3. Even though many people dislike spiders, spiders help people.

The first sentence includes important information, but not all the important information in the paragraph. The second statement is a detail that explains the first statement. The last statement includes all the most important information in the paragraph. It states the main idea.

As you read the next selection, look for the main ideas and the details that help to explain them. Some main ideas will be stated directly. You will have to state others in your own words.

LITTLE MONSTERS

M. JEAN CRAIG

STAR NOSED MOLE

It would be pretty frightening to wake up some night to find this enormous "monster" at the foot of your bed. But the star-nosed mole is not enormous. It could fit in the palm of your hand! It is not at all monstrous either, and it is almost never found in bedrooms!

The star-nosed mole digs tunnels in swamps or wet ground, hunting for insects to eat. It uses those twenty-two tentacles around its nose to help it find food. No one knows whether it smells with the tentacles or feels with them. There is no other furry animal in the world that has a nose quite like that.

The star-nosed mole can swim, too. Sometimes it catches a very small fish for its dinner.

This mole is found in North America, mostly in the northeastern parts.

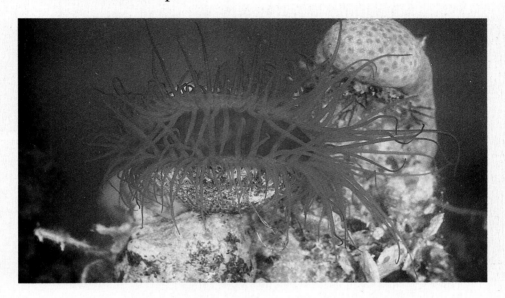

INFLATED FILE SHELL

An imaginary sea-monster? No, it is just an ordinary file shell, about the size of an egg. It is found almost anywhere in any ocean where it isn't very cold.

File shells are also called jumping shells. They jump about in the sea by squirting water through the two halves of their shell.

The long red fringes help the file shell find small sea-animals to eat.

SPICEBUSH SWALLOWTAIL BUTTERFLY LARVA

This is not a snake with enormous eyes. It is only a caterpillar, or larva, as long as the word "c a t e r p i l l a r" on this page. Soon it will become a butterfly.

Those huge "eyes" are not eyes at all, but colored spots on the caterpillar's skin. The real eyes are very small, and are hidden underneath the head. Perhaps the colored spots frighten away the birds or lizards that are the caterpillar's enemies.

The spicebush swallowtail butterfly larva is found in the eastern part of the United States and Canada.

JACKSON'S CHAMELEON

This could be a model for a monster in a horror movie, but it is actually a live chameleon (kə mēl′ yən).

Most kinds of chameleons look strange, and this kind is one of the strangest. Although those long spikes seem dangerous, they can't hurt anything. The male chameleon just uses them to push other male chameleons away when he is looking for a female.

A chameleon's tongue is longer than the chameleon is. (This chameleon is four inches, or

10 centimeters, long.) The tongue has a sticky tip, and the chameleon uses it for catching insects. When it sees an insect it wants to eat, it flicks its tongue out of its mouth and in again so fast that you can hardly see it move. The insect it swallows probably didn't see it at all.

A chameleon's skin changes color to match the branches or leaves it is sitting on. Then insects don't notice it waiting for them, and anything that might want to eat the chameleon has trouble finding it.

Chameleons are found in Africa, Asia, and Europe.

WOLF SPIDER

This savage wolf spider is only the size of a postage stamp—luckily!

The wolf spider does not make a web. It digs a hole in the ground, and then it builds a small tower of sticks and grass next to the hole. It sits on top of the tower and watches, with its eight eyes, for an insect or bug to come along. Then it pounces, and kills the insect with its poisonous fangs.

The wolf spider is a fierce hunter, but a good, careful mother. It carries its babies around on its back until they are big enough to take care of themselves.

Wolf spiders can be found all over the world. There are at least 2,000 kinds of them.

TEXAS BANDED GECKO

This *could* be a giant dragon breathing fire.
But there's no fire, of course, and this lizard is not
exactly a giant. In fact, it is just big enough to curl
up comfortably in a teacup.

This kind of gecko lives in Texas and some
other southwestern states. It hides among the rocks
in the daytime and runs about at night catching
insects and spiders.

If a Texas banded gecko is grasped by the tail,
it lets the tail break off in your hand and runs
away without it. It can grow a new tail again easily
and quickly.

Questions

1. How do file shells move through the water?
2. Use your ruler to measure the word *caterpillar* and find out how long the spicebush swallowtail butterfly larva is.
3. Would you expect to find the star-nosed mole living in areas where spicebush swallowtail butterflies live? Why or why not?
4. In what ways are the animals described in "Little Monsters" alike?

Applying Reading Skills

Number your paper from 1 to 4. Then write a complete sentence to answer each question below.

1. What is one supporting detail from the second paragraph under "Star-Nosed Mole"?
2. What is the main idea of the second paragraph under "Spicebush Swallowtail Butterfly Larva"?
3. How would you state the main idea of the third paragraph under "Jackson's Chameleon"?
4. What are two supporting details from the second paragraph under "Wolf Spider"?

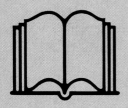

PREPARING FOR READING

Learning Vocabulary

1. Special effects for the movies are <u>created</u> by skilled artists and technicians.
2. Sculptors make models with moveable <u>joints</u> so they can bend the models into different positions.
3. Before <u>sculpturing</u> a model, sculptors often look at books and other <u>references</u>.
4. An artist may work alone or with other artists in a <u>studio</u>.

created   joints   sculpturing
references   studio

Developing Background and Skills
Main Idea

You know that the **main idea** is a statement that includes the most important information from a paragraph. That information may be found in one or two sentences. The other sentences explain the main idea. They give supporting details.

Read the paragraph on the next page. Think about how you would state the main idea.

The people who created the monsters for George Lucas's *Star Wars* movies call their workplace the Creature Shop. It's part of a company called Industrial Light and Magic, or ILM. ILM does most of the special effects for George Lucas's movies. Lifelike monsters and high-speed spaceships are some of the special effects that make these movies so exciting.

Which of the sentences below is a statement of the main idea? Which are supporting details for the main idea?

1. The *Star Wars* movies have many special effects, including lifelike monsters.
2. The Creature Shop is part of Industrial Light and Magic.
3. Industrial Light and Magic is a company that does most of the special effects for George Lucas's movies.

The first two sentences help to explain or give more information about the third sentence. They give supporting details. The third sentence is one way to state the main idea of the paragraph. You might have stated the main idea in a different way, but the information would have to be the same.

As you read the next selection, you will discover more about movies and special effects. Read carefully to find the most important information.

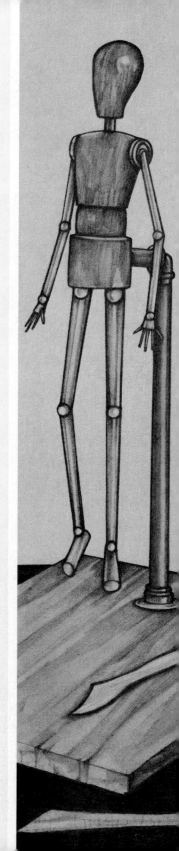

THE CREATURE SHOP

Lisa Yount

Where are movie monsters made? In a Creature Shop, of course!

The people who created the monsters for George Lucas's *Star Wars* movies call their workplace the Creature Shop. It's part of a company called Industrial Light and Magic, or ILM. ILM does most of the special effects for Lucas's movies. Lifelike monsters and high-speed spaceships are some of the special effects that make these movies so exciting.

"Creature Shops" in other places make monsters for other movies and television shows. Most are smaller than ILM, but they can be just as good at making movie magic. Tony McVey owns one of them.

Tony worked in ILM's Creature Shop a few years ago. He helped to make mon-

sters for the third *Star Wars* movie, *Return of the Jedi*. However, Tony does most of his work in his own "Creature Shop." It's a studio in San Francisco that he shares with his wife, Carla. Carla makes costumes and sometimes she and Tony work together.

Tony has been making monsters for about ten years now. He made his first ones in England, where he was born. It seemed a natural thing for him to do. "When I was young, I used to watch fantasy films all the time," he says. "I was always sculpturing and drawing, too." One of Tony's first jobs was making models of animals for the Natural History Museum of London. Later, he moved to California and got his chance to make monsters for the movies.

Before Tony builds a monster, he thinks about what he wants it to look like. If it's a real animal, he finds out as much about that kind of animal as he can. Recently, Tony

has been building models of dinosaurs. They will appear in a film he is making. Books about dinosaurs lie on several tables in his studio. "I always try to get enough references to do a good job," he says.

The next step is to draw the monster. Tony makes many drawings of the monster he is trying to create. The drawings show how the monster will look from the front, the side, and the back. They may show close-ups of its head or tail.

Most monster models have a skeleton, or armature. The armature is often made of wood, metal, and plastic. As Tony builds the armature, he compares it with his finished drawings. He uses tools called calipers to measure the drawing and the armature.

The armature has joints that let the monster's body bend in many places. A metal ball is part of each joint. The ball has

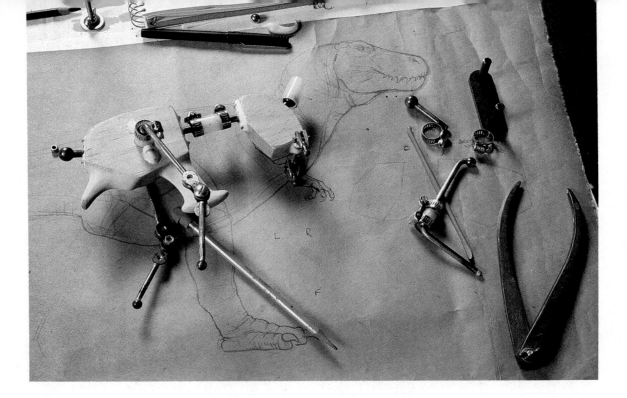

a hole in it so it can be welded onto the armature. Before Tony can drill the hole, he heats the ball with a torch. When the ball is very hot, it will become soft enough to drill.

The monster's joints help it stay in a certain position once it is set there. This will be important when the monsters are filmed. One common way of filming monsters is called stop-motion. In this technique, the model monster is set in position, and a picture is taken of it. Then the monster is moved a little bit. Its joints keep it in the new position while that, too, is filmed. The position is then changed a little more, and so on. When the pictures are run together as a movie, the monster seems to move by itself. Today, Tony says, computers and other new tools make stop-motion much more convincing than it was in older movies.

Once the monster's skeleton is finished, Tony may sculpture over it in clay. He builds up the monster's muscles and

body shape. Then he uses plaster to make a mold of the sculpture. The hollow mold is usually filled with a kind of rubber called foam latex. Sometimes, however, it is filled with soft plastic instead. The latex or plastic is covered with a rubber skin.

Tony paints and decorates the skin of the finished monster. He may add parts made from other materials. For instance, the teeth of his dinosaurs are made of a hard plastic called epoxy.

Tony made monsters for *Jedi* at ILM in much the same way that he makes monsters in his own studio. Many of the movie's monsters were already made when he began working there, but Tony designed one of them himself. It was the strange-looking "pet" that sat on the lap of Jabba the Hutt.

"I just fooled around with ideas for a couple of days and drew something up," Tony remembers. He showed the drawings to George Lucas, who liked them. Then Tony went ahead and built the "pet." Its head was made of latex. Its body had a rubber skin over an armature. When the movie was filmed, the "pet" was moved by a hand inside its body. "It was a hand puppet worked from below the stage," Tony says.

Tony also worked on masks for *Jedi*. Sometimes a mask had to fit tightly over an actor's face. Then the actor came down to the Creature Shop.

Tony mixed a special powder with water. He painted it over the actor's face. After five minutes, the coating hardened, and Tony peeled it off. The finished mask would be built from this mold.

The actors had an easier time during mask-making than they would have had in the older days of movies, Tony notes. Then the cast of their faces would have been made from plaster. They would have had to sit still for hours while the plaster hardened. During that time, they would breathe through a straw.

Tony has worked on many movies besides *Return of the Jedi*. He did models of Superman for some of the flying scenes in *Superman*. He built puppets for *Dark Crystal*. "And for *Gremlins*, I did the gremlin sculpture from which all the others were made," he says.

Tony also does work for TV commercials. Right now he is building a "frog creature" for a commercial for a radio

station. The frog creature has thick lips and a dinosaur-like frill on its neck. Drawings of it hang on the wall of Tony's studio. A partly finished model for it sits on a table.

One of the strangest creatures Tony ever made was for a TV commercial. The commercial told people all about dental care. The creature Tony made was a talking tooth!

Tony and Carla McVey remember that commercial very well. Both of them worked on it, and that was when they met. Carla made the costume for one of the actors in the commercial.

Today, their studio is filled with the signs of their work. The completed monsters are proudly displayed. Tony and Carla's "Creature Shop" is a busy place. They both work hard to bring to special effects "magic" an extra magic of their own.

Questions

1. What interests helped to prepare Tony McVey for his work making monsters?
2. How does the stop-motion filming technique work?
3. Why does Tony make drawings of a monster before he tries to make it?
4. Describe some special effects you have seen. How do you think they were done?

Applying Reading Skills

Number your paper from 1 to 4. Use complete sentences to answer each question below.

1. How would you state the main idea of the first paragraph on page 348?
2. What is one supporting detail from the same paragraph?
3. What is the main idea of the last paragraph beginning on page 349?
4. What are two supporting details from the same paragraph?

PREPARING FOR READING

Learning Vocabulary

1. Maria's <u>counselor</u> at camp was named Julie.
2. The campers set up their tents in a <u>clearing</u> next to a small stream.
3. During the days they spent at camp, the campers learned to <u>respect</u> nature.
4. When Carlos heard about a photograph of Bigfoot, he said that anybody could <u>fake</u> pictures.
5. He didn't even believe the talk about the <u>incident</u> at Chetco River.

counselor   clearing   respect
fake   incident

Developing Background and Skills
Make Judgments

Jamie can hardly wait to go to summer camp this year. The only problem is that the camp he went to last year is closed. Jamie's parents told him to find out about other camps. They gave him a list of things to find out about the camps.

1. location—The camp has to be within 60 to 100 miles of home.
2. price—The cost has to be about the same as the one charged by the camp Jamie went to last year.

3. activities—The camp has to offer a variety of activities such as swimming, horseback riding, and gymnastics.
4. recommendations—Jamie has to try to find people who know about the camp.

Once Jamie has gathered the information, he and his parents will have to **evaluate** it, or examine and decide its worth.

Evaluating information is an important part of making a **judgment** or decision. Jamie found that out as he and his parents looked through the booklets sent by several camps. It seemed that each camp was "the best" or "just the place you're looking for." Because Jamie knew what he was looking for, he could judge which camp was best for him.

As you read, you also evaluate information and make judgments about it. A writer may present information by using pictures, by quoting what someone says or reports, or by describing what witnesses have seen.

In the next selection, you will read about a creature called Bigfoot. As you read, notice how the writer presents information about Bigfoot. Evaluate the information and be ready to make a judgment about it.

My Bigfoot Weekend

Marilyn Z. Wilkes

"Everyone in the van," yelled Rick, "or you'll miss the camping trip of your lives!"

I swallowed my breakfast and ran out of the dining hall. I wasn't going to miss this trip!

I'm Maria Luisa Dolores Delgado—Maria for short—and this is my first time at sleep-away camp. I live in San Francisco, California, in the Mission District. My neighborhood is very old and beautiful, and I love it. Still, I always thought it would be great to live outdoors with the animals and cook over a fire the way the Indians did. So when my friend Tina said she was going to camp, I begged my mother until she said I could go, too.

Camp Redwoods is near Eureka (yū rē′ kə), California, about 280 miles north of San Francisco. At first, I was pretty disappointed. For one thing, everybody sleeps in log cabins with bunk beds and screened windows. I thought there would be tents. They don't cook over a fire, either. There's this big dining hall where we all eat. And the only wild animals I've seen are squirrels, which don't count because we have them at home.

So I got really excited when Julie, my cabin counselor, said there would be a weekend hike for those who were interested. I was the first one to sign up. Only six boys and six girls could go, and Rick and Julie would be in charge. Rick is a counselor for one of the boy's cabins. He knows all about hiking and what is called "campcraft" here. That means building campfires and knowing what roots are good to eat and stuff like that. Tina said count her out, she hated roots.

We drove to Highway 299 and headed east toward Willow Creek. As we turned north onto Highway 96, we saw a giant wooden statue by the side of the road. It looked sort of like a big ape.

"What's that, King Kong?" asked Carlos Ruiz. Carlos is from San Francisco, too. He goes to my school, and he's a real pain.

"That's Bigfoot," said Rick. "We're in Bigfoot country now."

"Is it real?" asked Kelly Fremont. "Will we see one?" Kelly was my best friend at camp, except for Tina, of course.

"Lots of people say they've seen Bigfoot," said Rick, "but no one has been able to prove it."

"That's because there's no such thing," said Carlos. "If there was, somebody would have caught one by now. That's the only way to prove it." That Carlos is such a know-it-all!

The van pulled off Highway 96 onto a dirt road and stopped. "We're here," said Julie. "Everybody out!"

"But where are we?" asked Pete Fox. "This looks like the middle of nowhere."

"It's the southern edge of the Hoopa Valley Indian Reservation," said Rick. "We're still three miles from where we make camp, so let's march!"

In case you're wondering, hiking through the woods with a backpack is hard work. Besides our own stuff, each person had to carry some of the food and equipment for the group. Just when everyone thought they couldn't go another step, Rick said, "Here we are!"

We were in a flat, pretty clearing next to a small stream. I said it looked as if no human had ever been there before.

"That's one of the rules of camping," said Rick. "Leave everything just the way you found it. No trash, no dead campfires. If we don't respect nature and take care of it, there won't be any nature left to enjoy."

The thought of everything around me disappearing forever made me feel just awful. I decided maybe I'd be a forest ranger when I grew up and help save nature.

I ate three cheese sandwiches and three granola bars for lunch. All that hiking really gives you an appetite! Then we set up the tents—two for the boys and two for the girls.

That night we cooked dinner over a fire. It was beef stew from a package—you just add water and boil—and some kind of vegetables in a sauce. By the time we were through it was dark, and the fire was going great.

"Let's tell ghost stories," said Randy Falco. "That's what you're supposed to do around a fire."

"Ghost stories are for kids," said Carlos.

"Then tell us about Bigfoot, Rick," said Randy. "What's he like? Does he really live around here?"

"Giant apemen have been seen around the world since ancient times," said Rick. "The best-known one is the Abominable Snowman, or Yeti (ye′ tē). They say he's covered with white hair and lives in the mountains of India. There have been stories about Bigfoot in the Northwest and Canada for more than a hundred years. The Indians call him Sasquatch."

"Does he really look like that statue?" asked Kelly.

"Bigfoot looks sort of like an ape, but he walks on two legs like a human," said Rick. "He's seven to twelve feet tall and weighs 600-1,000 pounds. Sometimes he's called Skunk Ape because he smells so bad. He has short ears and is covered with long

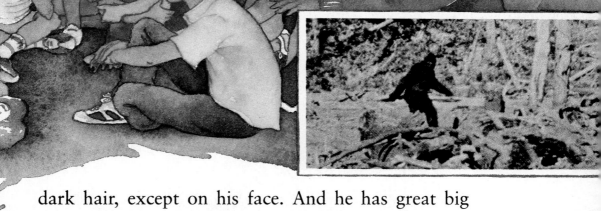

dark hair, except on his face. And he has great big feet with five short toes on each foot."

"There are also female Bigfoots," added Julie. "A man named Roger Patterson said he took pictures of one not far from here, in Bluff Creek, California, in 1967. People who saw his film weren't sure because it was so blurry, but it seemed to show an eight-foot-tall female with a very short neck, covered with dark hair. When she saw Patterson, she stared for a few minutes, and then ran off into the woods."

"Anybody can fake pictures," said Carlos.

"Some film experts from Hollywood swore the film hadn't been messed with," said Rick.

"It still could have been a big guy in a monkey suit," said Carlos.

"Maybe," said Julie. "But Patterson got interested in the first place because of a nature writer named Ivan Sanderson. Sanderson had heard of a road crew at Bluff Creek finding huge footprints around their equipment in 1958. They named it Bigfoot because of the size of the prints and even

made a plaster cast of one. Sanderson talked to people who had seen Bigfoot, including several Indians. Then he saw Bigfoot and some footprints himself. He wrote a magazine story and a book about it. Do you think a serious writer and scientist would make that up?"

"Maybe he was tricked," said Carlos.

"What about Albert Ostman?" said Julie. "He was looking for gold in British Columbia, Canada, in 1924. He said Bigfoot picked him up one day when he was sleeping, carried him to his den, and kept him there for days with Mrs. Bigfoot and their two kids."

"How did he get away?" asked Randy.

"Bigfoot ate Ostman's tobacco and got sick, and Ostman was able to run away."

"The poor thing," I said. "He shouldn't have made it get sick."

"Aw, the poor thing," said Carlos. "Maybe you'd like Bigfoot to come here so you could take it home as a pet."

That Carlos makes me so mad! "It doesn't sound as if it ever hurt anybody," I said. "Why should we hurt it?"

"In fact," said Julie, "one man said he was in a car accident on a mountain road, and a Bigfoot lifted the car off him and carried him to safety."

"See?" I said to Carlos.

"Of course, there was the Chetco River incident," said Rick. "It was about forty years ago, at a small logging camp on the Chetco River in Oregon, only

about 50 miles from Bluff Creek. People's garbage cans were being turned over at night. They thought it was bears. Then one morning they found huge footprints and heard strange whistling and terrible screams. They decided they were in danger, so some of the men took guns and followed the tracks into the woods. Everyone in camp heard shots and screams, and then silence. When the men didn't come back, the others went looking for them. They found them, all killed, and a trail of huge footprints leading into the woods. They were too scared to follow."

"There's your 'poor thing,'" said Carlos. "It killed people!"

"Well, they were shooting at it!" I said.

"I think that's enough about Bigfoot," said Julie. "Time to sleep."

"Who could sleep with giant ape-people running around?" said Kelly. She put her sleeping bag between mine and Rachel Randolph's.

I was too tired to be scared. Besides, I just knew that if there was a Bigfoot, it wouldn't hurt anybody. I almost hoped it would find us. At least that would prove to Carlos that Bigfoot was real.

It was still dark when I woke with a jerk. Someone was thumping and scuffling around outside and turning stuff over. Then there was a scream, and the most awful smell, and feet running, fast!

Rick and Julie came out of their tents with flashlights. Rick threw some wood on the fire.

"Skunk," he said, wrinkling his nose, "looking for food. I wonder what made it use its scent. They don't do that unless something scares them."

"Are you sure it was a skunk?" said Randy. "Look!"

There were footprints! Huge, *gigantic*, footprints. They were all around the clearing and led into the woods.

"Bigfoot!" screamed Kelly.

"The fruit's gone!" said Judd Washburn.

"So's Carlos!" said Pete. "Bigfoot got Carlos!"

"Now, wait a minute," said Rick. "Let's not jump to conclusions. I'm going to have a look around. The rest of you stay here next to the fire. I'll be right back."

"What if Bigfoot comes back?" cried Kelly.

"Bigfoot won't hurt anybody," I said.

"Oh, yeah?" said Randy. "Remember Chetco."

Pretty soon we heard footsteps in the woods. It was Rick, and he had Carlos with him.

"You're all wet!" Judd said to Carlos. "And boy, do you stink! Did Bigfoot get you? How did you get away?"

"A skunk got him," said Rick. "I found him upstream, trying to wash off the smell."

"But what about the footprints?" asked Kelly.

"And the fruit," said Judd.

"Carlos can tell you about that," said Rick. "Can't you, Carlos?"

Carlos looked pretty unhappy. "It's all *her* fault," he said, pointing at me.

"*My* fault!" I said. "What did I do?"

"You were so sure Bigfoot was real, and that it wouldn't hurt anybody. I just wanted to show you how easy it was to fool somebody with fake noises and footprints and stuff."

"How?" asked Rachel.

"I got a big flat stone from the stream and made tracks after everybody was asleep. Then I messed things up and hid the fruit. I was going back to bed when that skunk got me."

I started to laugh. I couldn't help it. Carlos looked so droopy, and he smelled so *bad*! If that's what a Bigfoot smells like, I'm glad we didn't meet one!

Carlos wasn't such a pain for the rest of the trip. That's because he had to stay about ten feet away from us the whole time. Rick says you can wash off skunk smell with tomato juice. Too bad we didn't have any.

Well, we didn't see Bigfoot, but who knows? Maybe someday when I'm a forest ranger, I really will see one. I hope I remember the tomato juice.

Questions

1. Why was Maria disappointed when she first arrived at camp?
2. How did Bigfoot get its name?
3. Carlos said that catching a Bigfoot was the only way to prove that there really were such creatures. Do you agree? Explain your answer.
4. Would you go camping in Bigfoot country? Why or why not?

Applying Reading Skills

Number your paper from 1 to 3. Then use complete sentences to answer each question below.

1. Roger Patterson said that he took pictures of a female Bigfoot. Evaluate the picture on page 363. What do you think it shows?
2. How did Ivan Sanderson get information about Bigfoot? What information about Sanderson might make people willing to believe his reports?
3. Based on what you have read in "My Bigfoot Weekend," do you think there are creatures like Bigfoot? What information supports your judgment?

FOOTPRINTS
Lilian Moore

It was snowing
Last night,
And today
I can see who came
This way.

A dog ran lightly here,
And a cat.
A rabbit hopped by and—
What was THAT?

A twelve-toed foot
Two yards wide?
Another step here
In just one stride?

It was snowing
Last night.
Who came past?
I'll never be knowing
For I am going
The OTHER way,
Fast.

WRITING ACTIVITY

WRITE AN EDITORIAL

Prewrite

Maria and her friends learned a lot about Bigfoot in the story "My Bigfoot Weekend." After reading the story, can you decide what are facts about Bigfoot and what are opinions? A fact is a statement that can be checked. An opinion is a statement that cannot be checked. Opinions are statements about what a person believes or feels. If you want people to respect your opinions, you must give reasons that explain your beliefs or feelings.

Imagine you are the editor of your local newspaper. A story about Bigfoot has been reported. You decide to write an editorial on the subject. An editorial states an opinion and then gives reasons that explain why the writer has that opinion. Read an editorial in your newspaper to help you get ready to write.

Before you start your editorial, write some sentences to answer the questions below.

1. What are some facts about Bigfoot? Check the story "My Bigfoot Weekend." You may want to read other books or magazines for more information.
2. What are some opinions about Bigfoot?
3. What is your opinion about Bigfoot?
4. What reasons can you give to explain why you believe in your opinion?

Write

1. Reread the sentences you wrote about Bigfoot.
2. Think about your audience, the people who will read your editorial. Some people will believe that Bigfoot exists, but others will not. Your editorial should make your readers want to support your opinion.
3. Think about how many paragraphs your editorial will have. State your opinion in the first paragraph.
4. Use the information you discovered to explain why you have the opinion that you do. Use the answer sentences you wrote.
5. Use your Glossary or dictionary for spelling help.

Revise

Read your editorial. Did you clearly state your opinion about Bigfoot? Did you give reasons that supported your opinion? If not, now is the time to rewrite the parts of your editorial that are unclear.

1. Did you indent the first sentence of each paragraph?
2. Did you use adjectives and adverbs that clearly describe the nouns and verbs in your sentences?
3. Did you use commas correctly?

PREPARING FOR READING

Learning Vocabulary

1. Loch Ness was an <u>isolated</u> lake before a road was built around it in the 1930s.
2. Since then many people have been trying to find <u>proof</u> that a monster in Loch Ness really <u>exists</u>.
3. Tim Dinsdale filmed an <u>object</u> that seemed to be a living creature.
4. One scientist used an <u>automatic</u> underwater camera that produced some interesting <u>results</u>.
5. Most people think that more <u>evidence</u> is still needed.

isolated   proof   exists   object
automatic   results   evidence

Developing Background and Skills
Make Judgments

When you read an article that describes or explains something, you discover much information. As you read, you should **evaluate** all the information carefully. Evaluating information is an important step in making a **judgment.**

One way to evaluate information is to think about where it comes from, or the sources that provide it.

Some sources of information are:

eyewitness accounts   reports by experts
photographs   results of scientific tests or
films   experiments

Books and articles may be based on one or more of these sources. Read the paragraph below. What sources of information does the writer refer to?

A monster hunter named Tim Dinsdale took a short film of what he thought was the monster. The "monster" was a long way from Dinsdale when he shot his film. All you can see is a little spot moving across the water. Yet Dinsdale was sure that he had something important. He gave his film to photo experts in the Royal Air Force. They looked at the film closely. Finally they decided that the object in the film was probably a living creature.

What information sources did you find? There are two: the film and the report of the photo experts. Dinsdale's evidence is not proof that a monster exists. The most you can say is that he probably photographed something living.

You will find out more about the "monster" in the next selection. As you read, think about the sources for the information the writer presents.

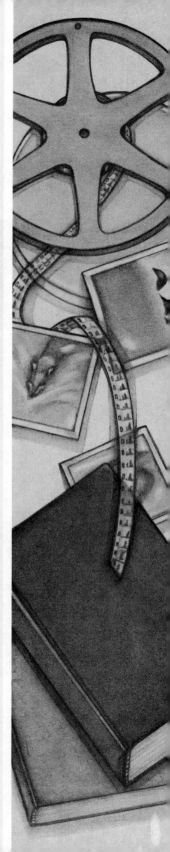

THE SEARCH AT

Loch Ness (lok nes) is a long lake in northern Scotland. Loch is the Scottish word for lake. Loch Ness is about 24 miles (38 kilometers) long and about a mile (1.6 kilometers) wide. The water is very deep—800 feet (244 meters) or more at some points. The water is also very cold, and very

DANIEL COHEN
LOCH NESS

dark. Even a strong light will allow you to see only about 15 feet (4.5 meters) into the dark water.

There have been tales of a monster in the loch for hundreds of years. Monster stories can be a lot of fun. But they are not proof that an unknown animal exists. The real hunt for Nessie, the Loch Ness monster,

377

began during the 1930s. That was when a road was built around the loch. Before that, Loch Ness had been very isolated. The road builders cut down a lot of trees and people could get a better look at the water.

Interest in the Loch Ness monster moves in jumps. Something exciting will happen, and there will be a jump in interest. Then people will forget about Nessie for a while. Then something else interesting will happen and there will be another jump.

The first big jump came in 1933 when a Scottish newspaper printed a story about two people who had seen a "monster" in the water. There was another big

jump in 1934. That was when a picture of what is supposed to be the Loch Ness monster was taken. The picture shows what appears to be the long neck and small head of a creature sticking out of the water. That is the most famous monster picture in the world. The photograph really sparked interest in Nessie. Then World War II came along. People had a lot of other things on their minds.

After the war people began drifting back to Loch Ness to look for the monster. All sorts of people reported that they had seen "something" in the loch. The first really important event after the war took place on April 23, 1960.

A monster hunter named Tim Dinsdale took a short film of what he thought was the monster. The "monster" was a long way from Dinsdale when he shot his film. All you can see is a little spot moving across the water. Yet Dinsdale was sure that he had something important. He gave his film to photo experts in the Royal Air Force. They looked at the film closely. Finally they decided that the object in the film was probably a living creature.

That news stirred up a lot of interest. People who had never believed in the Loch Ness monster before suddenly began to wonder if there might not be something to it after all.

During the late 1960s, groups were formed to look for the Loch Ness monster. Some of the groups

379

were able to buy modern equipment. They began using sonar (sō′ när).

Sonar is very useful at Loch Ness. If the monster exists, it spends most of its time underwater. Sonar allows you to "see" in the dark waters of the loch. Sonar works underwater the same way radar works in the air. Both allow people to find objects without the use of light. The sonar equipment sends out a burst of sound. If the sound hits something, it bounces off the object like an echo. Sonar is sometimes called "echo location."

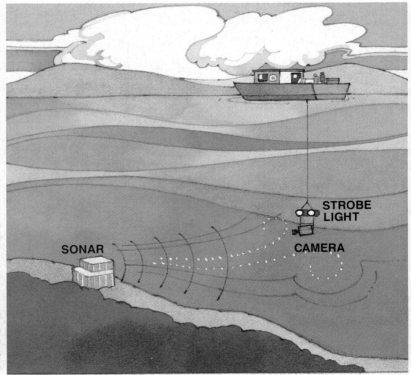

STROBE LIGHT

CAMERA

SONAR

A team of scientists from England used sonar equipment to try and locate the Loch Ness monster. Several times their equipment picked up echoes of what the scientists believe was the monster. In fact, these results seem to show that there are several large unknown animals in Loch Ness. At one point the sonar tracked a group of from five to eight large unknown creatures swimming together.

The name Loch Ness *monster* is a bit confusing. That sounds as if there is only one monster. But there can be no single monster that is hundreds of years old.

Scientists who believe in the creature know that there has to be more than one. There must be a group of unknown animals in the loch. They are born in the loch, grow up and breed there, and die in the loch.

Some scientists believe sonar has given us the most important evidence for the Loch Ness monster. But to the nonscientist, the records of a sonar contact don't look like a monster or anything else. Photographs are different. Everybody can look at a photograph. They can decide for themselves whether the thing in the photo looks like a monster or not.

Over the years there have been a lot of photographs and films taken of what is supposed to be the Loch Ness monster. However, all of those photographs were taken on the surface. But the creature spends most of its time underwater. The best place to take a picture of it should be underwater. But taking underwater pictures at Loch Ness presents all sorts of problems.

The biggest problem is the dark water. Even if you put a strong light on a camera, the object to be photographed has to be pretty close. It has to come within 15 feet (4.5 meters) or less of the camera. A photographer can't wait underwater for the monster to get close enough to take its picture.

You can put an automatic camera underwater. But how would the camera know when to snap the picture? An American scientist, Dr. Robert Rines, came up with one solution. He attached an automatic underwater

camera to sonar equipment. The sonar was on all the time. When the sonar picked up signs of a large object moving nearby, it triggered the camera. The camera would then begin taking pictures. In that way Dr. Rines hoped that he would be able to get a photograph of the large object located by the sonar. He hoped that the large object would be the Loch Ness monster.

On August 8, 1972, Dr. Rines's underwater camera took two of the most spectacular photos ever of the Loch Ness monster (or what he thought was the Loch Ness monster). The camera took two pictures of what appears to be a diamond-shaped flipper, and part of the rounded body of a large unknown animal swimming in the murky waters of Loch Ness.

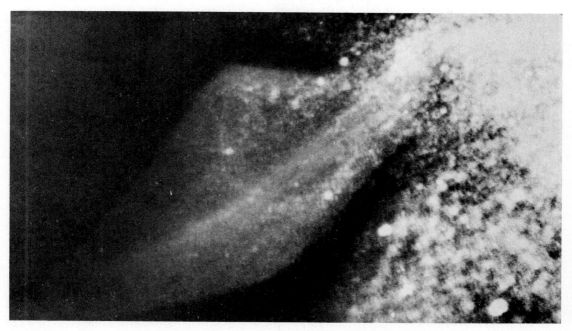

How big is the animal? It's not possible to tell. Most of those who have studied the pictures guess that the flipper alone is more than six feet (1.8 meters) long. Any creature that has such a flipper could be really huge. But we can't be sure of the size.

In 1975, Dr. Rines came back to Loch Ness. He had even better equipment. He had several cameras this time. Once again he got some spectacular pictures.

A picture taken on June 20, 1975, shows what looks like a creature with a very long neck swimming in the distance. Eight hours later something seems to have bumped into the same camera. The bump sent the camera rocking back and forth. One moment it was pointed upward and took a picture of the bottom

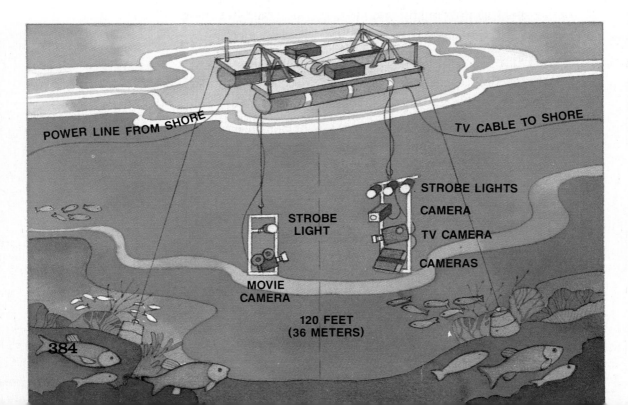

POWER LINE FROM SHORE

TV CABLE TO SHORE

STROBE
LIGHT

STROBE LIGHTS

CAMERA

TV CAMERA

CAMERAS

MOVIE
CAMERA

120 FEET
(36 METERS)

of the boat from which it was hung. Next it took a picture of what might be the rough hide of an animal swimming nearby. The next photo shows what might be the head of a truly monstrous animal.

The pictures are not very clear. They might also show a piece of a strangely shaped log. There is no way of telling for sure. Still, these photos created more excitement than ever before.

The biggest Loch Ness monster search ever was launched in 1977. All sorts of equipment was brought to the loch. There were more scientists gathered there than ever before in history. Yet the search came up with very little in the way of evidence. There were no worthwhile pictures at all.

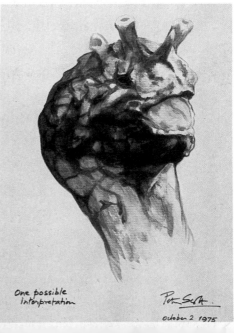

One possible interpretation

October 2 1975

That's the way it has always been with Nessie. Just when the proof seems at hand, it slips away. The monster remains what it has always been—a mystery.

After the disappointment of 1977, interest in the monster slipped. It was no longer big news. But that does not mean that serious monster hunters have given up on it. Not at all. Every year they come back to the loch with their cameras and binoculars, hoping to catch a glimpse of the creature.

The monster hunters are not discouraged. They say that with the photographs, the sonar, and the thousands of sightings by people, there is already more than enough evidence to be sure that the Loch Ness monster exists. It is only a matter of time, they say, before the searchers get close enough, and lucky enough, to figure out exactly what kind of animal it is.

Someday the monster hunters may be proven right. You may be around to see pictures of the real Nessie, the Loch Ness monster.

Questions

1. What makes Loch Ness such a difficult lake for scientists to work in?
2. How does sonar work?
3. If there is a Loch Ness monster, what do you think it looks like?
4. If a monster does live in Loch Ness, how do you think it will be found?

Applying Reading Skills

Copy the list of information sources below on your paper. Write an example of each that you read about in "The Search at Loch Ness." Then evaluate the example by telling whether or not you think it provides evidence supporting the idea that there is a monster in Loch Ness.

eyewitness accounts

photographs

films

reports by experts

results of scientific tests or experiments

PREPARING FOR READING

Learning Vocabulary

1. The Bobmobile <u>submerged</u> into the waters of Loch Ness.
2. Inside the submarine-like ship, Melvin and the Professor were <u>scanning</u> the lake in <u>pursuit</u> of a monster.
3. The trip would be a <u>failure</u> unless they found the monster.
4. Sometimes they <u>drifted</u> along on the surface of the lake.
5. When they did see the monster, there were <u>commotions</u> on land and water.

submerged   scanning   pursuit
failure   drifted   commotions

Developing Background and Skills
Plot, Setting, Mood

What is it that makes a good story?

Some readers like stories with plenty of action. They enjoy reading about exciting adventures. For those readers, the **plot** is very important. The plot includes events and actions. Whatever characters do is part of the plot.

Many readers like to read stories about a certain place or time. They may be very interested in stories that take place in Scotland. They may especially enjoy stories about frontier days or the future. For them, the **setting** is very important. Where and when a story takes place makes up the setting.

Other readers like a story no matter what kind of plot or setting it has. They are mainly interested in how a story makes them feel. They like to read something that will make them laugh, keep them in suspense, or even scare them. These readers care about the **mood** of a story. The general feeling a story creates is the mood.

What is it that makes you enjoy a story? Is it the plot, setting, or mood? Or are all three important?

As you read the next selection, think about its plot, setting, and mood. How has the writer tried to make all three interesting?

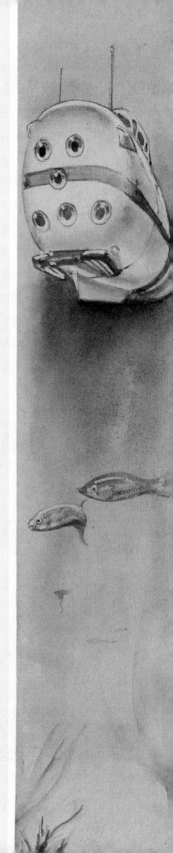

Melvin Spitznagle, with the help of his scientist friend Professor Mickimecki, has invented a submarine-like vessel that looks like a giant oyster shell. He calls it the Bobomobile. Two Scottish clubs gave Melvin the money to build the Bobomobile on the condition that he would come to Scotland and help them find out, once and for all, whether or not the famous Loch Ness monster exists. After months of hard work, Melvin and the Professor test the Bobomobile on their trip across the Atlantic. Once in Scotland, they meet their sponsors as well as other Loch Ness hunters. Finally, with the Nessie Doubting Society and the Surely There Lives Something Down There Fellowship looking on, Melvin and the Professor begin their search.

NESSIE AT LAST!

Jan Wahl

It was a sweet, clear day when at last Melvin and the Professor entered the loch. The Bobomobile submerged into the dark waters.

Professor Mickimecki was steering. Melvin carefully watched the loch. Both wore Infra Blue Ray Longseeing Loch Ness Goggles. The Nessie Feeder was filled with sea kelp. Melvin and the Professor dangled the bait.

The Bobomobile inched its way along the loch. Soon it was followed by the rowboat of Sir Desmond Bassett-Bone and Count Anatole Legume, the yacht of Miss Nelly Puffit, and the raft of Professor Toshiro von Silberklaus. They were all trying to learn the hunting technique of the newcomers.

Melvin thought about how to keep the other searchers away. He wanted to leave part of the loch free. He finally said to the Professor: "We have got to build a Nessie ourselves."

That same day their tent became a workshop. They offered a penny each for bottle caps, putting up a notice at the general store. Some people brought bottle caps in wheelbarrows.

The bottle caps became monster's scales. Broom straws were used as whiskers. The length of it was fifteen feet, with a five-foot neck. The head was something like a cow's head without the horns.

Melvin named it Fugwump.

Fugwump was sent out under cover of darkness. The team now was divided: one man in the Bobomobile at one end, or side, of the loch, the other controlling (by remote control) the actions of Fugwump, to get the attention of the other searchers; this would be done from the tent. The tent was moved to higher ground.

The first time, Melvin controlled Fugwump while the Professor roamed underwater through the loch. Melvin caught the attention of Nelly Puffit at once. Her yacht roared into action, all hands leaping on deck. Fugwump's neck glittered, then disappeared.

Melvin couldn't help letting the yacht draw close. Then the little monster would rise, look about, nod its head as if to say hello, and finally sink with a splash. Soon after, Fugwump's tail would come out of the water some fifty feet off. This gave the appearance that the monster must be of fifty-foot length.

Next Melvin took his turn alone in the Bobomobile. He was scanning the murky waters along the loch. Suddenly, on the Glub Box, it seemed to Melvin he heard a heavy breathing. Then, so quickly that he could describe nothing, something smashed into the Nessie Feeder and made off with a piece of sea kelp.

He was not sure, but he *believed* he had seen a huge pair of red-green eyes. He searched through each of the seventeen portholes, dashing from one to the next. He used the Infra Blue Ray Longseeing Goggles turned on to their highest power. He switched on the headlights also.

"It" was gone.

He zoomed in pursuit. But in which direction should he follow? Frustrated, Melvin surfaced the Bobomobile, wobbled into shore, and gazed out over the water.

At one end of the loch he could see something going on. The other searchers were circling around near Fugwump. Sir J. Wickwhuppity and Reverend Ham Barrow stood side by side shaking their fists at Professor Mickimecki, who appeared to be hiding in the tent. They were also pointing fingers at Melvin, who had beached the Bobomobile and was lying down, trying to rest. Every time he shut his eyes he saw those big blazing red-green ones. Was he mistaken?

That evening, everybody took dinner at the Hotel Grapplefoot. At one side of the room, at separate tables, sat the Nessie Doubting Society and the Surely There Lives Something Down There Fellowship. They were staring at Melvin and the Professor, who picked at their food at the other side.

In the middle fluttered Lord Desmond Bassett-Bone, Count Anatole Legume, Professor Toshiro von Silberklaus, and Nelly Puffit, excitedly discussing Fugwump.

In the morning Melvin and the Professor set Fugwump on automatic control, letting it go in a lazy underwater circle. Both boarded the Bobomobile. They talked, or read magazines. Noon came. They were directly in the middle of the loch. There was not a breath of breeze, and the water was smooth.

They drifted gently, staring out of the small round portholes. "Rock ahead!" noted the Professor, so Melvin steered around it. Melvin noted the position of the rock, so they wouldn't hit it in the future. The Professor softly played lullabies and folk dances on his ukulele. He opened one of the portholes to let some air in.

In response to the music, the brownish silver-blue rock—now behind them—started following. Neither Melvin nor the Professor noted this strange fact for a quarter of an hour.

Melvin happened to turn his neck, glancing over his shoulder. Out of the corner of his eye he realized the rock was in pursuit. He let the Bobomobile glide. Quietly, he took out his set of bells and started ringing them.

Then he and Professor Mickimecki played together while the rock followed, listening. Melvin, playing the bells, shut off the engines with a kick of his foot. The rock closed in and raised up.

Two very big, interested red-green eyes soon appeared. Next a long, lizard-like tail. Then a frizzy mane and whiskers sticking out about the head. The body, having short, stiff fur, was speckled. A rather long neck bent to and frō with the rhythm. There were two sets of paddling flippers, or feet. These splashed the loch into a froth.

"How long, Professor, would you say it is?" whispered Melvin.

"What, boy?" asked the Professor.

"Look."

Only then did the Professor notice. "Forty-five feet," he said, dropping the ukulele.

The music stopped. Nessie thrashed about, as if to catch it flying over her head. Melvin tried a chorus or two of "Jingle Bells."

A rain cloud suddenly shot over. The surrounding water now turned brownish-purple. So did Nessie; no silver and blue remained in her fur.

"The reason," whispered the Professor behind the back of his hand, "it is so hard to describe her. She changes color. Like some chameleon!"

"I hope our sponsors are watching!" said Melvin.

Unfortunately, they were not. Nelly Puffit had just landed Fugwump.

Upon reeling in the prize catch, she was enraged to discover that Fugwump was made of bottle caps, chicken wire, and junk machinery. There it lay, upon the deck of her yacht.

Sprinkles of rain dropped onto the loch.

Nessie flopped over, floating on her back, blue rain tickling her now-blue belly. She had thick light-blue lips and smiled sweetly.

Slowly her red-green eyes (the only part which did not change color) recognized that the rock *she* was gazing at was not a rock. She saw the Professor's and Melvin's heads poking out of the portholes.

She gritted her enormous teeth, hissed like a snake, and yowled. She dove to the bottom of Loch Ness forever.

Onshore, the Nessie Doubting Society and the Surely There Lives Something Down There Fellowship threw down their telescopes to fight fist-to-fist

in the rain and mud. The club members themselves were divided. Some had been watching Nelly Puffit's struggles while others had been watching the Bobomobile. The twin commotions from yacht and shore could be heard by people across the loch.

Melvin was all set to release a balloon to show where they had sighted Nessie. The Professor begged: "Put me ashore, boy! You search after her! I must calm them!"

Melvin did as the Professor suggested. Then he took the Bobomobile back to the meeting spot with Nessie. He submerged, turning on the headlights.

The Professor was chased by the angry club members and by the other searchers. They did not listen to him.

Lightning crashed. The scene was lit up in strong black-and-white. People of all kinds in shawls and raincoats crowded to watch.

In a while, the Bobomobile returned. It drove, dripping, with a bump, right onto a piece of land ahead of the fleeing Professor. The top sprang open.

"Race right in, Professor! It's *O.K.* We can leave now!"

"But! We do not have Nessie! We are a failure!" cried Professor Mickimecki.

Melvin, having a secret, just smiled mysteriously and put the machine on remote control.

They were leaving the mountains and hills and lochs and glens of Scotland. The rain stopped. The storm sun sank toward the far West as they entered the ocean, heading for home.

Crowds gathered up and down the coast, having run by foot to see them off. People climbed trees or rooftops to get a better view.

A brilliant rainbow leaped over red-pink waters. The pair steered straight towards it.

Not till then did Melvin climb to the top of the Bobomobile to display, to the crowds who waved wildly, what he had found in the loch. The Professor joined him.

Astonished, he helped the boy show the prize: An egg. A huge egg. A huge, warm, about-to-hatch Nessie egg!

The triumphant Bobomobile sped on under the rainbow and into the setting sun.

Questions

1. What was the Bobmobile?
2. Why did Melvin and the Professor build Fugwump?
3. Did Melvin and the Professor succeed in what they set out to do? Explain your answer.
4. What do you think will happen to the egg? What do you think Melvin and the Professor will do about it?

Applying Reading Skills

Number your paper from 1 to 4. Then use complete sentences to answer each of the questions below.

1. What are two settings described in the story?
2. How would you explain the mood of this story to someone who had never read it? What might you compare it to?
3. What are three events in the plot?
4. What characters play the most important parts in the plot?

The Slithergadee

Shel Silverstein

The Slithergadee has crawled out of the sea.
He may catch all the others, but he won't catch me.
No you won't catch me, old Slithergadee,
You may catch all the others, but you wo——

PREPARING FOR READING

Learning Vocabulary

1. The island of Komodo has a <u>harsh</u> climate of dry and rainy seasons.
2. Lizards called Komodo dragons are <u>graceful</u> and thin when they are young.
3. A Komodo dragon uses its <u>keen</u> sense of smell to find <u>prey</u>.
4. It needs sun and warmth to keep it <u>active</u>.
5. As a large Komodo dragon <u>strode</u> up to its food, younger lizards <u>lurked</u> in the brush nearby.

harsh	graceful	keen	prey
active	strode	lurked	

Developing Background and Skills
Main Idea

As you know, the **main idea** of a paragraph may not be stated in one sentence. Sometimes the main idea can be stated only by using information from two sentences. Ask yourself, "What are the most important points?" Then use the information to state the main idea in your own words.

Read the paragraph below. Think about the information you would use to state the main idea.

The largest lizards in the world live on the island of Komodo (kə mōd' ō). The island is part of Indonesia, which lies in the Indian Ocean north of Australia. It is twenty-two miles (35 kilometers) long and nine miles (14 kilometers) wide.

Which of the following sentences states the main idea of the paragraph?

1. The island of Komodo is twenty-two miles (35 kilometers) long and nine miles (14 kilometers) wide.
2. The largest lizards in the world live on the island of Komodo, which is part of Indonesia.
3. Indonesia is in the Indian Ocean north of Australia.

The second sentence states the main idea. It includes all the most important information in the paragraph.

As you read the next selection, look for the main ideas of the paragraphs. Sometimes the main idea will be stated directly. Other times you will have to state the main idea in your own words.

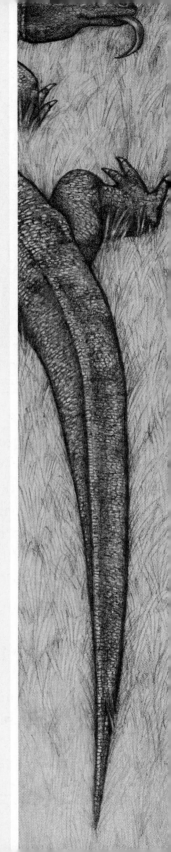

Biography of a KOMODO DRAGON

Alice L. Hopf

The largest lizards in the world live on the island of Komodo (kə mōd′ ō′). The island is part of Indonesia, which lies in the Indian Ocean north of Australia. It is twenty-two miles (35 kilometers) long and nine miles (14 kilometers) wide.

Few people live on this harsh land, which is ruled by strong monsoon winds. When the wind blows in one direction from November to early April, the island is pelted by rain. When it changes direction and blows the other way, a hot, dry summer begins.

Now it was April on Komodo, and a young lizard had found herself a safe perch up in a tree. She had only been out of the egg for a few days. She was graceful and thin, and no more than twenty inches (51 centimeters) long. Her dark greenish-black skin was covered with bright yellow

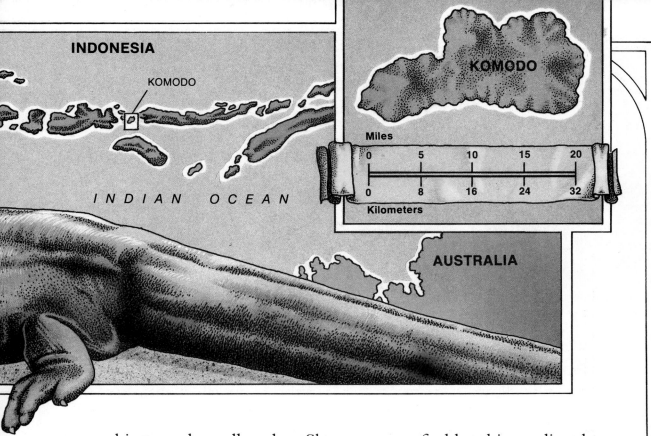

INDONESIA

KOMODO

INDIAN OCEAN

KOMODO

Miles

| 0 | 5 | 10 | 15 | 20 |

| 0 | 8 | 16 | 24 | 32 |

Kilometers

AUSTRALIA

markings and small scales. She looked as though she had passed through a shower of gold dust. But when she grew older, she would lose these bright colors. She would grow larger and heavier. Some people might consider her to be ugly and strange to look at. Because of this, the lizards on Komodo have come to be known as Komodo dragons.

The baby female stayed well up in the trees, out of the way of older, bigger lizards. She ran quickly from branch to branch. Her long neck snapped suddenly from one side to the other as she found lots to eat—beetles, ants, and spiders.

She used her long tongue not for catching her prey, but for finding it. Komodo dragons belong to a group of lizards called monitors. They are related to snakes. Like snakes, they have forked

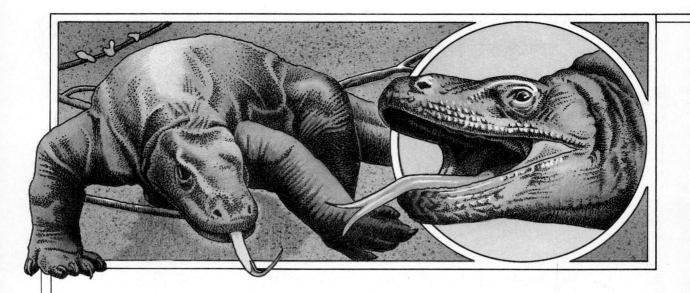

tongues, that, together with a smelling organ in the roof of the mouth, allow them to keep track of their prey from a distance.

Monitor lizards are also like snakes in the way their jaws work. The jaw can become disconnected while the animal is eating. This allows the lizard to swallow prey that is larger than its mouth—even larger than itself! A Komodo dragon weighing 110 pounds (49.5 kilograms) once swallowed 90 pounds (40.5 kilograms) of food in only seventeen minutes.

The young lizard grew fast. One day she found that she could no longer fit into her favorite tree hole. For several days she looked for a bigger tree hole, but she couldn't find one large enough. At last she left the trees for the ground and soon found a hole along a river bank. There was no water in the river, for it was the dry season and it had not rained for months. The lizard climbed up to the hole and stuck her head in. She couldn't smell any other animals, so she began to use her claws to make the hole larger.

Soon it was big enough for her to crawl through, and she curled up inside. She had found a new home.

But food was not so easy to find. Everything had dried up in the summer heat. Sometimes her keen sense of smell led her to a dead animal that had not survived the heat. Usually several other lizards of her size and age were already eating there. She hurried to get as much as she could. They all knew that the bigger lizards would come to the carcass, and when one of them arrived, the smaller ones ran away.

After each successful hunt, the female lizard returned to her den. But summer was ending, and the monsoon winds changed, bringing rain to the dry land. The river filled up with water. Then, one night, there was a big storm, and the water rushed down from the hills. The river rose several feet in a few hours, and water flowed into the dragon's hole.

She scrambled out and clawed her way up the bank. She did not like being out of her den at night, for lizards are daytime creatures. They

need sun and warmth to keep them active. Slowly, the female dragon made her way to the nearest tree and climbed up into the highest branch that would hold her. She slept for the rest of the night while the storm blew itself out.

In the morning the sun came out, but the water was still rushing down the riverbed. The water was much higher than she had ever seen it. It completely covered the opening to her den.

The female dragon climbed higher up the mountain slopes, and soon she saw a small hole in the side of a cliff. It was too small for her to enter, but she dug with her sharp claws. Finally she had a long tunnel with a round opening at the end. It was just big enough for her to curl up inside. Now she had two dens—one for the wet season and one for the dry.

By this time, the female had grown into a medium-sized lizard. When she stood up on her stout legs, she could run almost ten miles (16 kilometers) an hour. If there were smaller lizards already eating a carcass, she would push them aside and take the best place. But if the bigger lizards were eating, she waited in the underbrush, hoping that something might be left when they went away.

One day she was eating at a carcass with a male dragon who was only slightly larger than she. Suddenly, a huge male dragon, the strongest creature on the island, crashed out of the underbrush.

The giant dragon strode up to the carcass—hissing, opening his jaws. The female ran off into the bushes, but the male stood his ground. He had a good grip on the carcass and refused to let go. The giant dragon took hold of the other end, and both lizards pulled. But the giant did not

have as good a grip as the smaller male, who had already started to swallow the food. The big piece of meat popped out of the giant's jaws and disappeared down the throat of the smaller male.

For several minutes, the two stood and stared at each other. Then the bigger lizard went over to the smaller and began to bite at his jaw. The smaller male tried to back away, but he could not escape the giant. The huge lizard climbed onto the back of the smaller one, forcing him to the ground. The younger male collapsed under the weight of the giant. He lay there helpless until the stronger dragon finally climbed off and went back to eating.

The younger dragon lost no time in getting away. The female followed the smaller male. She understood that the giant was showing who ruled this territory.

One hot summer day, the smell of another dead animal reached the female, and she hurried to find it. It was a water buffalo—the largest creature on the island. There would be plenty of food for the lizards. But only one lizard was feeding on the buffalo when the female arrived—the big male.

Some smaller lizards lurked in the brush or dashed out to get a mouthful of food, but the big lizard warned them all away. When the female came, however, he let her eat from his kill. After a while, he stopped eating and moved over beside her. When she moved away from him, he followed her. She saw that he was not warning her away from the kill, so she kept still and stayed with him.

The female lizard went back to her cool place under the thick bush. She rested for two days while she digested her big meal. But another urge was growing in her. She must find a safe place to lay her eggs. At first, she went to her summer den in the river bank, but she wasn't satisfied. She remembered the rushing water that had come in and flooded her den. She left her hole and walked up into the hills.

When she reached her home in the side of the cliff, she was in a hurry. Egg-laying time had come. She made the little room at the end of the tunnel bigger by pushing the dirt and stones out with her claws and nose. Then she settled down to lay her eggs. When she had finished, there were seven eggs in the den.

Each one was about as large as a goose egg. The mother dragon curled herself about them and slept.

For several days the female stayed with her eggs, but soon she got hungry and went out looking for food. Every few days she came back to see if her eggs were safe. But as the weeks went by, she came less and less often. Finally, she stopped coming. When winter brought its floods and storms, she found shelter in the mountain bushes. She was a big dragon now, and she did not need the burrow to hide in.

In April, eight months after the female lizard laid her eggs, they hatched. One after another, the baby dragons found their way out of the tunnel and into the trees. There, the beautiful, gold-flecked young lizards began life on Komodo.

Questions

1. How does the appearance of a young Komodo dragon change as it grows older?
2. In what ways are Komodo dragons like snakes?
3. What was the advantage of the summer season for the Komodo dragon? What was the disadvantage?
4. Do you think the baby dragons will be able to survive on their own? Why or why not?

Applying Reading Skills

Number your paper from 1 to 4. Then write a complete sentence to answer each question below.

1. What is the main idea of the second paragraph on page 406?
2. How would you state the main idea of the first complete paragraph on page 409?
3. What are two supporting details in the third paragraph on page 410?
4. Use your own words to state the main idea of the paragraph that starts on page 413.

PREPARING FOR READING

Learning Vocabulary

1. Jane's father owned a shop filled with <u>antiques</u>.
2. Some of them were tiny figures <u>carved</u> from ivory and jade.
3. An old Chinese man named T'ang told Jane the <u>legend</u> of the dragon and the tiger.
4. The dragon was usually <u>sensible</u> and had very good <u>manners</u>.
5. Yet when the tiger dared to <u>insult</u> the dragon, the dragon <u>hurled</u> lightning at him.

antiques	carved	legend	sensible
manners	insult	hurled	

Developing Background and Skills
Plot, Setting, Mood

When writers plan their stories, they have to think about many things. They must decide on a **setting,** or time and place for the story. They have to figure out a **plot,** or series of events that will take place. Finally, they probably think about the **mood,** or general feeling the story will create for their readers.

Writers can use more than one setting or plot in a story. Sometimes they do this by telling one story within another story. The characters in the main story tell about characters in another story.

Read the story beginning below. What is the plot and setting of the main story? What will the story-within-the-story be about?

It was a cold, rainy afternoon. No one could go out for recess, so all the students had to return to their classrooms after lunch. Mr. Won saw the sad look on his students' faces.

"Don't look so gloomy," he said. "This is perfect weather for a story."

Just then a huge bolt of lightning flashed, and thunder boomed.

"Long ago," began Mr. Won, "there was a huge dragon that roared like thunder and breathed out bolts of lightning. . . ."

The setting of the main story is a classroom on a rainy afternoon. The plot has to do with a teacher telling a story to his students. The story-within-the-story will be about a dragon of long ago.

In the next selection, you will read a story-within-a-story. Notice when it begins and when it ends.

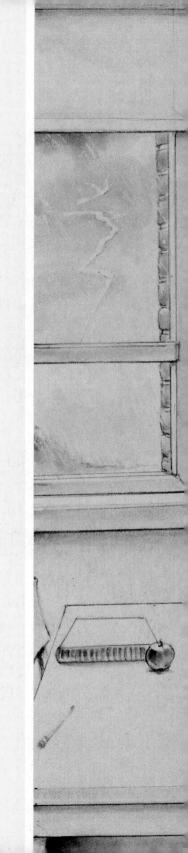

THE DRAGON AND THE TIGER

JEAN LEWIS

Jane Brooks could hardly wait for the school day to end. That morning a mysterious-looking packing case had been delivered to her father's shop just as she was leaving for school. The label read "Hong Kong." Could it be the dragon and the tiger at last?

Jane sprinted up Third Avenue. This part of New York City was crowded with antique shops. Jane passed three on the same side of the street as her father's shop.

"H. Brooks, Oriental Antiques," read the gold letters on the glass door. When Jane pushed it open a bell tinkled. In a moment an old Chinese man came into the front of the shop.

"Hello, T'ang! I'm home," said Jane breathlessly. They exchanged greetings the Chinese way: Jane clasped both hands together, bowing her head in a series of quick nods. T'ang returned her greeting.

Actually, Jane's home was the small apartment over the shop, which she shared with her father. But she thought of the rooms upstairs only as a place to sleep and have meals. It was here in the shop that Jane was really at home.

The shop was crowded with valuable oriental antiques. There were tiny figurines from China carved of ivory and jade. Jane loved to handle these. She often helped T'ang polish the huge brass trays and tinkling bells from India. Together they dusted the gleaming Japanese black lacquer boxes and bowls showered over with cherry blossoms.

"You haven't opened it yet, have you, T'ang?" Jane asked anxiously.

T'ang smiled. Stooping behind the counter, he lifted up a small packing case.

Jane sighed with relief and followed him to the back of the shop. Laying the case on a work table, T'ang picked up some pliers.

"The letters on the case say 'Hong Kong,' so we know that whatever it is, it's Chinese," said Jane, circling the table. "Oh, T'ang," Jane added eagerly, "*do* you think it could be the dragon and the tiger?"

"Only one way to find out," said T'ang, cutting the metal bands with the pliers and prying up the lid. Swiftly, but gently, he sifted through clouds of paper. Then, in the center of the case, he came to it.

Jane's eyes shone as she watched T'ang remove layer after layer of wrapping. At last he held in his hands a beautiful vase. The colors, rich gold, bright reds, brilliant greens and blues, gleamed like the finest silk.

"It *is*! It's the dragon and the tiger making the thunderstorm!" she exclaimed.

T'ang nodded, placing the vase on the table and standing back to admire it with her.

"Look!" said Jane. "The dragon's tail!" She pointed to one of two carved handles at the neck of the vase.

"And here—the paw of the tiger," said T'ang, touching the other handle. "Now we will have tea," he added, clearing more space on the work table.

Every afternoon when Jane came home from school she and T'ang had tea together here in the rear of the shop. That was when he told her tales of his homeland, stories she never tired of hearing.

Carefully, Jane poured the pale-green liquid into their cups. Each took a sip, and then, as Jane watched T'ang turn the colorful vase this way and that, he began to tell her the legend of the dragon and the tiger. He told it to Jane just as he had heard it from his grandmother years ago in China.

"Long, long ago, in ancient times, it was believed that thunderstorms were brought about by the battles of the dragon and the tiger.

"The mighty dragon hurled lightning bolts at the tiger that split open the skies. And in return the tiger roared thunderclaps that shook the earth. What

happened between the dragon and the tiger to cause such a fight, one that keeps breaking out so many hundreds of years later? I will tell you.

"One afternoon the dragon curled up for a nap in the shade of a mulberry tree. He was stuffed to bursting with a delicious meal of six kinds of noodles and three kinds of sauce. Soon the dragon was dreaming a most marvelous dream. Long lines of people were coming to bring him wonderful gifts.

" 'What is this?' he asked a smiling old woman. 'Can it be New Year's again so soon?'

" 'How very kind of you,' he said to a villager with a large package.

"As others in the line kept passing before him with their gifts the happy dragon said, 'Just what I wanted. . . . Thank you! . . . But this is my favorite sweet! How did you guess? . . . Thank you, thank you all!'

龍虎鬥龍虎鬥龍虎

"Best of all the dragon's gifts was a big, beautiful kite.

" 'I've never seen such a kite!' cried the dragon in delight.

" 'It's made in the shape of a tiger,' said the little boy who had brought it.

" 'Just so,' said the dragon. 'All gold and black stripes with snarling teeth and glowing eyes. And what a magnificent tail! Thank you! I shall fly it at once!'

"Clutching his beautiful kite, the dragon headed for the open fields.

" 'First, I'll get a good start by running up this hill,' said the dragon, puffing smoke and fire as he dragged the kite along behind him.

"As soon as he reached the top of the hill, he started down the other side, the kite sailing up, higher and higher.

" 'How real it looks!' puffed the dragon. 'The tail stretching out behind and the head turning this way and that!'

"Happily spouting great sheets of fire and clouds of smoke, the dragon was careful not to singe his kite.

"After running up and down hill several times, the dragon gasped, 'I must rest! I am very tired!' So he threw himself down in the shade of a mulberry tree and in no time he was asleep.

"Now, when the dragon awoke from his dream, he immediately began to search for his marvelous tiger kite. You see, his dream of the gifts people

brought him and of the kite had been so real to him that he quite forgot it *was* only a dream. Of course, he couldn't find the kite because there wasn't one. He was heartbroken.

" 'Someone's stolen my beautiful kite. Snatched it from me while I slept!' he cried. Then he stumbled over something soft. Something striped black and gold.

" 'What is this?' exclaimed the dragon. 'Why, it's my kite! The tail of my marvelous tiger kite!' And grabbing hold of the tail, the dragon raced up hill with it again.

"Only this time he found it much harder getting the kite into the air. He tugged and he pulled until suddenly he heard a great growling and hissing.

" 'All that noise!' said the dragon as he kept on tugging and pulling. 'A less sensible person might think my marvelous tiger kite was alive!' And he turned around to find himself looking into the very real teeth of a very real tiger! And a very angry one, too.

"The dragon let go of the tiger's tail at once. Then he tried to explain about his dream and the mistake he had made. But the tiger would not listen.

" 'Dream, indeed!' roared the tiger, lashing his tail about. 'What do you mean by waking a person from his rest and trying to drag him off by his tail?'

" 'If you haven't manners enough to listen to the truth—' began the dragon, drawing himself up to his full height.

" 'I know the truth when I hear it!' roared the tiger. 'And I can *smell* a pack of lies!'

" 'How dare you insult *me*!' snorted the dragon, breathing fire and smoke.

"And so the two fell to fighting there in the field near the big hill. They kept at it for hours. The dragon hurled lightning bolts at the tiger that split open the skies. The tiger roared thunderclaps that shook the earth. For miles around, people hid under their beds, shaking with fright.

"The truth is, they would still be at it if the wife of a giant, who lived at the top of the big hill, hadn't emptied an enormous washtub, soaking them both. As soon as they went away to dry themselves, the sun came out again and all was quiet.

龍虎鬪龍虎鬪龍虎

425

"But every now and again the tiger remembers how the dragon insulted him by pulling his tail and he snarls at him. Then they start in to battle all over again.

"Thunderclaps roar and lightning flashes until someone throws water on the dragon and the tiger."

Jane laughed as T'ang finished the story. She pointed at the face of the dragon on the vase. "He looks just as if he *would* make a mistake like that."

"And so he did," said T'ang. "How else would we have thunderstorms today?"

Jane looked closely at T'ang. Was he smiling at what he surely meant as a joke? Or was he just smiling at the face of the dragon on the vase?

Questions

1. Why was Jane eager to get back to her father's shop at the end of the school day?
2. What did the antique called the dragon and the tiger look like?
3. Do you think T'ang believed the legend? Give reasons to support your answer.
4. What legends do you know? How do legends differ from science articles and other nonfiction writing?

Applying Reading Skills

Number your paper from 1 to 4. Then use complete sentences to answer each question below.

1. What is the setting of "The Dragon and the Tiger"?
2. What is the setting of the story T'ang told Jane?
3. What were the main events in the plot of T'ang's story?
4. How would you describe the mood of "The Dragon and the Tiger"?

Thunder Dragon

Harry Behn

A somber dragon,
  Eyes agleam,
A baleful creature
  Out of dream,

Crept over the mountain
  Flashing flame
As down through the darkening
  Sky he came.

Over a cliff
  In coils of cloud,
Through winds that whistled
  Long and loud,

He dropped his scaly
  Carcass down
With a crash of thunder
  Across the town!

No one remembers
  So vast a noise
Since even the oldest
  Men were boys.

No one remembers
   When, if ever,
So wild a deluge
   Roiled the river!

But even a dragon
   Wearies at last,
And so his tempestuous
   Temper passed.

Now, in darkness,
   Away he crawls,
Up to his cave
   In the craggy walls,

Grumbling, growling,
   Back again,
Back he goes
   To his mountain den.

Oh, how his thunders
   Rumble and dim
As he nudges the deep earth
   Over him.

How feebly his lightnings
   Hiss and steam
As he flickers, and fades away
   To a dream.

429

THE Adventure OF Eustace

C.S. LEWIS

Eustace Clarence Scrubb was such a disagreeable child that when he heard that his cousins Lucy and Edmund were coming to spend the summer, he thought of all the ways he could give them a bad time. What Eustace had not planned on was that Lucy and Edmund would give him a time of their own.

One day the three children were looking at a painting of a sailing ship in Lucy's room. Suddenly they were magically transported onto the ship, and the waves, the wind, and the smell of the ocean became very real. The ship, called the Dawn Treader, belonged to Caspian, the king of Narnia, a kingdom Lucy and Edmund had visited before. Caspian and his sailors, along with the talking mouse Reepicheep, were in search of seven Narnian lords who had not returned from a journey. They welcomed their old friends, and Eustace, on the adventure.

After a rough storm, the crew docked at Dragon Island to rest. Eustace, who had become more disagreeable than ever, wandered off and lost his way in a fog. After stumbling down a mountain, Eustace waited for the fog to lift. It was then that his own adventure began.

Eustace stared around the unknown valley. It was so narrow and deep that it was like a huge pit or trench. About fifteen yards away from him was a pool of clear, smooth water. There was, at first, nothing else at all in the valley; not an animal, not a bird, not an insect.

Eustace realized, of course, that in the fog he had come down the wrong side of the ridge, so he turned at once to see about getting back. But as soon as he had looked he shuddered. Apparently he had by amazing luck found the only possible way down—a long green spit of land, horribly steep and narrow. There was no other possible way of getting back. But could he do it, now that he saw what it was really like?

He turned around again, thinking that he'd better have a good drink from the pool first. But as soon as he had turned, he heard a noise behind him. It froze him dead still where he stood for a second. Then he turned his head and looked.

At the bottom of the cliff, a little on his left hand, was a low, dark hole—the entrance to a cave perhaps. And out of it two thin wisps of smoke were coming. And the loose stones just beneath the dark hollow were moving (that was the noise he

had heard), just as if something were crawling behind them.

Something *was* crawling. And even worse, something was coming out. Edmund or Lucy or you would have recognized it at once, but Eustace had read none of the right books. The thing that came out of the cave was something he had never even imagined—a long lead-colored snout, dull red eyes, no feathers or fur, a long body that trailed on the ground, legs whose elbows went up higher than its back like a spider's, cruel claws, bat's wings that made a rasping noise on the stones, yards of tail. And the two lines of smoke were coming from its two nostrils. He never said the word *dragon* to himself. Nor would it have made things any better if he had.

But perhaps if he had known something about dragons he would have been a little surprised at this dragon's behavior. It did not sit up and flap its wings, or shoot out a stream of flame from its mouth. The smoke from its nostrils was like the smoke of a fire that will not last much longer. Nor did it seem to have noticed Eustace. It moved very slowly towards the pool—slowly and with many pauses. Even in his fear Eustace felt that it was an old, sad creature.

It reached the pool and slid its scaly chin down over the gravel to drink. But before it had drunk there came from it a great clanging cry, and after a few twitches it rolled around on its side and lay perfectly still with one claw in the air. The smoke from its nostrils turned black for a moment and then floated away. No more came.

For a long time Eustace did not dare to move. But one couldn't wait forever. He took a step nearer, then two steps, and halted again. The dragon remained motionless; he noticed too that the red fire had gone out of its eyes. At last he came up to it. He was quite sure now that it was dead. With a shudder he touched it; nothing happened.

The relief was so great that

Eustace almost laughed out loud. He began to feel as if he had fought and killed the dragon instead of merely seeing it die. He stepped over it and went to the pool for his drink, for the heat was getting unbearable. He was not surprised when he heard a peal of thunder. And before he had finished his drink big drops of rain were falling. Eustace ran for the only shelter in sight—the dragon's cave. There he lay down and tried to get his breath.

Most of us know what we can expect to find in a dragon's lair, but, as I said before, Eustace had read only the wrong books. That is why he was so puzzled at the surface on which he was lying. Parts of it were too prickly to be stones and too hard to be thorns, and there seemed to be a great many round, flat things, and it all clinked when he moved. There was light enough at the cave's mouth to examine it by. And of course Eustace found it to be what any of us could have told him in advance—treasure. There were crowns (those were the prickly things), coins, rings, bracelets, cups, plates, and gems. Eustace (unlike most boys) had never thought much of treasure, but he saw at once the use it would be in this new world. "They don't have any tax here," he said. "And you don't have to give treasure to the government. With some of this stuff I could have quite a decent time here. I wonder how much I can carry? That bracelet now— those things in it are probably diamonds—I'll slip that on my wrist. Too big, but not if I push it right up here above my elbow. Then fill my pockets with diamonds—that's easier than gold. I wonder when this rain's going to let up?" He got into a less uncomfortable part of the pile, where it was mostly coins, and settled down to wait. But a bad fright, when once it is over, and especially a bad fright following a mountain walk, leaves you very tired. Eustace fell asleep.

By the time he was sound asleep and snoring, the others had finished dinner and become seriously alarmed about him. They shouted, "Eustace!" until they were hoarse and Caspian blew his horn.

"He's nowhere near or he'd have heard that," said Lucy. "We'll have to send out a search party."

Meanwhile Eustace slept and slept—and slept. What woke him was a pain in his arm. The moon was shining in at the mouth of the cave, and the bed of treasures seemed to have grown much more comfortable. In fact he could hardly feel it at all. He was puzzled by the pain in his arm at first, but then it occurred to him that the bracelet which

he had shoved up above his elbow had become strangely tight. His arm must have become swollen while he was asleep (it was his left arm).

He moved his right arm in order to feel his left, but stopped before he had moved it an inch and bit his lip in terror. For just in front of him, and a little on his right, where the moonlight fell clear on the floor of the cave,

he saw a hideous shape moving. He knew that shape: it was a dragon's claw. It had moved as he moved his hand and became still when he stopped moving his hand.

"Oh, what a fool I've been," thought Eustace. "Of course, the brute had a mate and it's lying beside me."

For several minutes he did not dare to move a muscle. He saw two thin columns of smoke going up before his eyes, black against the moonlight, just as there had been smoke coming from the other dragon's nose before it died. This was so alarming that he held his breath. The two columns of smoke vanished. When he could hold his breath no longer he let it out stealthily. Instantly two jets of smoke appeared again. But even yet he had no idea of the truth.

Eustace decided that he would edge very cautiously to his left and try to creep out of the cave. Perhaps the creature was asleep— and anyway it was his only chance. But, of course, before he edged to the left he looked to the left. Oh horror! There was a dragon's claw on that side, too.

No one will blame Eustace if at this moment he shed tears. He was surprised at the size of his own tears as he saw them splashing onto the treasure in front of him. They also seemed strangely hot; steam went up from them.

But there was no good crying. He must try to crawl out from between the two dragons. He began extending his right arm. The dragon's foreleg and claw on his right went through exactly the same motion. Then he thought he would try his left. The dragon limb on that side moved, too.

Two dragons, one on each side, mimicking whatever he did! His nerve broke and he simply made a bolt for it.

There was such a clatter and rasping, and clinking of gold, and grinding of stones, as he rushed out of the cave that he thought they were both following him. He didn't dare look back. He rushed to the pool.

But just as he reached the edge of the pool two things happened. First of all it came over him like a thunderclap that he had been running on all fours—and why on earth had he been doing that? And secondly, as he bent towards the water, he thought for a second that yet another dragon was staring up at him out of the pool. But in an instant he realized the truth. That dragon face in the pool was his own reflection. There was no doubt of it. It moved as he moved. It opened and shut its mouth as he opened and shut his.

He had turned into a dragon while he was asleep. Sleeping on a dragon's hoard with greedy, dragonish thoughts in his heart, he had become a dragon himself.

That explained everything. There had been no two dragons beside him in the cave. The claws to right and left had been his

own right and left claws. The two columns of smoke had been coming from his own nostrils. As for the pain in his left arm (or what had been his left arm) he could now see what had happened by squinting with his left eye. The bracelet which had fitted very nicely on the upper arm of a boy was far too small for the thick, stumpy foreleg of a dragon. It had sunk deeply into his scaly flesh and there was a bulge on each side of it. He tore at the place with his dragon's teeth but could not get it off.

In spite of the pain, his first feeling was one of relief. There was nothing to be afraid of anymore. He was a terror himself now and nothing in the world but a knight (and not all of those) would dare to attack him.

Then he realized that he was a monster cut off from the whole human race. A terrible loneliness came over him. At last he decided he would try to find his way back to the shore. He realized now that Caspian would never have sailed away and left him. He felt sure that somehow or other he would be able to make people understand who he was.

He turned to climb out of the valley. He began the climb with a jump, and as soon as he jumped he found that he was flying. He had quite forgotten about his wings, and it was a great surprise to him—the first pleasant sur-

prise he had had for a long time. He rose high into the air and saw mountain tops spread out beneath him in the moonlight. He could see the bay like a silver slab, and the *Dawn Treader* lying at anchor, and campfires twinkling in the woods beside the beach. From a great height he launched himself down towards them in a single glide.

Lucy was sleeping soundly for she had sat up until the return of the search party in hope of good news about Eustace. It had been led by Caspian and had come back late and weary. Their news was disquieting. They had found no trace of Eustace but had seen a dead dragon in a valley. They tried to make the best of it, and everyone assured everyone else that there were not likely to be more dragons about, and that one which was dead at about three o'clock that afternoon (which was when they had seen it) would hardly have been killing people a very few hours before.

But later in the night Lucy was waked, very softly, and found the whole company gathered close together and talking in whispers.

"What is it?" said Lucy.

"We must all show great constancy," Caspian was saying. "A dragon has just flown over the treetops and lighted on the beach. Yes, I am afraid it is between us and the ship. And arrows are no use against dragons. And they're not at all afraid of fire. We must just keep close watch and, as soon as it is light, go down to the beach and give it battle. There are no other arrangements to be made. It will be light in a couple of hours. In an hour's time let a meal be served, and let everything be done silently."

The rest of the night was dreadful, and when the meal came, though they knew they ought to eat, many found that they had very poor appetites. And endless hours seemed to pass before the darkness thinned and birds began chirping and the world got colder and wetter than it had been all night and Caspian said, "Now for it, friends."

They got up, all with swords drawn, and formed themselves into a solid mass with Lucy in the middle and Reepicheep on her shoulder. A moment later they were marching. It grew lighter as they came to the edge of the wood. And there on the sand, like a giant lizard, or a flexible crocodile, or a serpent with legs, huge and horrible and humpy, lay the dragon.

But when it saw them, instead of rising up and blowing fire and smoke, the dragon retreated—you could almost say it waddled—back into the shallows of the bay.

"What's it wagging its head like that for?" said Edmund.

"And now it's nodding," said Caspian.

"And there's something coming from its eyes," said Drinian.

"Oh, can't you see," said Lucy. "It's crying. Those are tears."

"I shouldn't trust to that, Ma'am," said Drinian. "That's what crocodiles do, to put you off your guard."

"It wagged its head when you said that," remarked Edmund. "Just as if it meant *No*. Look, there it goes again."

"Do you think it understands what we're saying?" asked Lucy.

The dragon nodded its head violently.

Reepicheep slipped off Lucy's shoulder and stepped to the front.

"Dragon," came the mouse's shrill voice, "can you understand speech?"

The dragon nodded.

"Can you speak?"

It shook its head.

"Then," said Reepicheep, "it is idle to ask you your business. But if you will swear friendship with us raise your left foreleg above your head."

It did so, but clumsily because that leg was sore and swollen with the golden bracelet.

"Oh look," said Lucy, "there's something wrong with its leg. The poor thing—that's probably what it was crying about. Perhaps it came to us to be cured like in Androcles and the lion."

"Be careful," said Caspian. "It's a very clever dragon but it may be a liar."

Lucy had, however, already run forward.

"Show me your poor paw," said Lucy, "I might be able to cure it."

The dragon-that-had-been-Eustace held out its sore leg gladly. But he was disappointed. The fluid Lucy applied reduced the swelling and eased the pain a little but it could not dissolve the gold.

Everyone had now crowded round to watch the operation, and Caspian suddenly exclaimed, "Look!" He was staring at the bracelet.

"Look at what?" Edmund asked.

"Look at the device on the gold," said Caspian.

"A little hammer with a diamond above it like a star," said Drinian. "Why, I've seen that before."

"Seen it!" said Caspian. "Why, of course you have. It is the sign of a great Narnian house. This is the Lord Octesian's arm-ring."

"Villain," said Reepicheep to the dragon, "have you devoured a Narnian lord?" But the dragon shook his head violently.

"Or perhaps," said Lucy, "this *is* the Lord Octesian, turned into a dragon—under an enchantment, you know."

"It needn't be either," said Edmund. "All dragons collect gold. But I think it's a safe guess that Octesian got no further than this island."

"Are you the Lord Octesian?" said Lucy to the dragon, and then, when it sadly shook its head, "Are you someone enchanted—someone human, I mean?"

It nodded violently.

Then someone said—people disputed afterwards whether Lucy or Edmund said it first—"You're not—not Eustace by any chance?"

And Eustace nodded his terrible dragon head and thumped his tail in the sea and everyone skipped back to avoid the enormous and boiling tears which flowed from his eyes.

Lucy tried hard to console him, and nearly everyone said, "Hard luck," and several assured Eustace that they would all stand by him, and many said there was sure to be some way of disenchanting him, and they'd have him as right as rain in a day or two. And of course they were all very anxious to hear his story, but he couldn't speak. More than once in the days that followed he attempted to write it for them on the sand. But this never succeeded. In the first place Eustace (never having read the right books) had no idea how to tell a story straight. And for another thing, the muscles and nerves of

the dragon claws that he had to use had never learned to write and were not built for writing anyway. As a result he never got nearly to the end before the tide came in and washed away all the writing except the bits he had already trodden on or accidentally swished out with his tail. And all that anyone had seen would be something like this— the dots are for the bits he had smudged out—

I WNET TO SLEE . . . RGOS AGRONS I MEAN DRANGONS CAVE CAUSE ITWAS DEAD AND AINIG SO HAR . . . WOKE UP AND COU . . . GET OFFF MI ARM . . .

It was, however, clear to everyone that Eustace's character had been rather improved by becoming a dragon. He was anxious to help. He flew over the whole island and found that it was all mountainous and inhabited only by wild goats and wild swine. Of these he brought back many carcasses to supply the ship with food. And in the evening, if it turned chilly, as it sometimes did after the heavy rains, he was a comfort to everyone, for the whole party would come and sit with their backs against his hot sides and get well warmed and dried; and one puff of his fiery breath would light the most obstinate fire.

The pleasure (quite new to him) of being liked and, still more, of liking other people, kept Eustace from despair. For it was very dreary being a dragon. He shuddered whenever he caught sight of his own reflection as he flew over a mountain lake. He hated the huge bat-like wings, the saw-edged ridge on his back, and the cruel curved claws. He was almost afraid to be alone with himself and yet he was ashamed to be with the others. On the evenings when he was not being used as a hot-water bottle he would slink away from the camp and lie curled up like a snake between the wood and the water. On such occasions, greatly to his surprise, his

most constant comforter was Reepicheep. The noble Mouse would creep away from the merry circle at the campfire and sit down by the dragon's head, well to the windward to be out of the way of his smoky breath. There he would explain that what had happened to Eustace was an illustration of the turn of Fortune's wheel, and that if he had Eustace at his own house in Narnia (it was really a hole not a house and the dragon's head, let alone his body, would not have fitted in) he could show him more than a hundred examples of emperors, kings, dukes, knights, poets, astronomers, philosophers, and magicians, who had fallen from prosperity into the most distressing circumstances, and of whom many had recovered and lived happily ever afterwards. It did not, perhaps, seem so very comforting at the time, but it was kindly meant and Eustace never forgot it.

Eustace begins to become a better person after his adventure in the skin of a dragon. You can continue with the magical adventures of Eustace, Edmund, Lucy, and the other characters on board King Caspian's ship by reading **The Voyage of the "Dawn Treader."** *It is the third book in the series by C. S. Lewis,* **THE CHRONICLES OF NARNIA.**

Glossary

This glossary can help you to pronounce and find out the meanings of words in this book that you may not know.

The words are listed in alphabetical order. Guide words at the top of each page tell you the first and last words on the page.

Each word is divided into syllables. The way to pronounce each word is given next. You can understand the pronunciation respelling by using the key below. A shorter key appears at the bottom of every other page.

When a word has more than one syllable, a dark accent mark (′) shows which syllable is stressed. In some words, a light accent mark (′) shows which syllable has a less heavy stress.

The following abbreviations are used in this glossary:

n. noun   *v.* verb   *adj.* adjective   *adv.* adverb   *pl.* plural

The glossary entries were adapted from the Macmillan *School Dictionary*.

PRONUNCIATION KEY
Vowel Sounds

/a/	bat	/ō/	rope, soap, so, snow
/ā/	cake, rain ,day	/ô/	saw, song, auto
/ä/	father	/oi/	coin, boy
/är/	car	/ôr/	fork, ore, oar
/âr/	dare, hair	/ou/	out, cow
/e/	hen, bread	/u/	sun, son, touch
/ē/	me, meat, baby, believe	/ù/	book, pull, could
/ėr/	term, first, worm, turn	/ü/	moon
/i/	bib	/ū/	cute, few, music
/ī/	kite, fly, pie, light	/ə/	about, taken, pencil,
/ir/	clear, cheer, here		apron, helpful
/o/	top, watch	/ər/	letter, dollar, doctor

Consonant Sounds

/b/	bear	/s/	city, seal
/d/	dog	/t/	tiger
/f/	fish, phone	/v/	van
/g/	goat	/w/	wagon
/h/	house, who	/y/	yo-yo
/j/	jar, gem, fudge	/z/	zoo, eggs
/k/	car, key	/ch/	chain, match
/l/	lamb	/sh/	show
/m/	map	/th/	thin
/n/	nest, know	/th/	those
/p/	pig	/hw/	where
/r/	rug, wrong	/ng/	song

A

ac·count (ə kount′) *n*. **1.** a record of money spent or received. **2.** a spoken or written statement; report.

ac·tive (ak′ tiv) *adj*. full of action and energy; lively.

ad·ver·tise·ment (ad′ vər tīz′ mənt) *n*. a public announcement that describes an event, product, or service.

ad·vice (əd vīs′) *n*. an idea that is offered to a person about what he or she should do.

af·fec·tion (ə fek′ shən) *n*. tender feeling or fondness; warm attachment.

a·gree·ment (ə grē′ mənt) *n*. the state of agreeing, or having the same opinion or feeling; harmony.

a·lert (ə lėrt′) *v*. to make aware of; warn.

al·ti·tude (al′ tə tüd′, al′ tə tūd′) *n*. the height that something is above the ground or above sea level.

a·lu·mi·num (ə lü′ mə nəm) *n*. a light, soft, silvery-white metal.

A·mer·i·can Sign Lan·guage (ə mār′ i kən sīn′ lang′ gwij) *n*. a system of communication for the deaf in which hand movements are used instead of speech.

an·cient (ān′ shənt) *adj*. having to do with times very long ago; very old.

an·tique (an tēk′) *n*. a thing of special value that was made long ago.

ar·moured (är′ mərd) *adj*. protected by armour, or a metal covering.

ar·range (ə rānj′) *v*. **ar·ranged, ar·rang·ing.** to put in some kind of order.

art·ful (ärt′ fəl) *adj*. cunning; lying; tricky.

a·shamed (ə shāmd′) *adj*. upset or uncomfortable about having done something bad or silly.

as·sure (ə shûr′) *v*. **as·sured, as·sur·ing.** to tell positively.

at·ten·dance (ə ten′ dəns) *n*. the number of people present.

au·to·mat·ic (ô′ tə mat′ ik) *adj*. acting by itself; not operated by a person.

awk·ward (ôk′ wərd) *adj*. not graceful; clumsy.

B

bale·ful (bāl′ fəl) *adj*. full of danger.

bar·ren (bār′ ən) *adj*. having little or no plant life; not productive.

bear (bār) *v*. **bore, borne** *or* **born, bear·ing. 1.** to put up with; endure or tolerate. **2.** to hold up; support.

bi·noc·u·lars (bə nok′ yə lərz) *n. pl.* a device that makes distant objects look larger and closer. Binoculars are made up of two telescopes joined together, so that a person can look at distant objects with both eyes.

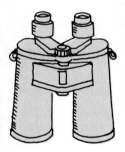

binoculars

blood pres·sure (blud′ presh′ ər) *n*. the force of the blood against the inner walls of the arteries and other blood vessels. It is created by the pumping action of the heart.

bolt (bōlt) *n*. **1.** a roll of cloth or paper. **2.** a rod used to hold things together. **3.** a flash of lightning.

bor·der states (bor′ dər stāts′) *n. pl.* the five slave states that bordered on the North at the time of the Civil War (Delaware, Maryland, Virginia, Kentucky, and Missouri).

brace (brās) *v.* **braced, brac·ing.** to make strong, firm, or steady.

breech·es (brich′ iz) *n. pl.* pants that reach to or just below the knees.

broad·ax (brôd′ aks′) *n., pl.* **broad·ax·es.** an ax with a broad, or wide, blade, used especially to cut logs.

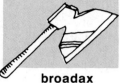

broadax

buck·skin (buk′ skin′) *n.* a strong, soft, yellowish-tan leather, made from the skins of deer or sheep.

Bu·reau of En·grav·ing and Print·ing (būr′ ō, en grāv′ ing) *n.* the department of the United States government that prints money. To *engrave* means to print something from a metal plate or other material that has been cut with letters or figures.

C

cal·i·co (kal′ ə kō′) *n.* a cotton material that has small, brightly colored designs on it.

cap·i·tal (kap′ it əl) *adj.* excellent; first-rate. —*n.* money used to start a business.

cap·sule (kap′ səl) *n.* a sealed cabin in a spacecraft, designed to support life during flight and be recovered after flight.

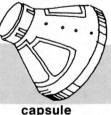

capsule

car·a·van (kär′ ə van′) *n.* **1.** a number of vehicles traveling together. **2.** a group of people traveling together for safety, especially through deserts or dangerous regions.

car·cass (kär′ kəs) *n., pl.* **car·cass·es.** the dead body of an animal.

carve (kärv) *v.* **carved, carv·ing.** to cut to make a design in things like ivory, wood, or stone.

cast (kast) *v.* **cast, cast·ing. 1.** to cause to fall; throw off. **2.** to throw through the air; hurl.

ca·tas·tro·phe (kə tas′ trə fē′) *n.* a great and sudden disaster or misfortune.

cer·e·mo·ny (sār′ ə mō′ nē) *n., pl.* **cer·e·mo·nies.** a formal act or set of acts done on special or important occasions.

chain gang (chān′ gang′) *n.* a group of prisoners or slaves who are chained together, usually while doing hard work outdoors.

chal·lenge (chal′ ənj) *n.* something that calls for work, effort, and the use of one's talent.

cham·pi·on·ship (cham′ pē ən ship′) *n.* a contest held to determine a champion, or winner of first place in a contest or game.

change·up (chānj′ up′) *n.* in baseball, a slow pitch delivered with the same motion as a fast pitch, usually following a fast pitch.

cir·cum·stanc·es (sėr′ kəm stan′ səs) *n. pl.* the conditions that surround and have an effect on a person or event.

cit·i·zen (sit′ ə zən) *n.* a person who lives in a town or city.

clasp (klasp) *v.* **1.** to hold or grasp closely or tightly. **2.** to fasten together with a clasp.

clear·ing (klir′ ing) *n.* a piece of land that is free of trees and brush.

clerk (klėrk) *n.* a person who keeps records and files in an office.

coach (kōch) *n., pl.* **coach·es. 1.** a person who leads and trains a sports team, or any other person or group. **2.** a large, closed carriage drawn by horses.

coat·tail (kōt′ tāl′) *n.* a pair of flaps or tails on the lower rear part of a coat.

col·i·se·um (kol′ ə sē′ əm) *n.* a large building or stadium used for sports or other entertainments.

coattail

col·o·nist (kol′ ə nist) *n.* a person who lived in one of the thirteen British colonies that became the first states of the United States.

com·mand (kə mand′) *n.* order; direction.

com·mand mod·ule (kə mand′ moj′ ül, mod′ ül) *n.* the section of a spacecraft that contains the control center, re-entry equipment, and living areas of the astronauts.

com·men·ta·tor (kom′ ən tā′ tər) *n.* a person who comments on, or explains or gives an opinion of, the news on radio or television.

com·mis·sar·y (kom′ ə sär′ ē) *n., pl.* **com·mis·sar·ies.** a store that sells food and supplies.

com·mit (kə mit′) *v.* **com·mit·ted, com·mit·ting. 1.** to devote; pledge. **2.** to do or perform.

com·mo·tion (kə mō′ shən) *n.* a noisy disturbance; confusion.

com·mu·ni·cate (kə mū′ ni kāt′) *v.* **com·mu·ni·cat·ed, com·mu·ni·cat·ing.** to exchange or pass along feelings, thoughts, or information.

com·pare (kəm pār′) *v.* **com·pared, com·par·ing.** to study or find out how persons or things are alike or different.

com·pute (kəm pūt′) *v.* **com·put·ed, com·put·ing.** to find out or calculate by using mathematics.

con·fess (kən fes′) *v.* to admit.

con·fu·sion (kən fū′ zhən) *n.* disorder or bewilderment.

con·so·la·tion prize (kon sə lā′ shən prīz′) *n.* a prize given to someone who does well but does not win in a contest.

con·sole (kən sōl′) *v.* **con· soled, con·sol·ing.** to comfort or cheer.

con·stan·cy (kon′ stən sē) *n.* a willingness to do or be something no matter what happens; loyalty.

con·struct (kən strukt′) *v.* to make by putting parts together; build.

con·tact (kon′ takt) *n.* a touching or meeting.

con·vince (kən vins′) *v.* **con·vinced, con·vinc·ing.** to cause a person to believe something; persuade.

co·op·er·a·tion (kō op′ ə rā′ shən) *n.* working with another or others for a common purpose.

cop·per (kop′ ər) *n.* a reddish-brown metal that is easy to form into different shapes. It is an excellent conductor of heat and electricity.

---

a b**a**t, ā c**a**ke, ä f**a**ther, är c**a**r, âr d**a**re; e h**e**n, ē m**e**, ėr t**e**rm; i b**i**b, ī k**i**te, ir cl**e**ar; o t**o**p, ō r**o**pe, ô s**a**w, oi c**oi**n, ôr f**o**rk, ou **ou**t; u s**u**n, u̇ b**oo**k, ü m**oo**n, ū c**u**te; ə **a**bout, tak**e**n

cord (kôrd) *n.* **1.** a quantity of cut wood, arranged in a pile 4 feet wide, 4 feet high, and 8 feet long. **2.** a string or thin rope made of several strands twisted or woven together.

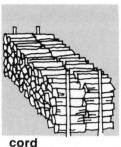

cord

cor·du·roy (kôr′ də roi′) *n.* a cloth with rows of ribs, usually made of cotton and used for clothing.

coun·se·lor (koun′ sə lər) *n.* a person who watches over children at summer camp.

cov·er·age (kuv′ ər ij) *n.* the reporting of a news event.

crag·gy (krag′ ē) *adj.* steep and rugged.

cre·ate (krē āt′) *v.* **cre·a·ted, cre·a·ting.** to cause something new to exist or happen; make.

crew (krü) *n.* a group of people who work together.

crock·er·y (krok′ ər ē) *n.* dishes, jars, and similar things made of baked clay; earthenware.

crockery

cross·roads (krôs′ rōdz′) *n. pl.* a place where roads cross.

cross·tie (krôs′ tī′) *n.* a log or beam laid crosswise to form a foundation or support.

cue (kū) *n.* a signal to begin or do something.

cus·tom·er (kus′ tə mər) *n.* a person who buys something or pays for a service.

cyl·in·der (sil′ ən dər) *n.* a solid or hollow object that is shaped like a roller or a soup can.

D

day·book (dā′ buk′) *n.* diary.

dead·line (ded′ līn′) *n.* a set time by which something must be finished; time limit.

debt (det) *n.* something that is owed to another.

dec·ade (dek′ ād) *n.* a period of ten years.

de·cent (dē′ sənt) *adj.* **1.** fairly good; satisfactory. **2.** proper and respectable.

de·ci·sion (di sizh′ ən) *n.* judgment; conclusion.

de·lib·er·ate·ly (di lib′ ər it lē′) *adv.* on purpose.

del·uge (del′ üj) *n.* **1.** anything that overpowers or rushes like a flood. **2.** a great flood.

de·mand (di mand′) *n.* the need or desire for something.

de·pen·da·ble (di pen′ də bəl) *adj.* able to be trusted and depended upon; reliable.

de·pot (dē′ pō) *n.* a railroad station or bus terminal.

de·pressed (di prest′) *adj.* low in spirits; sad.

de·rail (dē rāl′) *v.* to run off the rails; jump the tracks.

de·scent (di sent′) *n.* movement from a higher place to a lower one.

de·sign (di zīn′) *n.* an arrangement of different parts or colors; pattern.

de·spair (di spâr′) *n.* a complete loss of hope; hopelessness.

de·stroy (di stroi′) *v.* to ruin completely; wreck.

de·tail (dē′ tāl, di tāl′) *n.* a small or less important part of a whole; item.

de·ter·mine (di tėr′ min) v. **de·ter·mined, de·ter·min·ing.** to decide or settle definitely or ahead of time.

de·vour (di vour′) v. to eat; consume.

dis·be·lief (dis′ bi lēf′) n. lack of belief; refusal to believe.

dis·cuss (dis kus′) v. to talk over; speak about.

dis·pute (dis pūt′) v. **dis·put·ed, dis·put·ing.** to argue; debate; discuss.

dis·qual·i·fy (dis kwol′ ə fī′) v. **dis·qual·i·fied, dis·qual·i·fy·ing.** to declare to be unable to compete in or win a contest.

dis·qui·et·ing (dis kwī′ i ting) adj. making uneasy, anxious, or afraid; disturbing; alarming.

dis·solve (di zolv′) v. **dis·solved, dis·solv·ing.** to cause something to change from a solid into a liquid.

dis·tress·ing (dis tres′ ing) adj. causing or bringing suffering or sorrow; painful.

doc·u·men·ta·ry (dok′ yə men′ tər ē) n., pl. **doc·u·men·ta·ries.** a film whose subject deals with or is supported by actual facts.

do·nate (dō′ nāt) v. **do·nat·ed, do·nat·ing.** to give; contribute.

down·cast (doun′ kast′) adj. low in spirits; sad.

draft (draft) n. **1.** a current of air in an enclosed space. **2.** a device that·controls the flow of air in something.

drift (drift) v. **1.** to be moved or carried by moving water. **2.** to move or seem to move without a goal or purpose.

dry goods (drī′ gu̇dz′) n. pl. cloth, thread, lace, ribbons, and the like.

dry goods

due (dü, dū) adj. owed or owing.

E

ed·i·tor (ed′ ə tər) n. **1.** a person who reviews, cuts, and arranges something for presentation. **2.** a person who corrects, improves, and prepares something for publication.

elk (elk) n., pl. **elk, elks.** a large deer of the mountain regions of western North America.

elk

em·bark (em bärk′) v. **1.** to start out or set out; begin. **2.** to go on board a ship for a trip.

e·merge (i mėrj′) v. **e·merged, e·merg·ing.** to come into view, come out, or come up.

e·mer·gen·cy (i mėr′ jən sē) n., pl. **e·mer·gen·cies.** something serious that comes without warning and calls for fast action.

em·ploy·ee (em ploi′ ē, em′ ploi ē′) n. a person who works for a person or business for pay.

en·chant·ment (en chant′ mənt) n. **1.** a magic spell; charm. **2.** the act of casting a spell.

en·rage (en rāj′) v. **en·raged, en·rag·ing.** to make very angry.

---

a b**a**t, ā c**a**ke, ä f**a**ther, är c**a**r, âr d**a**re; e h**e**n, ē m**e**, ėr t**e**rm; i b**i**b, ī k**i**te, ir cl**e**ar; o t**o**p, ō r**o**pe, ô s**a**w, oi c**o**in, ôr f**o**rk, ou **ou**t; u s**u**n, u̇ b**oo**k, ü m**oo**n, ū c**u**te; ə **a**bout, tak**e**n

en·thu·si·as·tic (en thü′ zē as′ tik) *adj.* excited, interested, or eager about something.

en·try (en′ trē) *n.*, *pl.* **en·tries.** something that is entered in a contest.

es·ti·mate (es′ tə mit *for noun;* es′ tə māt′ *for verb*) *n.* an early judgment or opinion about something; guess. —*v.* **es·ti·mat·ed, es·ti·mat·ing.** to form an early judgment or opinion about something; guess.

ev·i·dence (ev′ ə dəns) *n.* something that can be used to prove or disprove a belief or conclusion.

ex·am·ine (eg zam′ in) *v.* **ex·am·ined, ex·am·in·ing.** to look at closely and carefully; check.

ex·as·per·a·ting (eg zas′ pə rā′ ting) *adj.* making very angry or annoyed; infuriating.

ex·change (eks chānj′) *v.* **ex·changed, ex·chang·ing.** to give in return for something.

ex·ist (eg zist′) *v.* to be real; live.

ex·pe·di·tion (eks′ pə dish′ ən) *n.* a journey made for a particular reason.

ex·pense (eks pens′) *n.* money spent in order to buy or do something; cost.

ex·pen·sive (eks pen′ siv) *adj.* having a high price; very costly.

ex·pert (eks′ pèrt) *n.* a person who knows a great deal about a particular thing.

ex·tend (eks tend′) *v.* **1.** to stretch out. **2.** to make longer; lengthen. **3.** to offer or give.

F

fail·ure (fāl′ yər) *n.* something that is unsuccessful or does not work out.

fake (fāk) *v.* **faked, fak·ing.** to make something seem real in order to fool others.

feeb·ly (fē′ blē) *adv.* weakly; without strength.

fel·low·ship (fel′ ō ship′) *n.* **1.** a group of people joined by common interests, beliefs, or goals; society. **2.** friendliness; companionship.

fe·male (fē′ māl) *adj.* relating to the sex that bears young or produces eggs.

fe·ro·cious·ly (fə rō′ shəs lē) *adv.* savagely, fiercely.

fer·ti·lize (fèrt′ əl īz′) *v.* **fer·ti·lized, fer·ti·liz·ing. 1.** to put fertilizer on. Fertilizer is a substance added to soil to make it more productive. **2.** to make fertile or productive.

fidg·et (fij′ it) *v.* to make quick, restless movements; be nervous or uneasy.

fierce (firs) *adj.* cruel or violent; ferocious; savage.

fier·y (fīr′ ē) *adj.* made up of fire; flaming.

fig·ur·ine (fig′ yə rēn′) *n.* a small carved figure; small statue.

Fi·ji (fē′ jē) *n.* a country made up of a group of islands in the southwestern Pacific Ocean.

flat·car (flat′ kär′) *n.* a railroad car without a roof or sides, used for carrying goods.

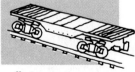
flatcar

flex·i·ble (flek′ sə bəl) *adj.* **1.** able to bend without breaking; not stiff. **2.** able to adjust easily to change.

foot·hills (fùt′ hilz′) *n. pl.* low hills at the foot of a mountain or mountain range.

foothills

force out (fôrs′ out′) *n.* in baseball, the act of causing a base runner to be put out by making a hit that forces him to move to the next base.

fore·leg (fôr′ leg′) *n.* one of the front legs of an insect or a four-legged animal.

fore·sail (fôr′ sāl′, fôr′ səl) *n.* the main sail on the bow, or forward end, of a ship.

foresail

fret (fret) *v.* **fret·ted, fret·ting.** to be upset, unhappy, or worried.

froth (frôth) *n.* a mass of bubbles formed in or on a liquid; foam.

fu·el (fū′ əl) *n.* something burned to provide heat and power, such as coal, wood, or oil.

ful·fill (fùl fil′) *v.* **1.** to meet or satisfy; live up to. **2.** to carry out or finish.

fund (fund) *n.* a sum of money set aside for a particular purpose.

G

gad·get (gaj′ it) *n.* a small, unusual tool or device.

gan·der (gan′ dər) *n.* a grown male goose.

gen·ius (jēn′ yəs) *n.* a person who has a great ability to think and to invent or create things.

gib·ber·ish (jib′ ər ish) *n.* meaningless speech; chatter.

glen (glen) *n.* a small, narrow valley.

glow (glō) *v.* to give off light.

glow·er (glou′ ər) *v.* to look at in an angry or threatening way.

goal (gōl) *n.* something a person tries to gain, make, or do; aim; purpose.

go·ing rate (gō′ ing rāt′) *n.* the current or existing price. See *rate.*

gol·den age (gōld′ ən āj′) *n.* a period of time in the history of a country or a people during which the highest level of wealth or achievement is reached.

gold·smith (gōld′ smith′) *n.* a person who makes or deals in objects of gold, such as jewelry.

gos·ling (goz′ ling) *n.* a young goose.

grace·ful (grās′ fəl) *adj.* smooth and beautiful in movement or action.

grad·u·al (graj′ ū əl) *adj.* happening little by little; moving or changing slowly.

grant (grant) *v.* to give or allow.

grasp (grasp) *v.* to take hold of firmly.

grat·ing (grā′ ting) *n.* a frame of iron bars set over a window or other opening, used to cover, guard, or screen.

grating

grit (grit) *n.* very tiny pieces of sand, stone, or other material. —*v.* **grit·ted, grit·ting.** to grind or press together hard.

groom (grüm) *v.* **1.** to make neat and pleasant in appearance. **2.** to wash, brush, and take care of horses.

grub·by (grub′ ē) *adj.* dirty; filthy.

guar·an·teed (gâr′ ən tēd′) *adj.* made sure or certain.

---

a **b**at, ā **c**ake, ä **f**ather, är **c**ar, âr **d**are; e **h**en, ē **m**e, ėr **t**erm; i **b**ib, ī **k**ite, ir **c**lear; o **t**op, ō **r**ope, ô **s**aw, oi **c**oin, ôr **f**ork, ou **o**ut; u **s**un, ù **b**ook, ü **m**oon, ū **c**ute; ə **a**bout, tak**e**n

H

harsh (härsh) *adj.* rough; unpleasant.

head·dress (hed′ dres′) *n., pl.* **head·dress·es.** a covering or decoration for the head.

hear·ing (hir′ ing) *n.* a formal gathering of people in a court of law to hear evidence; a trial.

heel (hēl) *v.* to follow closely.

hes·i·tate (hez′ ə tāt′) *v.* **hes·i·tat·ed, hes·i·tat·ing.** to wait or stop for a moment.

hind·quar·ters (hīnd′ kwôr′ tərs) *n. pl.* the rear part of an animal.

hire (hīr) *v.* **hired, hir·ing.** to pay for the work of a person or the use of a thing. —*n.* **1.** the act of hiring. **2.** payment for the use of something or work that is done.

hoard (hôrd) *v.* to save and store or hide away. —*n.* a thing or things stored up or hidden away for future use.

hoarse (hôrs) *adj.* having a harsh, deep sound.

hoist (hoist) *v.* to lift or pull up.

hol·low (hol′ ō) *n.* a hollow or empty space; hole.

Hong Kong (hong′ kong′) an island off the southeastern coast of China.

hor·i·zon·tal ve·loc·i·ty (hôr′ ə zont′ əl, hor′ ə zont′ əl vi los′ ə tē) *n.* speed of a vehicle that is moving on or over a surface, parallel to the horizon.

hub (hub) *n.* the middle part of a wheel.

hub

hurl (hėrl) *v.* to throw with great force.

I

i·den·ti·fy (ī den′ tə fī′) *v.* **i·den·ti·fied, i·den·ti·fy·ing. 1.** to connect closely; associate. **2.** to prove that someone or something is a particular person or thing.

i·dle (īd′ əl) *adj.* **1.** having little use or purpose; pointless. **2.** not working, in use, or busy.

ig·ni·tion se·quence (ig nish′ ən sē′ kwəns) *n.* the stages involved in preparing a rocket for lift-off.

im·i·tate (im′ ə tāt′) *v.* **im·i·tat·ed, im·i·tat·ing.** to act or behave like another person; copy.

im·mense (i mens′) *adj.* of great size; very large.

in·ci·dent (in′ sə dənt) *n.* an event; happening.

in·cline (in′ klīn′, in klīn′) *n.* a surface that slopes.

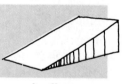

incline

in·come (in′ kum′) *n.* money received for work or services, or from the sale or rental of property.

in·cred·i·ble (in kred′ ə bəl) *adj.* hard or impossible to believe.

in·de·scrib·a·ble (in di′ skrī′ bə bəl) *adj.* impossible to describe in words; beyond description.

In·di·an res·er·va·tion (in′ dē ən rez′ ər vā′ shən) *n.* land that is set aside by the United States government for an Indian tribe to live on.

in·di·cate (in′ di kāt′) *v.* **in·di·cat·ed, in·di·cat·ing.** to point out; show.

In·do·ne·sia (in′ də nē′ zhə) a country in southeastern Asia made up of islands. The capital of Indonesia is Jakarta.

in·flat·ed (in flā′ tid) *adj.* swelled or puffed up with air, gas, water, or other liquid.

in·form (in fôrm′) *v.* to give information to; tell.

in·hab·it (in hab′ it) *v.* to live in or on.

in·sult (in sult′) *v.* to speak to or treat in a rude way.

in·te·grat·ed (in′ tə grā′ tid) *adj.* open to people of all races.

in·ter·est (in′ tər ist, in′ trist) *n.* money paid for the use or borrowing of money.

in·vest (in vest′) *v.* to put money to use in order to make a profit.

i·so·lat·ed (ī′ sə lā′ tid) *adj.* set apart; separate.

isth·mus (is′ məs) *n.*, *pl.* **isth·mus·es.** a narrow strip of land bordered by water and connecting two large bodies of land.

isthmus

i·vo·ry (ī′ vər ē) *n.*, *pl.* **i·vo·ries.** a smooth, hard, white substance that forms the tusks of elephants, walruses, and certain other animals.

J

jade (jād) *n.* a hard, green stone that is used for jewelry and carvings.

joint (joint) *n.* the place or part where two or more things are joined or fitted together.

jour·ney (jėr′ nē) *n.* a long trip.

K

keen (kēn) *adj.* sensitive; sharp and quick in seeing, hearing, or smelling.

keg (keg) *n.* a small barrel.

kelp (kelp) *n.* a kind of seaweed that grows along the coasts of the Atlantic and Pacific oceans.

kin·dle (kind′ əl) *v.* **kin·dled, kin·dling.** to set on fire; light.

L

lac·quer (lak′ ər) *n.* a substance that is painted on to form a shiny coat.

lair (lār) *n.* a place where a wild animal lives or rests; den.

land·slide (land′ slīd′) *n.* the sliding or falling down of a mass of soil or rock.

lar·va (lär′ və) *n.*, *pl.* **lar·vae** (lär′ vē). an early stage of an insect when it looks like a worm.

late (lāt) *adj.* recently dead; departed.

Lat·in (lat′ in) *n.* the language of the ancient Romans.

launch (lônch) *v.* **1.** to push or propel by force into the air; send off. **2.** to put a boat or ship into the water.

launch pad (lônch′ pad′) *n.* an area or structure from which a rocket or missile is launched.

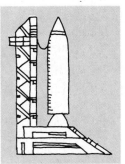

launch pad

---

a b**a**t, ā c**a**ke, ä f**a**ther, är c**a**r, âr d**a**re; e h**e**n, ē m**e**, ėr t**e**rm; i b**i**b, ī k**i**te, ir cl**e**ar; o t**o**p, ō r**o**pe, ô s**a**w, oi c**o**in, ôr f**o**rk, ou **ou**t; u s**u**n, ů b**oo**k, ü m**oo**n, ū c**u**te; ə **a**bout, tak**e**n

laun·dro·mat (lôn' drə mat') *n.* a self-service laundry with coin-operated washing machines and dryers.

league (lēg) *n.* **1.** a group of athletic teams that compete regularly with one another. **2.** a number of people, groups, or countries joined together for a common purpose.

leg·end (lej' ənd) *n.* a story that is passed down but that is not believed to be historically true.

lep·re·chaun (lep' rə kon') *n.* an elf who looks like a small man and plays tricks on people. Leprechauns appear often in the legends and folk tales of Ireland.

light me·ter (līt' mē' tər) *n.* a device used to measure the amount of light in a certain place in order to determine the correct exposure for photographing.

Lin·coln Me·mo·ri·al (ling' kən mə môr' ē əl) *n.* a large monument in Washington, D.C., that honors Abraham Lincoln, the sixteenth President of the United States.

Lincoln Memorial

lit·ter (lit' ər) *n.* **1.** young animals born at one time. **2.** scraps of paper or other rubbish scattered about; mess.

loan (lōn) *n.* something that is lent, or given to someone to use for a certain period of time.

lo·cate (lō' kāt) *v.* **lo·cat·ed, lo·cat·ing.** to find in a particular place.

lo·co·mo·tive (lō' kə mō' tiv) *n.* an engine that moves on its own power, used to haul railroad cars.

long drive (lông' drīv') *n.* in baseball, the act of driving a ball deep into the outfield.

lope (lōp) *v.* **loped, lop·ing.** a long, easy, often bounding stride.

lu·nar mod·ule (lü' nər moj' ül, mod' ūl) *n.* a section of a spacecraft used to land on the moon after separating from an orbiting spacecraft near the moon's surface.

lunge (lunj) *v.* **lunged, lung·ing.** to make a sudden forward movement. — *n.* a sudden forward movement.

lurk (lėrk) *v.* to hide; move around in a sneaky way.

M

ma·jor (mā' jər) *n.* an army officer ranked below a colonel but above a captain. —*adj.* greater in size, amount, value, or importance.

male (māl) *adj.* relating to the sex that can be the father of young.

man·ners (man' ərz) *n. pl.* polite ways of behaving or acting.

man·u·al con·trol (man' ū əl kən trōl') *n.* control by hand instead of machine.

mass pro·duc·tion (mas' prə duk' shən) *n.* the making of goods in very large amounts, especially by the use of machinery and assembly lines.

mast (mast) *n.* a tall pole on a sailing ship or boat that supports the sails and rigging.

ma·ture (mə chůr') *adj.* showing the qualities of a person who is fully grown or developed.

mer·chant (mėr' chənt) *n.* a person whose business is buying and selling things.

mes·sen·ger (mes' ən jər) *n.* a person who delivers messages or runs errands.

mi·cro·phone (mī' krə fōn') *n.* a device that changes sound waves into electronic signals to transmit sound or make it louder.

microphone

mid·day (mid' dā') *n.* the middle of the day; noon.

mid·way (mid' wā) *adv.* in the middle; halfway.

mill (mil) *n.* a machine that flattens, crushes, or grinds.

mim·ic (mim' ik) *v.* **mim·icked, mim·ick·ing.** to imitate, especially in order to make fun of.

mis·sion (mish' ən) *n.* a special job or task.

Mis·sion Dis·trict (mish' ən dis' trikt) a very old section of San Francisco, California. It is named for the Spanish missions, or settlements, that were established there in the late 1700s and early 1800s.

mix·ture (miks' chər) *n.* something made up of different things that are put together.

mold (mōld) *n.* a hollow form that is made in a special shape. A liquid takes on the shape of the mold after it hardens.

mold

mon·i·tor (mon' ə tər) *v.* to watch over; check.

mon·soon (mon sün') *n.* a seasonal wind that influences the climate of a large area.

mon·strous (mon' strəs) *adj.* horrible; like a monster.

mood (müd) *n.* a special quality or atmosphere, as of a place or work of art.

muf·fle (muf' əl) *v.* **muf·fled, muf·fling.** to soften the sound of something.

murk·y (mèr' kē) *adj.* dark, gloomy, or cloudy.

mur·mur (mèr' mər) *n.* a low, soft sound.

N

na·tion·al park (nash' ən əl pärk') *n.* an area of land, usually with great natural beauty or historical importance, maintained by the United States government for public use.

net·work (net' wèrk') *n.* a system of lines or structures that cross.

news·cast·er (nüz' kast ər, nūz' kast ər) *n.* a person who presents the news on a radio or television program.

no·ble (nō' bəl) *adj.* **1.** having or showing great character; worthy. **2.** having high rank or title.

numb (num) *adj.* lacking or having lost feeling or movement.

O

o·be·di·ence (ō bē' dē əns) *n.* the act of obeying, or doing what one is told to do; willingness to obey.

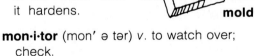
a **ba**t, ā **ca**ke, ä **fa**ther, är **ca**r, âr **da**re; e **he**n, ē **me**, èr **te**rm; i **bi**b, ī **ki**te; ir **cl**ear; o **to**p, ō **ro**pe, ô **sa**w, oi **coi**n, ôr **fo**rk, ou **ou**t; u **su**n, ú **boo**k, ü **moo**n, ū **cu**te; ə **a**bout, tak**e**n

ob·ject (ob′ jikt) *n.* anything that can be seen or touched; thing.

ob·li·ga·tion (ob′ lə gā′ shən) *n.* a duty, or something that a person is bound to do.

ob·sti·nate (ob′ stə nit) *adj.* wanting strongly to have one's way; not giving in to argument or reason; stubborn.

oc·ca·sion (ə kā′ zhən) *n.* an important or special event.

oc·cu·py (ok′ yə pī′) *v.* **oc·cu·pied, oc·cu·py·ing. 1.** to live in; inhabit. **2.** to take up space or time.

of·fi·cial (ə fish′ əl) *adj.* coming from or approved by a proper authority.

op·er·a·tion (op′ ə rā′ shən) *n.* an action or mission including its planning and carrying out.

or·i·gin (ôr′ ə jin, or′ ə jin) *n.* the source from which something begins or comes.

out·do (out′ dü) *v.* **out·did, out·done, out·do·ing.** to do better than; surpass.

o·ver·all (ō′ vər ôl′) *adv.* as a whole; generally.

o·ver·take (ō′ vər tāk′) *v.* **o·ver·tak·en, o·ver·tak·ing.** to catch up with.

P

par·a·chute (pär′ ə shüt) *v.* **par·a·chut·ed, par·a·chut·ing.** to descend by parachute. A parachute is a device that is similar to an umbrella, used for slowing the speed of a body falling through the air.

par·cel (pär səl) *n.* a thing or group of things packed together; package.

parcel

par·tial·ly (pär′ shəl ē) *adv.* not completely or totally; partly.

par·tic·i·pate (pär tis′ ə pāt′) *v.* **par·tic·i·pat·ed, par·tic·i·pat·ing.** to take part in.

Pa·tri·ot (pā′ trē ət) *n.* an American colonist who supported independence from Great Britain. **patriot.** a person who loves his or her country and loyally defends or supports it.

pa·trol (pə trōl′) *n.* a group of people who go through or around an area to guard it or make sure everything is all right.

pave (pāv) *v.* **paved, pav·ing.** to cover or put a surface on a road or street.

pay·ment (pā′ mənt) *n.* something that is paid.

peal (pēl) *n.* a loud, long sound or series of sounds.

peas·ant (pez′ ənt) *n.* a person who works on or owns a small farm.

pelt (pelt) *v.* **1.** to beat against heavily over and over. **2.** to attack or strike with something over and over.

pen·nant (pen′ ənt) *n.* a long, usually triangular flag that symbolizes a victory or championship, especially in baseball.

pennant

perch (pėrch) *n.* **1.** any raised place for sitting or standing. **2.** a bar, branch, or anything else a bird can come to rest on. — *v.* to sit or rest on.

per·mit (pėr′ mit, pər mit′) *n.* a written order giving permission to do something.

pi·geon (pij′ ən) *n.* a bird that has a plump body, a small head, and thick soft feathers. Pigeons are found in nearly every city of the world.

pig·let (pig′ lit) *n.* a small pig.

pitch (pich) *v.* **1.** to throw or toss. **2.** to sway wildly back and forth or to and fro; lurch.

plan·ta·tion (plan tā′ shən) *n.* a large farm where usually one crop is grown, such as cotton, tobacco, or sugar.

plaque (plak) *n.* a flat plate of hard material that is decorated or engraved.

pli·ers (plī′ ərz) *n. pl.* a tool made for gripping or bending things.

pon·der (pon′ dər) *v.* to think over carefully.

pop fly (pop′ flī′) *n.*, *pl.* **pop flies.** in baseball, a high fly ball hit into or near the infield.

port·a·ble (pôr′ tə bəl) *adj.* easy to carry from place to place.

port·hole (pôrt′ hōl′) *n.* a small, usually round opening in the side of a boat or ship for letting in air and light.

porthole

pos·i·tive·ly (poz′ ə tiv′ lē) *adv.* without question; undoubtedly.

post·pone (pōst pōn′) *v.* **post·poned, post·pon·ing.** to put off until later; delay.

pot·bel·lied stove (pot′ bel′ ēd stōv′) *n.* a stove that has the shape of a potbelly, or a large, bulging middle section. It burns coal or wood.

potbellied stove

pounce (pouns) *v.* **pounced, pounc·ing.** to spring or swoop suddenly in order to catch something.

press con·fer·ence (pres′ kon′ fər ence) *n.* an interview given to a group of newspeople by a public official.

prey (prā) *n.* any animal hunted or killed by another animal for food.

pride (prīd) *n.* one's feeling of worth and importance; self-respect.

pro·duce (prə düs′, prə dūs′ *for verb;* prō′ düs, prō′ dūs *for noun*) *v.* **pro·duced, pro·duc·ing.** to make or bring into being; create. — *n.* **1.** farm products. **2.** something that is produced.

pro·duc·tion (prə duk′ shən) *n.* the act of making or creating something.

pro·fes·sion (prə fesh′ ən) *n.* a job that requires special schooling or training.

pro·fes·sion·al (prə fesh′ ən əl) *adj.* for those who are experienced and highly skilled.

pro·fes·sor (prə fes′ ər) *n.* a teacher of the highest rank in a college or university.

prof·it (prof′ it) *n.* the amount remaining after all business expenses are paid.

proof (prüf) *n.* facts or evidence that show something is true.

prop (prop) *v.* **propped, prop·ping.** to support, hold up, or hold in place by putting something under or against.

pros·per·i·ty (pros pār′ ə tē) *n.* success, wealth, or good fortune.

---

a b**a**t, ā c**a**ke, ä f**a**ther, är c**a**r, âr d**a**re; e h**e**n, ē m**e**, ér t**e**rm; i b**i**b, ī k**i**te, ir cl**ea**r; o t**o**p, ō r**o**pe, ô s**a**w, oi c**oi**n, ôr f**o**rk, ou **ou**t; u s**u**n, u̇ b**oo**k, ü m**oo**n, ū c**u**te; ə **a**bout, tak**e**n

pulse (puls) *n.* the regular in-and-out movement of the arteries caused by the beating of the heart.

pur·suit (pər süt') *n.* the act of chasing, following, or pursuing.

Q

Quak·er (kwā' kər) *n.* a member of the Society of Friends, a Christian group founded in the seventeenth century.

R

ra·dar (rā' där) *n.* a device used to find and follow distant objects by bouncing radio waves off them.

rage (rāj) *n.* very great anger; fury.

rap (rap) *v.* **rapped, rap·ping.** to knock or tap sharply.

rasp·ing (ras' ping) *adj.* making a rough, grating sound.

rate (rāt) *n.* the price or charge for something.

raw ma·te·ri·al (rô' mə tir' ē əl) *n.* a substance in its natural state, that has not yet been treated, processed, or manufactured.

re·cite (ri sīt') *v.* **re·cit·ed, re·cit·ing.** to repeat from memory.

re·cord (ri kôrd') *v.* **1.** to set down in permanent form. **2.** to put music or other sounds on a phonograph record or magnetic tape.

re·cov·er (ri kuv' ər) *v.* to get back something that was lost or stolen.

ref·er·ence (ref' ər əns) *n.* a person or thing that is referred to; source of information.

re·fresh·ments (ri fresh' mənts) *n. pl.* food and drink taken as a snack.

re·lay (rē' lā') *n.* a race involving a group of runners in which each person in turn covers a part of the total distance.

re·lease (ri lēs') *v.* **re·leased, re·leas·ing. 1.** to let go of. **2.** to set free or loose.

re·mark·a·ble (ri mär' kə bəl) *adj.* worthy of being noticed; extraordinary; unusual.

re·mote con·trol (ri mōt' kən trōl') *n.* control of a machine or device from a distance, especially by means of radio signals.

rep·re·sent (rep' ri zent') *v.* to be a sign or symbol of; stand for.

res·i·dent (rez' ə dənt) *n.* a person who lives in a particular place.

re·spect (ri spekt') *v.* to show care and consideration for. — *n.* high regard for or appreciation of the value of someone or something.

re·spond (ri spond') *v.* **1.** to act in return; react. **2.** to give an answer.

re·spon·si·ble (ri spon' sə bəl) *adj.* able to be trusted; reliable.

re·sult (ri zult') *n.* something that happens or is made to happen because of another action; outcome; effect.

re·tire·ment (ri tīr' mənt) *n.* the act of withdrawing oneself from a job or a business.

re·treat (ri trēt') *v.* to draw or move back.

ridge (rij) *n.* **1.** a long and narrow chain of hills or moun- tains. **2.** the long and narrow upper part of some- thing.

ridge

rig·ging (rig' ing) *n.* all the lines of a boat or ship, such as the ropes, chains, and wires, used for supporting the mast or working the sails.

rigging

rile (rīl) *v.* **riled, ril·ing.** to annoy; bother. **to rile up.** to stir up; excite.

rim (rim) *n.* the outer edge or border of something.

ri·ot (rī' ət) *n.* a noisy and sometimes violent disorder caused by a group or crowd of people.

road·bed (rōd' bed') *n.* **1.** the foundation or suface of a road. **2.** a foundation or bed for the ties and rails of a railroad.

roil (roil) *v.* to stir up a liquid; unsettle.

Ro·man (rō' mən) *adj.* of or having to do with ancient or modern Rome, its people, or their way of life.

Roy·al Air Force (roi' əl ãr' fôrs') **R.A.F.** *or* **RAF.** the air force of Great Britain.

ru·ble (rü' bəl) *n.* the basic unit of money of the Soviet Union.

ru·mor (rü' mər) *n.* a story or statement that is passed from one person to another as truth without anything to prove it.

ru·ral ar·e·a (rür' əl ãr' ē ə) *n.* an area that is in or like the country.

rus·tling (rus' ling) *n.* a series of soft, fluttering sounds.

rut (rut) *n.* a groove or track made in the ground by a wheel or by constant use.

S

sar·sa·pa·ril·la (sas' pə ril' ə) *n.* a plant whose roots are dried and used as a medicine, and as a flavoring for syrup and soft drinks.

sav·age (sav' ij) *adj.* cruel or violent; ferocious; fierce.

scan (skan) *v.* **scanned, scan·ning.** to look closely; search carefully.

scarce (skãrs) *adj.* difficult to get or find.

scheme (skēm) *n.* a plan or plot for doing something.

scout (skout) *n.* a person who is sent out to find and bring back information.

sculp·ture (skulp' chər) *v.* **sculp·tured, sculp·tur·ing.** to carve, model, or cast figures or designs.

sec·ond de·gree burn (sek' ənd di grē' bẽrn) *n.* a burn in which blisters are formed.

self·ish (sel' fish) *adj.* concerned for or serving one's own desires and interests above all others.

sen·si·ble (sen' sə bəl) *adj.* having or showing good judgment and sense.

ser·pent (sẽr' pənt) *n.* a very large snake.

serpent

ser·vice (sẽr' vis) *n.* any useful work other than the production of goods; for example, work done by doctors, lawyers, and teachers.

ses·sion (sesh' ən) *n.* a meeting.

shield (shēld) *v.* to defend or protect.

---

a b**a**t, ā c**a**ke, ä f**a**ther, är c**a**r, ãr d**a**re; e h**e**n, ē m**e**, ẽr t**e**rm; i b**i**b, ī k**i**te, ir cl**e**ar; o t**o**p, ō r**o**pe, ô s**a**w, oi c**o**in, ôr f**o**rk, ou **ou**t; u s**u**n, u̇ b**oo**k, ü m**oo**n, ū c**u**te; ə **a**bout, tak**e**n

sift (sift) *v.* **1.** to look at closely. **2.** to separate large pieces from small pieces by using a sieve, or a utensil with many holes in the bottom.

sil·ver·smith (sil′ vər smith′) *n.* a person who makes or repairs objects of silver.

singe (sinj) *v.* **singed, singe·ing.** to burn slightly.

site (sīt) *n.* the position or location of something.

slang (slang) *n.* an informal way of speaking.

slash (slash) *v.* to make a forceful, sweeping stroke with a knife or other instrument.

so·ci·e·ty (sə sī′ ə tē) *n., pl.* **so·ci·e·ties.** **1.** a group of people gathered together for a common purpose or interest. **2.** people as a group; all people.

som·ber (som′ bər) *adj.* dark and gloomy.

so·nar (sō′ när) *n.* a device used to find underwater objects by bouncing sound waves off them or by picking up sound waves given off by the objects themselves.

sound track (sound′ trak′) *n.* a narrow strip along one edge of a motion picture film that carries the sound recording.

sou·ve·nir (sü′ və nir′, sü′ və nir′) *n.* something that is kept as a reminder of a person, place, or event.

space shut·tle (spās′ shut′ əl) *n.* a space vehicle for transporting passengers and material to a space station.

spe·cial ef·fects (spesh′ əl i fekts′) *n. pl.* visual or sound effects in a movie or other show.

Spe·cial O·lym·pics (spesh′ əl ō lim′ piks) *n. pl.* a special athletic event for persons who are handicapped.

spec·tac·u·lar (spek tak′ yə lər) *adj.* having to do with a spectacle, or an impressive or unusual sight.

spec·ta·tor (spek′ tā′ tər) *n.* a person who watches something but does not take part; observer.

spend·thrift (spend′ thrift′) *n.* a person who spends money wastefully.

spike (spīk) *n.* **1.** a large, heavy nail. **2.** any sharp, pointed object.

spit (spit) *n.* **1.** a narrow point of land extending into the sea. **2.** a slender, pointed rod on which meat is roasted.

spit

spon·sor (spon′ sər) *n.* a person or group who is responsible in some way for another person, group, or thing.

sprint (sprint) *v.* to run at full speed, especially for a short distance.

spur (spur) *n.* a sharp metal piece worn on the heel of a rider's boot, used to make a horse go faster.

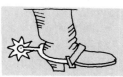

spur

stage (stāj) *n.* **1.** part of a journey. **2.** a single step, period, or degree in a process or development.

stage whis·per (stāj′ hwis′ pər) *n.* a whisper that is meant to be heard by persons other than the person addressed.

stag·ger (stag′ ər) *v.* to move unsteadily or with a swaying motion; totter.

sta·tus (stā′ təs, stat′ əs) *n.* the condition or situation of a person or thing.

stealth·i·ly (stel′ thə lē) *adv.* without being noticed; in a secret way.

stern·ly (stẽrn′ lē) *adv.* feeling or showing displeasure; harshly.

stout (stout) *adj.* **1.** having strength; strong. **2.** thick and heavy; fat.

stride (strīd) *v.* **strode, strid·ing.** to walk with long, sweeping steps.

stu·di·o (stü′ dē ō′) *n.* a place where a painter or other artist works.

style (stīl) *n.* a particular way of doing or making something.

sub·merge (səb mẽrj′) *v.* **sub·merged, sub·merging.** to go under water; become covered with water or another liquid.

sug·ges·tion (səg jes′ chən) *n.* something suggested, or offered as something to think about.

sus·pect (sə spekt′) *v.* to think that something is possible or true.

sus·pi·cious (sə spish′ əs) *adj.* feeling or showing suspicion; not trusting.

swap meet (swop′ mēt) *n.* an outdoor market where people can buy, sell, or trade goods.

swift (swift) *adj.* moving or able to move with great speed; fast; quick.

swine (swīn) *n., pl.* **swine.** a pig or hog.

sym·bol (sim′ bəl) *n.* something that stands for, or represents, something else.

sys·tem (sis′ təm) *n.* an orderly method.

T

tale (tāl) *n.* a story.

tar·pau·lin (tär pô′ lin) *n.* a waterproofed canvas or other material that is used as a protective covering for boats, athletic fields, or other objects exposed to weather.

tax (taks) *n., pl.* **tax·es.** a charge, usually of money, put on things for the support of the government.

tech·nique (tek nēk′) *n.* a method or way of bringing about a desired result.

tem·pes·tu·ous (tem pes′ chü əs) *adj.* stormy; raging; wild.

ten·sion (ten′ shən) *n.* **1.** mental or emotional strain. **2.** the act of stretching or the state of being stretched.

ten·ta·cle (ten′ tə kəl) *n.* a long, thin growth of certain animals, used to feel, grasp, and move.

ter·rar·i·um (tə rãr′ ē əm) *n.* a small container, usually of glass, that is used for growing small plants or raising small land animals such as lizards.

terrarium

ter·ri·fy·ing (tãr′ ə fī′ ing) *adj.* very frightening or alarming.

Te·ton Sioux (tē′ tən sü′)

thong (thông, thong) *n.* a narrow strip of leather or other material, used especially as a fastening.

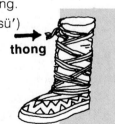
thong

---

a b**a**t, ā c**a**ke, ä f**a**ther, är c**a**r, âr d**a**re; e h**e**n, ē m**e**, ẽr t**e**rm; i b**i**b, ī k**i**te, ir cl**ea**r; o t**o**p, ō r**o**pe, ô s**a**w, oi c**o**in, ôr f**o**rk, ou **o**ut; u s**u**n, u̇ b**oo**k, ü m**oo**n, ū c**u**te; ə **a**bout, tak**e**n

thor·ough (thėr′ ō) *adj.* leaving nothing out; careful and complete.

tilt (tilt) *v.* to raise one end or side of; tip.

time con·sum·ing (tīm′ kən sü′ ming) *adj.* taking up a great deal of time.

tip (tip) *n.* **1.** a small piece of useful information or advice. **2.** the end part or point.

tor·rent (tôr′ ənt, tor′ ənt) *n.* a violent, fast-flowing stream, especially of water.

tot·ter (tot′ ər) *v.* to walk or move with weak or unsteady steps.

tra·di·tion (trə dish′ ən) *n.* **1.** a custom or belief that is handed down. **2.** continuing customs or ways of doing things.

trans·con·ti·nen·tal (trans′ kon tə nent′ əl) *adj.* crossing a continent.

trans·port (trans′ pôrt) *n.* a ship used to carry soldiers.

trans·por·ta·tion (trans′ pər tā′ shən) *n.* the act or means of carrying or moving something from one place to another.

tread (tred) *v.* **trod, trodden** *or* **trod, tread·ing.** to walk on; step upon.

Treas·ur·y De·part·ment (trezh′ ər ē di pärt′ mənt) *n.* a part of the United States government that is in charge of the country's money supply and the collection of taxes.

treat·ment (trēt′ mənt) *n.* the way something or someone is treated.

trem·ble (trem′ bəl) *v.* **trem·bled, trem·bling.** to shake with cold, fear, weakness, or anger.

trench (trench) *n., pl.* **trench·es.** a long, narrow ditch.

tri·um·phant (trī um′ fənt) *adj.* successful or victorious.

troops (trüps) *n. pl.* groups of soldiers.

U

u·ku·le·le (ū′ kə lā′ lē) *n.* a small guitar having four strings.

um·pire (um′ pīr) *n.* a person who rules on plays in baseball or certain other sports.

umpire

un·ac·cus·tomed (un′ ə kus′ təmd) *adj.* not used to; not in the habit of.

un·bear·a·ble (un bār′ ə bəl) *adj.* unable to be stood or put up with; intolerable.

un·der·brush (un′ dər brush′) *n.* bushes and other plants growing beneath big trees in a forest or woods.

u·nit (ū′ nit) *n.* a single person, thing, or group, especially one that is a basic part of a larger group.

urge (ėrj) *n.* a strong desire or impulse.

ush·er (ush′ ər) *n.* a person who leads people to their seats in a theater, stadium, or other place.

V

val·ue (val′ ū) *n.* the worth, usefulness, or importance of something.

van·ish (van′ ish) *v.* to pass from sight, especially suddenly or quickly; disappear.

va·ri·e·ty store (və rī′ ə tē stôr′) *n.* a store that has many different kinds of goods for sale.

var·y (vār′ ē) *v.* **var·ied, var·y·ing. 1.** to be different; differ. **2.** to change.

vast (vast) *adj.* very great in size or amount.

ven·dor (ven′ dər) *n.* a person who sells things.

vexed (vext) *adj.* annoyed; irritated.

vic·tim (vik′ təm) *n.* a person who is injured, killed, or ruined.

vic·to·ry (vik′ tər ē) *n., pl.* **vic·to·ries.** success; triumph.

vi·o·lent·ly (vī′ ə lənt lē) *adv.* in a rough or violent way; fiercely.

vi·tal (vī′ təl) *adj.* necessary to or supporting life.

W

wage (wāj) *n.* payment for work done.

wa·ter buf·fa·lo (wô′ tər buf′ ə lō′) *n., pl.* **buf·fa·loes, buf·fa·los, buf·fa·lo.** an African or Asian buffalo that has large, spreading horns.

water buffalo

wa·ver (wā′ vər) *v.* to move in an unsteady way up and down or from side to side.

weld (weld) *v.* to join pieces of metal or plastic by heating until soft enough to be hammered and pressed together.

whip·poor·will (hwip′ ər wil′) *n.* a plump North American bird with brown, black, and tan feathers. Its call sounds like its name.

whippoorwill

whop·ping (hwop′ ing) *adj. Informal.* very large or great.

wid·ow (wid′ ō) *n.* a woman whose husband is dead and who has not married again.

wis·dom (wiz′ dəm) *n.* learning; knowledge.

wit·ness (wit′ nis) *v.* to see or hear something in person.

won·der·ment (wun′ dər mənt) *n.* wonder; astonishment; surprise.

Y

yacht (yot) *n.* a small ship used for pleasure trips.

Z

zinc (zingk) *n.* a grayish-white metal.

a b**a**t, ā c**a**ke, ä f**a**ther, är c**a**r, âr d**a**re; e h**e**n, ē m**e**, ėr t**e**rm; i b**i**b, ī k**i**te, ir cl**ea**r; o t**o**p, ō r**o**pe, ô s**a**w, oi c**oi**n, ôr f**o**rk, ou **ou**t; u s**u**n, u̇ b**oo**k, ü m**oo**n, û c**u**te; ə **a**bout, tak**e**n

This section of *Bold Dreams* is a review of letters and the sounds they stand for. Good readers know that letters in a word are clues. Looking carefully at these letters is one way to figure out how to say a word. Some words may look new, but once you *say* them you may discover that you already know them.

Lessons

Word Work

Beginning Sounds

> Letters stand for sounds at the beginning of words.

__eter __iper __icked a __eck of __ickled __eppers.

Without the letter that makes the beginning sound in the words above, the sentence makes no sense. What letter could you use to finish the sentence?

Number your paper from 1 to 10. Copy the sentences below. Fill in the missing letters. Choose the letters from those in the box. Be sure the words make sense in the sentence.

> b d g l m p qu t v w y z

1. Carla __oke up __ery early one Saturday __orning.
2. She couldn't sleep __ecause it __asn't __iet.
3. There were __oud noises __oming from __own __elow!
4. "What's __oing on?" Carla __ondered with a __awn.
5. She __ot out of __ed and __ickly ran to the __indow to get a __iew.
6. When Carla __ooked out, she saw a __arade going __ast her house!
7. There was a __and __arching by.
8. The players had uniforms of __ellow and __urple.
9. Carla wasn't __oo __ired any __ore.
10. "I'm __oing to join them," she said, as she __ashed __ownstairs.

467

Same Sound - Different Spellings

> Some beginning sounds can be spelled more than one way.

Read the words below. Look at the underlined letters.

furnace	hole	kerchief	sailor
photo	whole	collar	ceiling

What ways can you spell the sound you hear at the beginning of *furnace*?

What sound can the letters *wh* stand for?

Does the beginning sound in *ceiling* sound like the beginning sound in *collar* or *sailor*?

Number your paper from 1 to 12. Read each group of words. Write the two words from each group that begin with the same sound.

1. hero
   whose
   window

2. phone
   piano
   final

3. candle
   season
   cellar

4. kitchen
   cereal
   cabbage

5. Carol
   Ken
   Cindy

6. kettle
   center
   cover

7. whether
   whoever
   highway

8. porch
   finish
   photograph

9. salad
   certain
   course

10. who
    hammer
    wheel

11. feather
    Phyllis
    Peter

12. connect
    circle
    second

One Sound - Two Spellings

> Some beginning sounds can be spelled more than one way.

Read the words below. Look at the underlined letters.

note	right	join
knock	wrong	giant

What two letters together can spell the sound you hear at the beginning of *note*?

What letters can stand for the sound you hear at the beginning of *right*?

What letters can stand for the sound you hear at the beginning of *jump*?

On your paper make a chart like the one below.

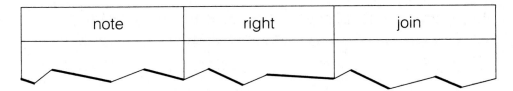

note	right	join

Add these words to your chart. Write each word in the column under the word that has the same beginning sound. HINT: You will *not* use *all* of the words.

kneel	wrist	gift	night	knob
kettle	keep	round	wrinkle	general
gem	napkin	gentle	knight	weather
wrote	jungle	geese	ginger	wrap

Ending Sounds

> Letters stand for sounds at the end of words.

Choose a letter to complete this word.
   bu___

You could have chosen many different letters. Each letter made a different word.

Read each word below. Look at the underlined letters.

scru<u>b</u>	mu<u>d</u>	pai<u>l</u>	bu<u>dge</u>	we<u>t</u>
clea<u>n</u>	ra<u>g</u>	war<u>m</u>	rela<u>x</u>	wra<u>p</u>

The letters *dge* stand for the sound you hear at the beginning of *jar*.

The letter *x* stands for the sound you hear at the end of *sacks*.

Number your paper from 1 to 10. Each sentence below is missing one word. Notice the sound at the end of the under-lined word in each sentence. Then find the word in the box above that ends with that same sound. Write both words on your paper.

1. My dog Flax wouldn't ___ from the <u>ledge</u>.
2. It started to rain, and she <u>got</u> all ___.
3. By the time we got home, she was <u>covered</u> with ___.
4. That sad <u>dog</u> looked like a ___!
5. <u>Karen</u>, Bob, and I had to ___ her.
6. Flax started to <u>howl</u> when she saw the ___ of suds.
7. Karen held Flax down while <u>Bob</u> helped me ___.
8. We had to ___ her in a towel so she wouldn't <u>drip</u>.
9. <u>Mom</u> put Flax's bed near the stove so Flax would be ___.
10. With <u>Flax</u> settled, we could all ___!

Spelling Ending Sounds

> Some ending sounds can be spelled more than one way.

Read the words below. Look at the underlined letters.

lea<u>f</u>	shoo<u>k</u>	bu<u>s</u>
cu<u>ff</u>	traffi<u>c</u>	pa<u>ss</u>
gra<u>ph</u>	bla<u>ck</u>	

Number your paper from 1 to 10. Copy the sentences below. Fill in the missing letters. Choose the letters from those in the box. Be sure the words make sense in the sentence.

> f   ff   ph   k   c   ck   s   ss

1. My brother's name is Jeffrey, or Je__ for short.
2. We were stu__ indoors because it was raining.
3. "I know," I said, "let's go up to the atti__."
4. "Ye__!" Jeff said. "That's a terrifi__ idea!"
5. We couldn't believe what a me__ it was upstairs.
6. There was stu__ everywhere!
7. In one corner there was a broken clo__ and an old phonogra__.
8. We couldn't even wor__ our way acro__ the room!
9. Finally Jeff said, "How about i__ we sit right here on this sta__ of books?"
10. "O.K." I said. "We can look for an old photogra__ of u__ in this scrapboo__!"

Short Vowel Sounds

> There are five short vowel sounds.

Read each word below. Look at the underlined letter that spells each short vowel sound.

a	e	i	o	u
gr<u>a</u>b	n<u>e</u>st	f<u>i</u>sh	st<u>o</u>p	pl<u>u</u>m

A. Number your paper from 1 to 5. For each sentence, decide which vowel will fit *all* of the blanks. Use the same vowel to complete each word. Write the sentence on your paper.

1. K__m was going on a tr__p to v__sit her grandparents.
2. Her m__m dr__pped her off at the bus st__p.
3. Wh__n the bus came, Kim climbed the st__ps, sat down n__xt to a window, and put her seatb__lt on.
4. In j__st a minute, the b__s was h__mming down the highway.
5. Kim s__t b__ck, and looked out __s the bus p__ssed everything by f__st.

B. Number your paper from 1 to 5. Write the words below. Next to each word, write three words that rhyme.

     1. man **2.** ten **3.** pin **4.** hot **5.** bug

C. Now try to write a sentence using one group of rhyming words that you have written. For example:

The man ran to the van.

Consonant Clusters with *l*

> The sounds of some letters blend together. These letters are called consonant clusters.

Read this riddle.

> What is the same about <u>blue</u> and <u>blow</u>,
> About <u>clear</u> and <u>flash</u> and <u>glow</u>?
> It is also true of <u>plenty</u> and <u>slow</u>.
> <u>Please</u> tell me, if you know.

Notice that the two letters at the beginning of each underlined word blend together. *Bl, pl, sl, fl, gl,* and *cl* are consonant clusters.

Number your paper from 1 to 10. Read each word clue below. Write your answer. Use one of the consonant clusters in the box below to finish each word.

bl	cl	fl	gl	pl	sl

1. You can ride me down a snowy hill.   ___ed
2. I can be shaped into almost anything.   ___ay
3. I am a reddish-purple fruit.   ___um
4. I'll cover you when you sleep.   ___anket
5. You walk on me all the time.   ___oor
6. I can fix your leaky faucet.   ___umber
7. I am round, and I can show you the earth.   ___obe
8. You can mix me with water to make dough.   ___our
9. I am a very harsh snowstorm.   ___izzard
10. You wear me on your hand.   ___ove

Consonant Clusters with *r*

> Consonant clusters are made up of two or more letters whose sounds blend together.

Read the poem below. The underlined words begin with a consonant cluster.

Would you like to ride on a <u>train</u>,
To <u>cross</u> the miles from Georgia to Maine?
Or would you <u>prefer</u> <u>driving</u> a <u>brand</u>-new <u>truck</u>,
<u>Greeting</u> <u>friends</u> as you pass, and wishing them luck?

What letter is part of each consonant cluster in the poem?

Number your paper from 1 to 8. Read the sentences below. The underlined words do NOT make sense. Think of rhyming words that DO make sense. Write the sentences with the new words on your paper. Circle the consonant cluster at the *beginning* of each new word.

1. The train runs on a <u>crack</u>.
2. Peter <u>dried</u> the lid open with a spoon.
3. I woke up and then I got <u>pressed</u>.
4. We wore hats and mittens so we wouldn't <u>breeze</u>.
5. The tree's leaves were green, but the trunk was <u>frown</u>.
6. Dad mowed the <u>brass</u> in our yard.
7. Nancy is <u>crushing</u> her hair.
8. The <u>grow</u> flew to its nest.

Consonant Clusters with *s*

> Consonant clusters can be two or three letters whose sounds blend together.

Many consonant clusters begin with *s*. Look for consonant clusters as you read the story below.

Thanks to a screeching storm last night, I had to do my report all over. That's why I'm not smiling today.

You see, the lights went out, and I spilled juice all over my paper. "Oh, swell," I thought as I hunted for the switch. Of course, I squashed the cat, who streaked out of the room hissing at me. "Scaredy cat!" I snarled back.

When Dad saw me sprawled flat on my face, he asked, "Oh, is your report about skating or swimming?"

A. Number your paper from 1 to 11. Write the consonant clusters below. Next to each, write the word or words from the story that begin with the cluster.

1. sc	2. sk	3. sm	4. sn
5. sp	6. st	7. sw	8. scr
9. spr	10. squ	11. str	

B. Write the two consonant clusters that stand for the same sound.

C. Number your paper from 1 to 4. Read each group of words below. Write the two words in each group that begin with the same sound.

1. scratch	2. spell	3. squirt	4. snap
scrap	scout	smell	smooth
stripe	still	squat	swift
stem	scarf	swing	sway

Ending Consonant Clusters

Consonant clusters can come at the beginning or at the end of words.

Tell me, my <u>friend</u>,
How can <u>worst</u> be like <u>best</u>
And <u>mild</u> be like <u>wild</u>?
Both answers are right at the <u>end</u>.

Look at the underlined words in the poem again. Each ends with a consonant cluster.

Some important ending consonant clusters are listed in the box below.

ld   nd   nk   sk   mp   ft   lt   nt   st

Number your paper from 1 to 9. Copy the sentences below. Fill in the blanks of each incomplete word with the same consonant cluster. Use the consonant clusters in the box.

1. Dad se__ the re__ when it was due.
2. I thi__ I'll get a dri__ of water.
3. I got a bu__ on my head when I hit the la__.
4. Did you hear a sou__ coming from the po__?
5. I lo__ my be__ baseball mitt.
6. Ho__ that end of the blanket and help me fo__ it.
7. We bui__ a pen for the co__.
8. I le__ my ra__ in the pool.
9. I'll a__ John if I can wear his ma__.

Short Vowel Sounds

> Some short vowel sounds can be spelled more than one way.

Read each word below. Look at the underlined letters.

a	e	i	o	u
b<u>a</u>t	m<u>e</u>n	tr<u>i</u>p	m<u>o</u>p	s<u>u</u>n
	br<u>ea</u>d			w<u>o</u>n
				t<u>ou</u>ch

Number your paper from 1 to 6. Complete each sentence below by choosing a word that has the same vowel sound as the underlined word. Write the word on your paper. Underline the letter or letters that spell the short vowel sound.

1. My ____ brother <u>Russ</u> is only four.
   cute   small   young

2. Still, he asks <u>some</u> ____ questions.
   strange   tough   wrong

3. Each day he pops out of <u>bed</u> with a ____ full of questions.
   mind   brain   head

4. "How many <u>tons</u> does the ____ weigh?"
   moon   Earth   sun

5. "<u>Can</u> you tell me why the ____ is green?"
   grass   sky   sea

6. Mom and I have to ____ hard to answer <u>him</u>!
   study   think   look

Long Vowel Sounds

> Many words that end in e have a long vowel sound.

How can you change —

tap	to	tape?
pin	to	pine?
rob	to	robe?
cut	to	cute?

The magic e will do the trick.

A. Number your paper from 1 to 8. Write each word below. Then make a new word by adding the magic e. Use each new word in a sentence.

1. plan	**2.** cod	**3.** rip	**4.** can
5. not	**6.** hid	**7.** mad	**8.** cub

B. Number your paper from 1 to 10. Read the story below. Write each word in the story that has a long vowel sound. Underline the vowels.

Pete came home late. There was nothing left of the cake his mother baked. Poor Pete! His sister Kate ate the whole thing!

Long *a* Vowel Sound

> The long *a* vowel sound can be spelled more than one way.
>
> p<u>a</u>n<u>e</u>   p<u>ai</u>l   p<u>ay</u>

Read the poem below. As you read, listen for the long *a* vowel sound.

My friend, <u>Ray</u>,
loved to <u>play</u>.
"Let's <u>play</u> <u>games</u> all <u>day</u>," he'd <u>say</u>.
"Let's <u>make</u> a <u>plane</u>,
<u>Race</u> my toy <u>train</u>,
Or would you rather <u>skate</u> in the <u>rain</u>?"

A. The underlined words in the poem show three ways to spell the long *a* vowel sound. Write *a-e*, *ai*, and *ay* at the top of your paper. Write the underlined words from the poem under the headings that spell the long *a* vowel sound the same way.

B. Number your paper from 1 to 8. Read each group of words. Write the two words from each group that have the long *a* vowel sound.

1. stay	2. blade	3. true	4. sled
sun	grass	give	stray
sand	shade	brave	chain
wade	tree	aid	bike

5. path	6. flake	7. dine	8. clay
straight	story	ate	buddy
state	raid	bean	grain
past	read	bay	clap

Long e Vowel Sound

The long e vowel sound can be spelled more than one way.
beep   beak   bury   be   believe

Read each word below. Look at the underlined letters.

queen	dream	city	she	thief
kneel	teach	daily	we	shield

There is a long e vowel sound in each word.

Number your paper from 1 to 6. Find the word or words with the long e vowel sound in each sentence below. Write the long e words on your paper. Underline the letter or letters that stand for this sound.

1. The nation of Greece has had a long history.
2. We remember ancient Greece each time the modern Olympic games take place.
3. The Greeks shared many of our beliefs, such as freedom.
4. We can still read many plays and stories written in Greece long ago.
5. Many tourists visit the cities and beaches of Greece today.
6. They discover the wonders of this sunny land by the sea.

Long *i* Vowel Sound

The long *i* vowel sound can be spelled more than one way.

str<u>i</u>k<u>e</u>   m<u>igh</u>t   sk<u>y</u>   p<u>ie</u>

Sly Spy?

If you were a <u>spy</u>,
Just how would you dress?
In a jacket and <u>tie</u>,

Or any old mess?
Would you <u>try</u> to blend in
And fade out of <u>sight</u>?
Or <u>like</u> lots of noise
From morning till <u>night</u>?

Read each underlined word in the poem again. The words
show different letters that stand for the long *i* vowel sound: *igh*,
ie, *y*, and *i-e*.

Number your paper from 1 to 21. Read the story below. Then
write each word that has a long *i* vowel sound. Underline the
letter or letters that stand for the long *i* vowel sound.

> This spy story is true. It happened in a tiny town on the
> coast of Maine.
> Soon after high tide, a woman saw two strangers going
> by. "Something's not right," she said. "They dress like folks
> from far away. They have fine briefcases, too, but they look
> *too* new. I must notify the FBI."
> "Don't pry," was her husband's reply.
> Meanwhile, the spies did not hide. They got a ride to
> New York and started living quite the life. They were
> caught—can you guess why?
> It does not always pay to advertise!

Long *o* Vowel Sound

> The long *o* vowel sound can be spelled more than one way.
>
> r<u>o</u>s<u>e</u>   b<u>oa</u>t   g<u>o</u>   thr<u>ow</u>

Read the poem below. Listen for the long *o* vowel sound.

Where does this beautiful rainbow go?
If I follow this road of stone will I know?
Or are leprechauns and pots of gold,
Only stories I've been told?

A. Number your paper from 1 to 9. Write the words from the poem that have the long *o* vowel sound. Underline the letter or letters that stand for the long *o* vowel sound.

B. Number your paper from 1 to 8. Look at each group of words. Write the two words from each group that *rhyme*.

1. done	**2.** spoke	**3.** rode	**4.** above
hoe	town	load	crow
shoe	boss	pod	stop
no	cloak	good	go
5. throat	**6.** tool	**7.** hood	**8.** doll
root	coal	groan	round
cost	book	hound	goat
note	pole	flown	wrote

Long *u* Vowel Sound

> The long *u* vowel sound can be spelled more than one way.
>
> c<u>u</u>te   f<u>ew</u>   m<u>u</u>sic

A. Number your paper from 1 to 6. Write each word below. Underline the letter or letters that stand for the long *u* vowel sound.

1. cute
2. compute
3. ewe
4. used
5. future
6. unit

B. Number your paper from 1 to 10. Choose the word from the box that makes sense in the sentence. Then write the complete sentence.

mule	pew	menus	humor	fuel
huge	refused	musical	confused	perfume

1. When we entered the restaurant, the waiter gave us ____.
2. Our teacher has a good sense of ____.
3. A ____ is a good pack animal.
4. During choir practice I sat in the last ____.
5. Gasoline is a ____ used to run cars.
6. That ____ you're wearing smells like roses.
7. Was that a ____ bear I saw?
8. The violin is a ____ instrument.
9. Sarah ____ to let me help her with her homework.
10. Do you understand the math problem now, or are you still ____?

Review: Short and Long Vowel Sounds

A. Read the two underlined words in each sentence below. Notice that they look almost the same but sound different. Write the headings *Short Vowel* and *Long Vowel* on your paper. List each underlined word under the correct heading.

Notes in My Diary

1. <u>Sam</u> eats the <u>same</u> lunch every day.
2. I love my new <u>cap</u> and wool <u>cape</u>.
3. I owe Mom a <u>huge</u> <u>hug</u> for that.
4. Should I <u>read</u> the book about the <u>Red</u> Cross?
5. I shall <u>not</u> write <u>notes</u> anymore in class.

B. Number your paper from 1 to 10. Read each sentence and the two words that follow it. Write the sentence with the word that makes sense.

1. My friend Rosa looks ____. (pale, pal)
2. She was sick in ____ for a week. (bead, bed)
3. We ____ she can come to the party. (hop, hope)
4. It's a Halloween party, so we're hanging scary paper ____ all over the place. (bats, baits)
5. Miguel says they are ____, not scary. (cut, cute)
6. My lion costume has a golden ____. (man, mane)
7. It's shaggy and ____ looking. (mean, men)
8. It's not a very pretty ____. (sit, sight)
9. Don't worry, I won't ____! (bit, bite)
10. See you ____ the party, right? (at, ate)

Beginning Consonant Digraphs

> Two or three consonants that stand for one sound are called consonant digraphs.

Read the words below. Look at the underlined letters. They are consonant digraphs.

<u>ch</u>oose	<u>sh</u>eep	<u>wh</u>ale	<u>th</u>rew	<u>th</u>ick	<u>th</u>is

Notice that the letters *th* can stand for two different sounds.

A. Copy the words in the box on your paper. Then, next to each word, write the two words from the list below that begin with the same sound.

throat	think	champion	them
whisper	three	short	cheer
shovel	there	white	thorn

B. Number your paper from 1 to 6. Add a consonant digraph to complete each word below. Write the complete word on your paper. Be sure it makes sense in the sentence.

1. Yesterday Dad and I were looking __ough a magazine.
2. Guess __at we saw in one of the pictures.
3. Clue #1: __ese things transported goods all over the world.
4. Clue #2: They had many sails and very __ick ropes.
5. Clue #3: Their huge anchors hung from __ains with links bigger than your arm.
6. You __ould have guessed "clipper ship" by now!

Ending Consonant Digraphs

Consonant digraphs can come at the end of words.

Read the words below. Look at the letters that spell the ending consonant digraphs.

ri<u>ch</u>   fi<u>sh</u>   sti<u>ng</u>   pa<u>th</u> di<u>tch</u>

Read the story below. Look at the consonant digraph at the *end* of each underlined word.

    A <u>month</u> ago my cousin <u>Edith</u> and I found a robin chick under a <u>bench</u> on the lawn. So, we put the cat on a <u>leash</u>, fed it a huge <u>dish</u> of food, and checked the gate <u>latch</u>. Then we set to work. Since it is <u>wrong</u> to <u>touch</u> a fallen bird, we slipped large leaves <u>beneath</u> it. Very gently, we carried it <u>along</u>. It gave a weak chirp as we put it back. Was it a thank-you <u>song</u>?

    When it is time for the birds to <u>hatch</u>, step carefully, and <u>watch</u> where you are going. Please!

Number your paper from 1 to 5. Write each word below. Next to each word, write the words from the story that end with the same sound and are spelled the same way.

1. sou<u>th</u>   2. da<u>sh</u>   3. bri<u>ng</u>   4. in<u>ch</u>   5. ba<u>tch</u>

Syllables

> Some words can be divided into parts called syllables.
> You can hear a vowel sound in every syllable.

Sometimes two or more vowel letters stand for one vowel sound. For example, in the word *rain*, you see two vowels, but you hear only one vowel sound. The word *rain* has only one syllable.

A. Number your paper from 1 to 20. Read each word below. The number of vowel sounds is the same as the number of syllables. How many syllables does each word have? Write your answers.

1. pen	2. pencil	3. traffic	4. list
5. department	6. monster	7. tracks	8. banana
9. leader	10. important	11. revolution	12. ridiculous
13. regular	14. river	15. fantastic	16. hesitate
17. froze	18. which	19. squash	20. pretend

When you say a word that has more than one syllable, you stress, or emphasize, one syllable more than another. In a dictionary or glossary, the stressed syllable is followed by an accent mark (').

truth' ful   cre a' tive

B. Number your paper from 1 to 9. Read each word below. Which syllable is stressed: the first, second, or third? Write your answers.

1. creature	2. decision	3. above
4. dinosaur	5. heavy	6. remember
7. gorilla	8. cotton	9. pretend

487

Schwa

The schwa is a special vowel sound. It can be spelled with *a, e, i, o,* or *u*. The schwa is often heard in the unstressed syllable of a word.

Read the words below. The underlined letters stand for the schwa vowel sound.

carniv<u>a</u>l   shov<u>e</u>l   pup<u>i</u>l   ribb<u>o</u>n   hopef<u>u</u>l

The schwa vowel sound can also be at the beginning of a word, as in *ago* and *upon*.

Number your paper from 1 to 10. Write each underlined word below. Underline the vowel that stands for the schwa vowel sound.

1. A bad dream <u>awoke</u> me in the night.
2. Since I was up, I decided to go to the <u>kitchen</u> for a snack.
3. I tiptoed down the stairs, trying to be very <u>quiet</u>.
4. When I went to <u>open</u> the door, I noticed the light was on!
5. "What could be the <u>reason</u> for that?" I wondered.
6. I didn't go in just then; I wanted to be <u>careful</u>.
7. I listened for <u>about</u> a minute.
8. It sounded like someone was eating a crunchy <u>salad</u>.
9. "There's only one <u>person</u> that could be," I decided.
10. "My sister—she's on a <u>diet</u>!"

Vowel Combinations

> Some vowel combinations make the same sound but are spelled with different letters.
>
> join round
> boy crown

A. Write the words *boy* and *crown* at the top of your paper. Under each word, write six words from the list below that have the same vowel sound.

clown	soy	crowd
boil	brown	ahoy
found	spoil	ground
mouth	point	royal

B. *Ou* and *ow* do not always stand for the vowel sound you hear in *crown*. Read the words below. Only six of them have the vowel sound you hear in *crown*. Which six are they? Write them on your paper.

shout	power	prowl
would	glow	sound
proud	four	enough
know	owe	gown

C. Number your paper from 1 to 5. Read the word clues below. Each answer will have the vowel sound you hear in *boy*.

1. This is another word for dirt. ____
2. This word describes someone who is faithful and true. ____
3. A snake can wind itself into this shape. ____
4. This is something you can play with. ____
5. A nickel is one, and so is a dime. ____

Vowels + *r*

> The letter *r* changes the sound of the vowel it follows.

Look at each word pair below. Are the vowel sounds the same in—

Cat and car?
Flame and flare?
Plain and pair?
Went and were?
Fit and fir?
Honey and horn?
Bun and burn?

A. Number your paper from 1 to 5. From each list write the two words that *rhyme*.

1	2	3	4	5
soup	burst	fair	worm	dark
sir	pencil	burn	sunny	tack
churn	first	bet	penny	spark
chip	coil	square	germ	spool

B. Number your paper from 1 to 5. From each list write the two words in which *r* changes the vowel sound.

1	2	3	4	5
present	really	chart	roof	rein
curl	work	crate	rail	glare
twirl	stair	curve	barn	hairy
track	brim	crazy	squirt	scribble

r-Controlled Vowels

> Some *r*-controlled vowel sounds can be spelled in different ways.

Read the two groups of words below. Listen for the rhyming sounds in each group.

f<u>or</u>	d<u>ear</u>
ch<u>ore</u>	d<u>eer</u>
r<u>oar</u>	h<u>ere</u>

The first list shows three ways of spelling the vowel sound you hear in *board*. The second list shows three ways of spelling the vowel sound you hear in *near*.

A. Write the words *board* and *near* at the top of your paper. Under each word, write the eight words from the list below that have the same vowel sound.

tore	rear	mere	steer
appear	porch	soar	severe
nearly	shorten	organ	morning
cheerful	aboard	gear	snore

B. Sometimes two words sound exactly alike even though they are spelled differently. In each sentence below, the underlined word does NOT make sense. Number your paper from 1 to 4. Write a word that sounds the same and DOES make sense.

1. This morning I woke up with a <u>soar</u> throat.
2. Did you <u>here</u> the news?
3. Rob had <u>for</u> dollars to spend.
4. We <u>road</u> the bus to school.

Schwa + *r*

The letter *r* can follow and change the schwa vowel sound.

Read the words below. Look at the underlined letters.

coll<u>ar</u>   driv<u>er</u>   mot<u>or</u>

A. Number your paper from 1 to 7. Complete each sentence by choosing the word that ends with the sound you hear at the end of *collar*. Write the word on your paper.

1. My great uncle ＿＿ is from Sweden. (Sven, Oscar)
2. He is a very important ＿＿ of my family. (person, member)
3. He tells stories to my ＿＿ and me. (sister, cousin)
4. As a ＿＿, he sometimes helped on a fishing boat. (child, youngster)
5. The cook had him test the ＿＿ of everything. (flavor, taste.)
6. Even today, Uncle Oscar can tell what is in food just by its ＿＿. (smell, odor)
7. We think his nose is just ＿＿. (super, great)

B. Find the words below that name a job. Write them on your paper. Underline the letters that make the ending sound of each job name.

farmer   baker
toast   doctor
scarf   perfect
tailor   dancer
interest nervous

Review: Short and Long Vowel Sounds

> The letters *a*, *e*, *i*, *o*, *u*, and sometimes *y* can be used alone or together to spell short or long vowel sounds.

A. Number your paper from 1 to 8. Copy the sentences below. Complete the sentence by finding a word at the right that has the same vowel sound as the underlined word.

Fifth Grade Sale

1. Bud's mom gave knit _____.   box
2. Lisa sold green _____.   clips
3. Skip brought magnet _____.   gloves
4. They sold as fast as the baseball _____.   beads
5. John gave a _____ for computer disks.   ties
6. Violet brought six striped _____.   tray
7. "How bright!" said Gail, who gave a _____.   bows
8. Gloria gave _____ that glowed in the dark.   caps

B. Read these words: cloudy   gray   sky
   All three words end with the letter *y*, but each ends with a different vowel sound. On your paper, make a chart like the one below.

long *e*	long *a*	long *i*
cloudy	gray	sky

Add these words to your chart. Write each word in the column that tells its ending sound.

sunny	February	stay	okay	May	someday
chilly	firefly	snowy	July	fry	reply

Syllables and Short Vowel Sounds

Learning to divide words into syllables can help you read new words. When you come to a difficult word in your reading, you can work on one small part at a time.

Read these one-syllable words.

<blockquote>
bat   hen   pig   rod   tub
</blockquote>

Now read these words.

<blockquote>
butter   window   center
</blockquote>

How many vowel sounds are in each word?
How many syllables does each word have?

Below are the same words divided into syllables.

<blockquote>
but ter   win dow   cen ter
</blockquote>

Notice that a vowel comes between two consonants in the first syllable of each word. Do you hear a short or a long vowel sound?

> When two consonants stand between two vowels, the word is usually divided between the consonants. The vowel in the first syllable is often short.

Number your paper from 1 to 12. Write each word, leaving a space between the syllables.

1. monkey	2. rabbit	3. reindeer	4. sunfish
5. parrot	6. penguin	7. sparrow	8. puppy
9. walrus	10. donkey	11. collie	12. tortoise

Syllables and Long Vowel Sounds

My brother <u>Milo</u>
    is <u>tidy</u> and neat.
He cannot stand clutter
    under his feet.

One day I found hanging
    on the door of my room,
A sign—DANGER! KEEP OUT!—
    a mop and a broom.

I icily answered
    to Milo (that tease),
"Enough is enough! No <u>humor</u>,
    please."

Read the underlined words above. How many vowel sounds does each have? How many syllables?

This is how the words are divided into syllables.

Mi lo   ti dy   hu mor

Notice that a vowel is at the end of the first syllable of each word. Do you hear a short or a long vowel sound?

> When one consonant stands between two vowels, the consonant usually goes with the second syllable. The vowel in the first syllable is often long.

A. Number your paper from 1 to 8. Write each word, leaving a space between the syllables.

1. cozy   2. notice   3. lazy   4. tuba
5. broken   6. recent   7. major   8. truly

B. Number your paper from 1 to 6. Find six words below that have a long vowel sound in the first syllable. Write them on your paper, leaving a space between the syllables.

sofa	finish	silence	honor	paper
center	human	silly	ocean	packet

Syllables, Consonant Digraphs, and Consonant Clusters

Read the words below. How many sounds do the underlined letters stand for?

su<u>ch</u>	<u>sh</u>ine	<u>th</u>ink	de<u>ck</u>	<u>th</u>ese
<u>wh</u>ere	<u>th</u>roat	wa<u>tch</u>	stro<u>ng</u>	

Did you recognize the consonant digraphs? Remember that consonant digraphs are two or three letters that stand for one sound.

Bl, cl, pr, br, tw, st, lf, and *nk* are some of the consonant clusters you know. In a consonant cluster, the separate sounds of the consonants blend together.

Look out for these letter combinations when you are dividing a word into syllables.

In most cases, do not divide between the letters in consonant digraphs or consonant clusters.

Number your paper from 1 to 12. Write the words below on your paper. Underline the consonant digraph or consonant cluster in each. Then draw a line between the syllables in each word.

1. kerchief
2. bucket
3. between
4. butcher
5. mushroom
6. weather
7. halfway
8. lobster
9. handful
10. ashamed
11. apron
12. purchase